LIFE AND THOUGHT IN OLD RUSSIA

THE
PENNSYLVANIA
STATE
UNIVERSITY
PRESS

LIFE AND THOUGHT
IN OLD RUSSIA
BY MARTHE BLINOFF

Copyright © 1961 by The Pennsylvania State University
Library of Congress Catalog Card No. 61-11415
Printed in the United States of America by
Kurtz Bros., Clearfield, Pennsylvania
Designed by Marilyn Shobaken

To the memory of my parents

■ ■ ■ I should like to thank my friends at the University of Minnesota who were patient and helpful with problems of translation or interpretation. I owe a special debt of gratitude to Professor T. F. Magner, Chairman of the Department of Slavic Languages, The Pennsylvania State University, for his constant encouragement.

CONTENTS

7. NATIONAL CONSCIOUSNESS AND IDEOLOGIES

A BRIEF HISTORY OF RUSSIA, 1147-1881

CHRONOLOGICAL TABLES

ILLUSTRATIONS

PREFACE

This anthology offers a selective view of the material and intellectual life of Russia between the late fifteenth and the end of the nineteenth centuries, four hundred years beginning with the centralization of power in Moscow and closing with the assassination of Alexander II in 1881. The scope of the book is limited geographically as well as historically, only Great-Russian civilization being considered.

Except for the introductory remarks at the beginning of each section, the editor has let the Russians speak for themselves. The texts which have been chosen describe, illustrate, or interpret Russian life through Russian eyes, although a few revealing reports by foreign observers have also been included. Though some of the originals possess great literary value, they were chosen only for their ability to convey feelings or ideologies or to provide factual information. Thus, in addition to government decrees, official reports, and chapters from chronicles, the anthology includes passages from autobiographies, philosophical or historical essays, art criticism, and texts that are merely descriptive. In each of the seven sections of the book the order is roughly chronological. Since many of the texts could have been included in more than one section, some arbitrariness of classification was unavoidable, which accounts for the difference in length—more apparent than real—of the various sections.

In translating the texts the editor anglicized familiar words instead of transliterating them: thus *izbas, tsar* (but *khaty, Batyi*). Since, however, the word *Kremlin* has connotations which do not accord with "citadel," its meaning in the early texts, the transliterated form *Kreml'* has been used.

For the reader unfamiliar with Russian history, "A Brief History of Russia, 1147–1881" has been included in the appendix. Chronological tables relating events in Russia to concurrent events of importance in other parts of the world also appear in the appendix.

MAP OF OLD RUSSIA   Original drawing by S. Shakhovskoy
Nizhny-Novgorod: now Gorky. Rybinsk: now Shcherbakov. Tsarev-
Kokshaysk: now Yoshkar-Ola. Tver: now Kalinin. Vyatka: now Kirov.

1

**PEOPLE
AND
PLACES**

The broad expanses of the northern or central Russian landscape, with their faint relief and the uniformity of their prospects, afford at best only a mild esthetic pleasure to the foreign eye. To the Russian, this space, with its traditional elements of river, forest, or steppe, arouses emotions that the very sameness and monotony of the scene seem to magnify. Much has been said —to the point of triteness—on the affective resonance of the word *prostor* (space) as well as on the sentimental value of birch and river to the Russian heart. The French say that a landscape is "a state of the soul," a mood; this is eminently true of the Russian landscape. There is a profound association between a Russian and the nature of his native land. It has often been remarked that, in contrast with the European landscape, the Russian, like the American, is not humanized. Humanization in western Europe is obvious, evidenced by names, landmarks, boundaries, hedges, habitations. Such signs are not so visible in Russia or North America. But the link forged by the unconscious memories of stubborn conflict with poor soil and cruel climate, of agelong sufferings, of endless wanderings and forced marches, in a land predominantly peasant until a very recent past, may be stronger than in western Europe, if not as immediately apparent. Thus, though the Russian language had no word of its own for landscape until it borrowed one from the German in the eighteenth century (and, for good measure, another from the French), life itself, and not only romantic feeling, has bred the powerful attachment of the Russian people to their land.

The human dwellings, at first clustered along the river roads or in the forest clearings, were built of wood. Medieval—and even modern— Russia had a wood civilization, in contrast with the stone civilization of western Europe. The Great-Russian soil is poor in stone. In reading Russian documents of the Middle Ages the word *kamen* (stone) must often be interpreted as "brick," while what we call stone is distinguished by the addition of the adjective "white." Song and poem celebrated "whitestone" Moscow because of its Kreml' churches and inner city walls, first built in the fourteenth century as a sign of defiance to the Tatar overlords, and an object of wonder to the inhabitants.

The wealth of wood made the Russian peasant the most skilled carpenter in the world. His axe—the saw was little used—could, as Tolstoy observed, build a house or whittle a spoon. Until the nineteenth century every man was his own carpenter, and no specialized man of the craft could be found in a Russian village. The izba was built functionally, quickly, and, in spite of its rather dreary aspect and primitive appointments, often aroused the admiration of foreign travelers. Hardly changed from the eleventh to the eighteenth century, its traditional division into warm room or izba proper, storeroom, and anteroom can still be found in many peasant houses of Russia and western Siberia, and the style is, of course, preserved in

1

"Peter's cottage" in Petersburg. Its design inspired that of the native wooden or brick churches as well as the gentry's manors, which were usually no more than glorified izbas. Both city and village, until the eighteenth century, were essentially loose agglomerations of such manors or farms, though in the cities the tradesmen's and craftsmen's districts presented a more urban appearance.

Things changed with the eighteenth century. The building of a European city, St. Petersburg, created a new model for towns as well as for private dwellings. After the reign of Catherine II, and chiefly under Alexander I and Nicholas I, administrative centers of provincial cities put on a modern uniform, one that altered only slightly until recent times. And the "houses with columns" of country squires sprouted all over the country, much as did colonial houses in North America at about the same period.

Meanwhile, though some izbas put forth citified embellishments—porches and upper rooms with balconies—the old manner of life persisted among the peasants, timelessly conditioned by the nature of soil and climate, by the necessities of working for the squire and paying taxes, and by the customs of a still largely patriarchal family tradition. When the land did not feed the peasant the year around—and in many of the central and northern provinces it did not—family resources were eked out by home crafts or by a seasonal migration of individuals or groups. Thus the Vyatka makers of clay figures, the Bogorodskaya village (Moscow province) carvers of wooden toys, the weavers of the Vladimir region, the bootmakers of the Tver province, to mention only a few, became famous. A link with city life was established. But, until the nineteenth century at least, the real civilization of Russia remained essentially a peasant civilization, and the peasant remained the chief character in the drama of Russian history. His relationship to river, forest, marsh, or steppe shaped the pattern of Russian life. Urban civilization, mostly imported, stayed on the surface. Whenever it reached the mass of the people, it became so deeply modified as to lose much of its original character.

RUSSIAN PEASANTS IN THE SEVENTEENTH CENTURY

Olearius' "Voyages and Travels"

From *Istoriya Moskvy* (Moscow, 1952), Vol. I

VIEW OF THE PALACE EMBANKMENT FROM THE PETER AND PAUL FORTRESS, ST. PETERSBURG   Painting by F. A. Alexeev, 1794
From an album of reproductions of paintings in the Tretyakov gallery, Moscow

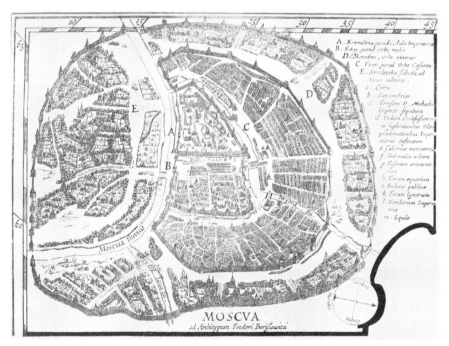

THE GODUNOV PLAN OF MOSCOW—1604–05
From *Istoriya Moskvy* (Moscow, 1952), Vol. I

MY NATIVE LAND

M. Yu. Lermontov

> The ageless features of the Russian landscape appear in this poem by Lermontov, expressing the traditional but deep-felt emotion of love for the native land. It was written in 1841, the last year of his short life.

■ ■ ■ I love my native land, but with a strange love! My reason cannot conquer it. Neither the glory blood has bought, nor the tranquillity bred of a proud confidence, nor the sacred legends of its shadowy past can stir in me pleasurable dreams.

But I love—why, I can not tell myself—the cold silence of her steppes, the waving of her boundless forests, the ocean-like expanse of her flooded rivers. . . . I love to speed in a telega[1] along the country road, when, as I sigh for the night's lodging, my slow gaze pierces the shadows of the night and glimpses the trembling lights of melancholy villages.

I love the smoke of the burnt stubble, the wagons bivouacking at night in the steppe; and on the hill, among the yellow fields, a couple of white-glimmering birches. With a gladness unfamiliar to many, I see the heaped threshing-floor, the thatch-roofed izba with its carved shutters; and on a holiday, in the dewy evening, I am ready to spend half the night looking at the dancers as they whistle and stamp, and listening to the tipsy peasants' talk.

—*Polnoe sobranie sochinenii* (Moscow, 1947–48)

NOTES: [1]A four-wheeled country wagon.

■ ■ ■

VILLAGES AND CITIES

A. I. Nekrasov

■ ■ ■ Leaving aside for the moment both the distinctive villages and izbas of the North and the *khaty*[1] of the Ukraine, let us turn to the central Russian area, to the provinces of Moscow, Smolensk, Tver, Yaroslavl, Kostroma, Nizhny-Novgorod, Vladimir, Ivanovo-Vosnesensk, Ryazan, and

5

Kaluga, and see what a Great-Russian village with its homesteads looks like.

We approach the village from the road and finally enter it. From a distance, we can already see the rows of ridged roofs on the izbas which face the street in a line, while at their sides and at the back various outbuildings are irregularly scattered. When we enter the village, this arrangement becomes still more noticeable. Sometimes, of course, the village is laid out on both sides of a main road; but even when this is not the case, the izbas are still built along the street. This street is comparatively straight and runs from one end of the village to the other, with bypaths and alleys branching off right and left.

On the periphery lie the back lanes which circle the village; but the village has a face: the street, on which the peasant homestead always looks with the front of its izba and the eyes of its customary three windows. . . .

There are frequent and rather obvious signs of contemporary city culture: little fenced-in gardens in front of the izbas, entrance steps that sometimes spread into terraces, doors that used to be garret windows opening now on tiny balconies. The izba is ready to turn into a chalet, obviously in accordance with the new needs and economy of the village. We can easily disregard the recent additions; we can find older types of izbas in remote locations; but, on the whole, izba and village produce the impression indicated above.

Was this always so? What was the evolution in the forms of the izbas? How did the changes come about? In other words, what is original and what is borrowed in peasant architecture?

No villages have been preserved whose topography would allow us to ascertain the old traditions. But we have one important piece of evidence: the well-known Russian writer and expert on Russian life (in central Russia particularly) Melnikov-Pechersky[2] mentions in his autobiographical essays that during the first half of the nineteenth century villages were being rebuilt everywhere and that new planning was adopted.

The former pattern of Russian settlements may be discovered by studying the plans of cities. These, being more important because of both their area and the complexity of their economic life, were more conservative, even when they had to be rebuilt after ravaging fires. The comparative simplicity of the village, its greater submission to local powers, have doubtless changed its outer aspect. True, this can also be observed, say, in the "Merchant" district of Novgorod,[3] whose streets now conform to a regular chequered pattern, crossing at right angles. But in most cases the old Russian cities have kept their ancient concentric disposition. Among these are Moscow, Novgorod, Kostroma (partly rebuilt in the seventeenth century according to the old plan), and others. Even when a city was built in a location that did not lend itself conveniently to concentric planning, the official buildings and houses were set in a semicircle; this is the case for

Yaroslavl, which is hemmed in on a promontory between the Volga and the Kotorost, and for the central part of Pskov, between the Velikaya and the Pskova rivers. The reason for this must be sought in the urge to have a compact settlement, so that help might be rapidly obtained from all quarters in case of attack. The city wall emphasized the usual plan of the settlement, but did not originate it. We know that settlements in western Europe followed the same pattern. If we meet with any exception, it can always be explained by the presence of some overwhelming exterior obstacle. For instance, the city of Vladimir stretches out in length because it is hemmed in between the steep bank of the Klyazma and a deep ravine running parallel to the river. Even so, in this as in other ancient cities, the main street did not run from one end of the city to the other, but abutted on the Cathedral of the Assumption and the Prince's Palace. . . .

It would be interesting to know how the homestead, with izba and outbuildings, looked in old times: whether the izba fronted the street, whether the barns and sheds were concealed behind it, whether the street was composed of a group or a row of izbas. This is difficult to ascertain; however, we have some indications on this point too: the sketches and reports of foreigners in the sixteenth and seventeenth centuries: Barberini, Chancellor, Herberstein, Mayerberg, Palmquist, Olearius[4]—also a few drawings by our own artists, plans of fortresses and the remarkable plans of the Tikhvin[5] monastery, and the icons of the Alexander Svirsky[6] monastery in the seventeenth century. The plan of Moscow, made under Boris Godunov, is interesting. Unfortunately, foreigners were nearly always concerned with cities, not villages, and the same can be said of our old drawings. However, the cities of old Russia, in their planning, were essentially like large villages, and in this respect Moscow in particular has, nearly up to our own days, been contrasted with European cities. . . .

Fortunately, Mayerberg has left some sketches of villages which correspond to what we can see in the Tikhvin monastery plans, Godunov's plans of Moscow, and Olearius' drawings. These sketches show that in many cases the izba did not face the street: its location was hardly noticeable, lost among the mass of farm buildings. The street was frequently bordered either by the side wall of the izba, or one of the farm buildings, or simply a fence. As the city was built in a circle, so, more or less, was the farm-enclosure. Consequently its role was more independent, and the street consisted of a gathering of homesteads rather than of izbas proper with their outbuildings concealed at the back.

The architectural ensemble was organized around a center; the settlement consisted of a system of individually centered groups, which in turn formed a whole—the village—around a common center. A self-contained immobility, such was the artistic character of a Russian village in the past: the static circle and not the dynamic line. Indeed, the evidence of foreigners, the Italian Barberini in the sixteenth century, Chancellor

7

and Olearius in the seventeenth,[7] points to a circular planning of Russian villages. It also indicates that Russian settlements were very compact, and that each family had its own independent enclosure, lived in its own establishment. . . .

But this old and fundamental character of Russian villages is now changed. We do not think that the forced alterations that took place early in the nineteenth century are exclusively to blame. It is probable that the villages had already begun to change at an earlier period: the general disposition of the modern village reveals the influence of the Russian cities that were built in the European style in the eighteenth century. The symmetrical stretch of a contemporary Russian village can no more be attributed to the Russian peasant's invention than the wide roads that were built and planted with birches or willows under Catherine II.

—*Russkoe narodnoe iskusstvo* (Moscow, 1924)

NOTES: [1]A khata is built of clay or turf, generally roofed with reeds or thatch; the northern or central Russian izba is a log hut.

[2]Melnikov-Pechersky: see "Beyond the Volga," pp. 10–13.

[3]Old Novgorod was divided into two main districts or "sides," the Sophia side and the Merchant side, separated by the river Volkhov. The Kreml' or "Detinets" was on the Sophia side; it held the Cathedral of St. Sophia.

[4]R. Barberini traveled in Russia and the Scandinavian countries in the sixteenth century; Richard Chancellor came to Muscovy by the northern route (White Sea and northern Dvina) to establish trade relations between Moscow and England (1553–54); Sigismund Herberstein was the envoy to Moscow of Emperor Maximilian in 1517 and 1526; Augustine Mayerberg was in Moscow in 1661–62 as an Austrian diplomat; Eric Palmquist came to Moscow as a military attaché from Sweden in 1673; Adam Olearius was a member of the Schleswig-Holstein embassy to Moscow, 1635–39. All wrote narrations of their stay in Russia, the most detailed being those of Olearius and Herberstein.

[5]The Tikhvin monastery was founded in 1560, on the trade route from the Volga to the Onega region and abroad; the Tikhvin fairs were very important in the sixteenth and seventeenth centuries.

[6]The monastery of Alexander Svirsky is located on the river Svir, Leningrad region.

[7]Chancellor was in Russia in the sixteenth, not in the seventeenth century (see note 4 above).

■ ■ ■

ALONG THE ONEGA

N. Nikitin

8

■ ■ ■ All the villages along our northern rivers are alike. People here have always huddled near the water. The riverbanks are well populated, but behind them stretches the wilderness. And so it is too on the Onega river.

The low-lying bank of the Onega, with sandy-clayish hills, isolated granite crags, and bare rocks in the north, rises gradually toward the south and seems to clothe itself with thicker timber at every step. The fir trees crowd each other. The birch grows here too, but it has a hard time surviving the frigid weather. It is not green before June, and by late August it already shivers and sheds its leaves. And sometimes a hard September frost will veil it under such a white shroud that it cannot recover. The pine, now, does not care: marsh, sand, stone, it will grow anywhere. All it needs is a little light. Its roots clutch the soil like those of a radish. The izbas built from the sturdy massive pine that grows on the hills in dry places can stand for centuries.

The forests here are full of grouse that sit in the forest thickets, do not migrate, build no nests, are satisfied with the sun's rare appearances.

In the old times these regions gave birth to the phrase: "Sea before you, grief behind you, moss to the left of you, woe to the right of you." "There's only one hope—God," added the old people with a smile.

These forests have always been there.

When, a thousand years ago, the Russian people spread to the north, they hit a dark wall of forests, rising fantastically as it seemed to them from earth to sky. "No passage for the runaway's foot, none for the adventurer's horse." But the adventurers, the Novgorod men, followed the rivers, hewed villages and towns out of the forest, set them up along the water.

In the last century nearly half the population of the Onega were timberworkers. The others hunted sea game, fished for lamprey and navaga[1] at the river mouths, spread floating nets to catch salmon. Squirrel, ermine, polar fox, fox, marten, and hare were hunted in all seasons. Some men went off to work as carriers or shipbuilders.

All the timberyards were situated near the mouth of the Onega. Foreign steamers often stood in the deep harbor, loading wood. The port of Onega, like that of Arkhangelsk, exported timber for the English market in various countries, as far away as Africa.

The peasants also worked the land and raised cattle. They planted rye, millet, oats, hemp, potatoes, and peas. Since the Onega soil cannot boast any fertility, the people produced only enough for their own food.

The people of the north have always been of an independent spirit. Besides the tradition of freedom, they have cherished, up to our times, old and even ancient notions bound with religion, which have reached our days through the centuries. The memory of Archpriest Avvakum[2] was still alive in this taiga[3] country, and though there were Orthodox churches everywhere, many people secretly clung to the old faith and, cursing Patriarch Nikon,[4] respected and honored only the old church books and the old church rites.

9

Taiga forest, bogberries, hummocky peat fields, sullen people, and a cold wind eternally blowing in spite of the summer sun—thus did the Onega land appear. . . .

—*Severnaya avrora*[5] (Moscow, 1951)

NOTES: [1]A sea fish of the cod family.
[2]See "The Life of Avvakum," pp. 90–96.
[3]The broad belt of forest (chiefly coniferous) covering the northern regions of Russia and Siberia.
[4]Nikon was the chief enemy of the Old Believers during the seventeenth-century schism.
[5]The novel *Northern Aurora* is concerned with the fighting between pro- and anti-revolutionary forces in the north of Russia in 1918.

■ ■ ■

BEYOND THE VOLGA
P. I. Melnikov-Pechersky

P. I. Melnikov-Pechersky (1819–83) is the author of two long novels, *In the Forests* and *In the Hills*, in which he lovingly describes the manner of life of Old Believers of the region. However, in his official capacity as assistant to the governor of the Nizhny-Novgorod province, he contributed to their persecution.

■ ■ ■ The upper Trans-Volga is a free, spacious land. The people there are talented, brisk, sharp, and clever. Such is the land from up beyond Rybinsk down to the mouth of the Kerzhenets.[1] Downstream the picture changes: deep forests, the meadow Cheremis, Chuvash,[2] and Tatars. Still lower down, beyond the Kama, the steppes spread wide and the population is different: Russians, true, but unlike those on the upper reaches. They are recent settlers, while inhabitants of the upper Trans-Volga forests and marshes have been Russian for centuries. Judging from the speech of the region, the Novgorodians must have settled here in the remote Rurik[3] times. Legends of Batyi's[4] devastations are still fresh. You will be shown "Batyi's path" and the site of the invisible city of Kitezh on Lake Svetly Yar.[5] The city is still intact, with white stone walls, gold-topped churches, venerable monasteries, ornate terems[6] for the princesses, stone mansions for the boyars, and houses built of massive unrotting timber. All intact—but invisible. The sight of glorious Kitezh is not for sinners. It vanished miraculously, by the Lord's will, when godless Tsar Batyi, after destroying Suzdal, moved to attack

Kitezh. The Tatar tsar advanced on the great city of Kitezh, wishing to set its houses on fire, to slaughter its men or drive them into captivity, to take its women and maidens as concubines. But God did not allow the infidel to defile the Christian sanctuary. Ten days, ten nights did Batyi's hordes seek the city of Kitezh, but they could not find it; blinded they were. And to this day the city stands invisible, to be revealed on the eve of Christ's dreadful Doomsday. But on Lake Svetly Yar on a quiet summer evening one can see the walls, churches, monasteries, the princely terems, the boyars' mansions, the homesteads of the townspeople, all reflected in the water. And at night one can hear the dull melancholy ringing of the Kitezh bells.

Thus goes the story in the land beyond the Volga. This is old Russia, ancestral and sturdy. Since the time when the Russian land began, no alien settlers have lived in these regions. Here Russia stands pure; as it was in our forefathers' days, so it remains in our time. A good land, though it looks askance at outsiders.

In the forested upper Trans-Volga, villages are small but many, one or two versts apart. The soil is cold, unfruitful; it's a good year when the peasant can make his grain last till Shrovetide. Toil as you like on your lot, sweat and suffer as you like, the bread of your labors will not feed you the year around. That's how the land is!

Anyone but the Trans-Volga man would have starved to death long ago, but he's no lie-a-bed; he's a sharp fellow. What the land doesn't give he takes by his skill. The peasant of the Zavolzhe[7] doesn't wander off to remote parts for his livelihood, like his neighbor the Viazniki man, who trudges the wide world peddling buttons, ribbons, and other wares to feed his family. He doesn't roam distant regions carpentering, like his other neighbor from the Galich district. No, he has managed to find profitable work at home. He knits mittens, crushes felt and makes hats and boots from the material, he makes fur hats, axes and nails, beams for scales that sell nearly all over Russia. And what beams! You can weigh drugs at the pharmacy on them, they're so finely made!

The forests feed the Zavolzhe peasant. He carves and paints spoons, bowls, cups, and dishes; he makes combs, spindles and other wooden implements, pails, buckets, tubs, spades, boxes, oars, watering pots, ladles; nothing that can be got from the forest escapes his hand. He boils resin with tar, or he pays the timber rights and cuts trees in the state forests to send logs, beams, rafters, stakes, joists, and any other timber goods down the Volga to Astrakhan. The Volga is just a step away, but the Zavolzhe man never goes boat-towing. There's no worse job than that. Beyond the Volga, people tell you that "it's more honest to beg for bread in Christ's name at the village windows than to strain at the towman's strap." And they're right too.

The Zavolzhe man works hard for his living, but he suffers no lack. The men wear boots, the women high shoes. Bast shoes are unknown, though not unheard-of. Timber is plentiful, bark costs nothing, but you

11

won't see braiding-hooks in many houses, unless there's an old fellow who has not left his bed on the stove for several years and so, to while the hours away, he plaits bast shoes either to give passing beggars or to wear himself when he's laid out in his coffin. That's the custom: leather boots for summer, felt boots for winter, and bast shoes for the journey to the next world!

The Trans-Volga man never lies down at night without hot food; on Sundays he has meat; his izba has five walls[8] and a stove with a chimney; "black izbas"[9] and thatch roofs are things he only knows from hearsay: they're to be found somewhere "in the hills." And the neatness of the homes! People praise the Germans for cleanliness and blame Russians for dirt and slovenliness. Let those praise-singers come to the Trans-Volga, they'll change their tune. If a man knows only our steppe and black-soil villages, it can't enter his head how neatly, how cleanly people live beyond the Volga.

The Volga is right there. What the peasant has made over the week he carries off immediately to the landing stage, or if he's lazy to the neighboring market. He won't make a big profit; not everyone gets to be a "thousand-ruble man," even beyond the Volga; but no matter how poor the work is, how few workers there are in the family, the Zavolzhe peasant is fed, clothed, and shod all his life long, and there are no tax arrears to his name. What more would you have? Praise the Lord for this much! Not everyone's lot is to walk in gold and carry silver in his hands, even though every Russian boy's nurse or nanny foretells him such a future when he is still in the cradle.[10]

—*V lesakh* (Academia: Leningrad, 1936–37)

NOTES: [1]The Kerzhenets is a tributary of the Volga, east of Nizhny-Novgorod (Gorky). There were many Old Believers' chapels and convents in the region.

[2]Finno-Ugrian tribes: the Cheremis (now Mari) are traditionally divided into "meadow Cheremis," on the low left bank of the Volga, and the "hill Cheremis," on the high right bank.

[3]Legendary founder of the Kievan dynasty.

[4]The Mongol khan who devastated the Middle Volga lands, Moscow, Suzdal, Vladimir, from 1236 to 1238 and finally took Kiev in 1240.

[5]"Bright Bluff," a small volcanic lake in the province of Nizhny-Novgorod.

[6]Terem originally meant a tall and rich mansion; the most frequent meaning, as here, is the women's apartments, generally situated in the upper part of the house.

[7]Russian form for Trans-Volga lands.

[8]A five-walled izba has an inner log wall, not a mere partition, between its various rooms.

[9]"Black izbas" have no smokestack.

[10]In contrast to this picture of prosperous peasant life in the nineteenth century, see the following description by Radishchev of an izba in a village north of Moscow at the end of the eighteenth century: "Four walls, half-covered, as was the whole ceiling, with soot; a cracked floor crusted with at least two inches of dirt; a stove with no smokestack which, however, was still their best protection against the cold; smoke which

fills the izba every morning, winter or summer; bladder skins stretched across the windows, filtering a dull light, even at midday; two or three pots (fortunate the izba when even one of these is filled every day with meatless cabbage soup!). A wooden bowl and porringers that go by the name of plates; a rough-hewn table, scraped clean on holidays; a trough to feed the pigs or calves (if there are any) who sleep with the people, all together breathing an air so thick that the candle seems to burn in a fog or behind a curtain. . . . With luck, a tub filled with kvas that tastes like vinegar, and a bathhouse outside, in which the cattle sleep when the people are not sweating in it. A homespun hemp shirt, the footwear given by nature, and leggings and bast shoes for going out." —*Journey from Petersburg to Moscow (1790)*.

■ ■ ■

SUZDAL, PAST AND PRESENT

V. Soloukhin

■ ■ ■ **The twenty-sixth day:** . . . We raised our eyes and stood still, spellbound. The road curved slightly and cut into the rye that grew tall and thick. High above the rye gleamed white a sharp-pointed turret topped by a blue onion-shaped cupola; beside it rose another turret with a gold cupola, and then a cluster of five turrets and five domes together, while to the left stood a lofty slender bell tower, then the rosy fortress-like walls of a monastery, also topped by turrets, and farther, more and more bell towers rising from the rye. They straggled in a long line, so that the eye could not catch them all at once and we had to turn our heads left and right. The sky over them had turned quite blue, and so, apart from half tones, the fairy-like picture was composed of three fundamental colors: the green-gold of the rye field, the rich blue background of the sky, and the gleaming white of the many Suzdal churches. . . .

From the twenty-seventh to the thirtieth day: . . . So we stopped in Suzdal. It is generally thought that a city must have outskirts; that it normally possesses a railway station; that it can hardly exist without some sort of a factory or industry. Suzdal has none of these.

Without factory stacks, without a railroad, without large city buildings, Suzdal hides among the cornfields of the Vladimir *opole*[1] region. The turrets and bulbs of the churches can be glimpsed among the rye. Grainfields surround the city, advancing upon its outer houses as in the approaches to a village. And the meadows that push on beside the Kamenka river burst right into the heart of the city.

Aside from the main street you will now and again find lanes overgrown with grass. Where you might expect sidewalks winds a narrow

13

track hemmed in by green. . . . The short lanes abut as a rule upon the wall of a monastery or a church. Because of this you remember them as quiet dead ends. The windows have carved frames; on the window sills are flowers, flowers, endlessly. Nearly every house has its vegetable and its flower garden, and the enclosures in front look like baskets full of lilac.

Some of the main streets are paved, others are being paved now. The city has been decreed a national reserve and is preparing to receive numerous tourists.

It is said that there are fifty-eight churches in Suzdal, and since the city is small, they are all compactly clustered together. . . .

Suzdal is older than a number of Russian cities; Vladimir for instance, to say nothing of Moscow. We do not know when it first arose, just as we do not know why it is called Suzdal. The Slavophil conjecture that the name comes from the word *sudit, osuzhdat, rassuzhdat* (to judge, to reason), is of course a beautiful dream. On sober consideration, we must admit that Suzdal is a word of pre-Slavic origin, like the names of the Nerl, which flows near by, and the Klyazma. Like these, the word Suzdal has not been deciphered and its meaning eludes us.

However, if we cannot shed light on this question, a more important one is quite clear to us: why it was here that the city first arose and later grew to be the capital of a vast principality.

If you have imagination, and no doubt you do, you can rise with me to a certain height and from there cast a look at the lands of central Russia. Among sandy infertile soils which provide nourishment to dense forests lies a small wedge of black soil. Its origin is obscure. Well, Suzdal is the center, the capital of this fertile land surrounded by forests.

On the other hand, by rising higher still, we shall see that Suzdal does not lie away from the main trade roads, but right on a busy, brisk traffic route. Now of course it has been by-passed; the trade routes have changed; but earlier, there were two such roads: one from Novgorod to the Black Sea, the other from Novgorod to the Caspian. Suzdal arose on the latter.

Where we now see fine yellow water lilies, flowed the river Kamenka, deep enough for the merchants' skiffs to sail on. Four versts off, the Kamenka joins the Nerl. The Nerl takes its waters to the Klyazma, the Klyazma to the Oka, the Oka to the Volga. And there, in a blue haze, already glimmers the legendary East of incense, carpets, spices, and all the luxuries.

Where the Volga-Don canal now is there was a portage to the Dniepr, and there, in a blue haze, glimmer oversea lands—Byzantium, Venice, Arabia. This is why excavations in the black soil of Suzdal bring to light Persian, Indian, Arabian coins.

Suzdal arose in pagan times. Right ahead of us we see a hill with a church on top. This is no ordinary hill; in pagan days it was named "the Fair Hill." It thawed earlier than other places, and for this reason the Suzdalians of old gathered there in the sun to celebrate the *yariliny*[2] or love

14

games. On the other hill to the right, where now you can see clearly the brick structure of a school, games were acted in honor of another god. Other peoples call him Bacch, Dionysos, Bacchus, but among the Suzdalians he went by the simpler name of Oblupa. Oblupa was honored with drinking and rejoicing.

Christianity, when it came from Kiev, did not take root in Suzdal immediately or peacefully. We know of a sorcerers' uprising. The first mention of Suzdal in the old chronicles is connected with that uprising which took place in 1024.

Vladimir Monomakh[3] came to quell the rebellion, and at the same time he had the church of the Nativity of the Virgin erected. But the builders were southerners, Kiev men; they did not allow for the frosts and dampness of the northern climate; they laid light foundations and the church collapsed.

However, it was restored. We are now entering it. Recently excavations reached Vladimir Monomakh's pavement, which now lies two meters and ninety-six centimeters deep. . . .

When Suzdal was a flourishing and powerful city, to the west, in deep forests, the smoke of a dozen chimneys rose from the little village of Moscow. . . .

The doors of the church, bound with bronze, black as coal, glimmered with gold ornament. This is the famous gold foil, which is laid once for all time. The doors have survived the Batyi ravages, and this was deemed to be a church miracle.

"Look here," our guide nodded at the lower corner of the doors, "I walked by here for twenty years, and one day I decided—Let's clean it! I cleaned a corner, and there was Samson tearing open the lion's jaws." Pure Byzantium! The walls of the church are painted with religious subjects. The outer layer has no interest, explained our guide. But under the paintings, if you clean them off, are frescoes of the seventeenth century, and if you clean those off, you find the decorations of Monomakh's time.

A fresco, of course, must be laid on the damp plaster. It has to be painted in four hours, before the plaster dries. Some artists used to outline their drawing first with a nail. And our guide showed us circles outlined in the plaster; in one place a number were scratched haphazardly: the artist couldn't manage to find the center.

"Was he inexperienced?" we wondered.

"In his cups, I'd say. That's why he spoiled the plaster. Rublev[4] painted straight away, without any nails.[5] That was a master!"

—"Vladimirskie proselki," *Novy mir*, Vol. X (1957)

NOTES: [1]The eastern part of the plain *(pole)* between the Koloksha and Nerl rivers, south of Suzdal.

[2]From Yarilo, the sun god.

[3]Vladimir Monomakh reigned in Kiev from 1113 to 1125.

[4]Andrey Rublev (1360?–1430): the greatest Russian icon painter, a monk of the Troitsa and of the Andronicus monasteries. His greatest work, "The Trinity," is now in the Tretyakov gallery in Moscow.

[5]The Russian phrase "no nails" still means "without fuss or complications."

■ ■ ■

THREE DECREES ON THE BUILDING OF PETERSBURG—1714

Peter the Great

■ ■ ■ 1. On the City island and the Admiralty island in Saint Petersburg, as likewise on the banks of the greater Neva and its more important arms, wooden buildings are forbidden, only adobe houses being allowed. The two above-mentioned islands and the embankments excepted, wood may be used for building, the plans to be obtained from the architect Trezzini.[1] The roofs are to be covered either with two thicknesses of turf laid on rafters with cross ribs (not on laths or boards), or with tiles. No other roof covering is allowed under penalty of severe fines. The streets should be bordered directly by the houses, not with fences or stables.

2. The most illustrious and mighty Peter the Great, Emperor and Autocrat of all Russia, has commanded his imperial decree to be proclaimed to people of all ranks. Whereas stone construction here is advancing very slowly, it being difficult to obtain stonemasons and other artisans of this craft even for good pay; for this reason all stone buildings of any description are forbidden in the whole state for a few years, until construction has sufficiently progressed here, under penalty of confiscation of the offender's property and exile. This decree is to be announced in all the cities and districts of the Saint Petersburg province, except this city, so that none may plead ignorance as an excuse.

3. The following is ordered: no building shall be undertaken in Petersburg on the grounds of houses, between neighboring back yards, until all the main and side streets are entirely built up. However, if after this any person needs more buildings, he may build on his grounds, along the neighbor's lot. No stables or barns may be built facing the street, but only inside the grounds. Along the streets and side streets all the space must be filled by residences, as ordered. In the locations where, as ordered by

16

previous decrees, wooden houses may be built, they must be made of squared logs. If the logs are used as they are, the walls must be faced with boards and coated with red, or painted to look like brick.

—I. Grabar, *Istoriya russkogo iskusstva* (Moscow, 1909)

NOTES: [1]A Swiss-Italian architect who came to Russia in 1703 and stayed thirty years. For the first nine years he ruled practically alone, until architects from various other countries came in ever greater numbers.

■ ■ ■

DESCRIPTION OF THE NEW CAPITAL—1720
Member of the Polish Embassy

An extract from the notes of a member of the Polish Embassy in Petersburg.

■ ■ ■ To describe Petersburg properly, one should have been here before its foundation and have seen, as it then appeared, the site where now stands a large stone city. The several arms of the Neva, a wide and deep river, flow across it. The city is intersected by broad canals along whose banks it has spread regularly.

I am informed that fifteen hovels, the homes of Swedish fishermen, used to stand here. When Muscovy took over this region, the village was burnt, and the Tsar had a small house of two rooms built for his own residence.[1] This house is still standing, with a tile roof, but no windows; for better preservation it is surrounded by a fence. It is situated on the riverbank, between the Senate and the Gagarin Palace. There the Tsar drew the plans for the city, had the river's banks, its arms, and the canals surveyed. The city is large already, and if the Tsar lives a few years more, he will extend it tremendously. On the far side of the river, on the way to the monastery,[2] there used to be a small fort at which ships sailing from Muscovy through Ladoga would stop before reaching the open sea. This fort has been wrecked, and in its place are izbas of medium size and windmills. Many people are building there now.

. . . Near Petersburg, the Tsar has reinforced the riverbanks, built dams and locks, had canals dug, so that the excess of water driven by a storm from the sea may find an exit: had this not been done, the waves

17

would flood the buildings. There are boardwalks over the locks, and it is possible to ride across them. The bed of the Neva broadens as it nears the sea, and it separates into several arms which flow in different directions. Piles are now being driven along those arms; their banks are aligned and their beds broadened, evened, and deepened when necessary for ships to accost.

The city stretches over a huge area. Each senator, state minister, and boyar is obliged to have a palace here; some were ordered to build three. Those who were allotted a dry site were lucky; but the poor fellow who was assigned a boggy swampy place had to sweat before the foundations could be laid and the trees cleared, since the nearer the sea, the lower and marshier the soil. Even now, though the houses are completed, they still shake whenever a carriage drives by, owing to weak foundations. The area has a city look already: there are houses, locks, and enormous edifices with annexes and all conveniences. Farther off, toward Kronstadt, there is still a vast open space where people are starting to build and where a few thousand commoners have already settled right by the sea.

Petersburg has churches, offices, palaces, and shops where everything can be obtained; these shops are to be found in a square building, on either side of which live the merchants. The palaces are huge edifices of stone, with annexes, kitchens, and all conveniences; but they were built so hurriedly that the tiles fall off at the least wind. This is probably due to poor material—or perhaps the work was done in winter, since summer is very brief in these parts. Half the city is still unbuilt.

On this side of the Neva, the river is bordered by houses that stretch right up to the Tsar's palaces. There are three of these: two for summer and one for winter. The gardens are beautiful. The Tsar himself has told us: "If I live three more years, I'll have a finer garden than the French king at Versailles." Indeed, a number of marble statues have been brought here by sea from Venice, Italy, England, and Holland; a whole summerhouse of alabaster and marble was even brought from Venice for the garden that is laid out between canals on the riverbanks.[3] You can see many remarkable things there: arbors, galleries, fountains, and amazingly fine trees. A stone wall encloses the garden on the river side; galleries lead to the river, on which you can take a boat or galley or yacht for a trip to the sea or along the canals and the broad river.[4] In the river is an island on which they are erecting buildings to which the Kunstkamera[5] will be transferred.

—*Russkaya starina*, Vol. VI (1879)

18

NOTES: [1]Peter's house is still one of the historic sights of Leningrad. It is an izba-style wooden house, with its walls patterned to imitate brick.
[2]The Alexander Nevsky Monastery.
[3]This is the Summer Garden in Petersburg.

⁴Peter took measures to encourage the love of life on the water among the residents of his new capital. Each house owner had to have a boat, keep it in good repair, and take part regularly in water parades and parties, under penalty of fines.

⁵The Kunstkamera, which first housed the freaks and monsters for which Peter had a passion, later became a museum and library which were ultimately taken over by the Academy.

■ ■ ■

MOSCOW IN THE MIDDLE OF THE EIGHTEENTH CENTURY

I. E. Zabelin

I. E. Zabelin (1820–1908), a self-taught student of Russian life and manners, was one of the founders of the Historical Museum in Moscow. He wrote several important works on Russian history.

■ ■ ■ In the middle of the eighteenth century many things in Moscow were still reminiscent of Alexey Mikhailovich's[1] times. The past was preserved not only in the physical aspect of the city, but also in the social and family ways of the inhabitants, in their lives and habits. Peter the Great's reforms, energetic as they had been, especially at first, in relation to Moscow, had yet been unable to change its ancient character to any great extent. For nearly three hundred years Moscow had lived an independent life, it had gathered all Russia into one, it had "governed and ruled" the land, it had elaborated in toil and sweat its own system in which it had become rooted with the passage of time, and had assumed the title of oldest sovereign city. The lines along which it had grown had not been drawn by chain and compass, but by life itself, freely and spaciously. For this reason, Peter the Great's wish to give his ancient capital a European appearance met obstacles at nearly every step.

If by comparison with Petersburg the Moscow of our days reveals many original, spacious, even rustic traits, one can easily imagine what it was a hundred years ago. It was essentially a village-like city; wood was not only the material for most of the houses, it also served to pave the causeways. The streets were irregular, either too broad, like open squares, or too narrow, making it difficult for two carriages to pass each other. There were many dead ends. The greater number of the houses were ordinary peasant izbas, large and small, which not only were unpainted, but frequently were "black," that is with no smokestacks, or with wooden smokestacks, and roofed with boards and laths or even, in the carriers' districts and in the outskirts,

19

with thatch (it was only in 1753 that this was strictly forbidden). Under the windows of such shacks you could nearly always find an earth-bank or a bench, which played quite a part in the social life of Moscow's common people. On holidays they would come out at the gates, onto the street, to sit and talk with the neighbors on those earth-banks, eat nuts, observe the passers-by, and generally have a good time. This is still done in many remoter districts of Moscow. Such shacks and izbas generally stood flush with the street, as in villages, and sometimes they were built close together. In contrast, all buildings of some importance, such as the residences of substantial and wealthy people, were concealed deep in the courtyards, so that fences stretched endlessly along some streets, broken at rare intervals by gates which still kept their ancient architecture; that is, they were covered by small ridged roofs under which a small icon or a bronze cross was nearly always fixed. Sometimes the groups of buildings were separated by huge spaces: pleasure or vegetable gardens, wastelands, meadows, ponds, and so forth; all this was protected by palings or twig-fences, while some areas remained open, and strict measures were sometimes needed to compel the owners to enclose their property. The open spaces were finally confiscated. Elsewhere, even in the center of the city, along the course of the Neglinnaya,[2] where now are the Trubny Boulevard, the Kuznetsky Bridge, the beautiful Theater Square, and the Kreml' gardens, there still existed long, nearly impassable stretches of mud and bog, always full of refuse, dung, and filth of all kinds. This was true also for the ditches near the Kreml' gardens and the vicinity of the Kitay-Gorod[3] walls. Many old inhabitants who lived in Moscow before 1812 still remember this. In the streets themselves, especially in the remoter districts, there were perpetual puddles, the haunts of geese, ducks, and other domestic fowl. Only the larger carriage-streets were paved with stones, many being still covered in the old manner with wooden logs or fascines, while most were not paved at all. The mud of Moscow streets, turning with time into rich black soil, made excellent fertilizer; several hundred carts of this soil were used every year for the tsar's gardens. One must read extensively the decrees and various edicts on this subject to realize the efforts and constant concern of the government to maintain some cleanliness in the city. Indeed, all Moscow had a picturesque country look which only faintly resembled a city as we understand it. We have not yet spoken of stone buildings; but, apart from churches (and not all of these, since some were built of wood) and the city walls and towers, stone buildings were very few. They all belonged to the state or to eminent or wealthy persons, and they generally stood deep in large grounds used for annexes, gardens, and the various appurtenances of a spacious gentry life.

20   Compared with the little one-story wooden houses around them, these residences looked like country manors in the midst of a village population, so that in this respect Moscow resembled a cluster of villages and hamlets. And indeed, even according to the official evidence of *The Descrip-*

tion of the Plague in 1770–1772, there were then in Moscow "many houses of the nobility that by their plan, spaciousness, and the great and excessive number of servants, constituted, rather than city establishments, whole villages where lived a self-contained population of commoners of various conditions and trades."

—*Opyty izucheniya russkikh drevnostey i istorii* (Moscow, 1873)

NOTES: [1]Alexey Mikhailovich reigned from 1645 to 1676. Peter the Great was his son.
          [2]Tributary of the Moskva river, now running in a tunnel under the street of the same name.
          [3]The district of Moscow east of the Kreml', along the river. It was surrounded by stone walls in the sixteenth century.

■ ■ ■

A PROVINCIAL TOWN IN
THE EARLY NINETEENTH CENTURY
F. F. Vigel

> F. F. Vigel (1786–1856), a talented but embittered man, described Russian life and manners of the first third of the nineteenth century in his *Memoirs* (1863–65). He knew most of the personalities of his time and has given some excellent portraits of writers and politicians.

■ ■ ■ On the very crown of the high hill on which Penza[1] is built, higher than the main square on which stand the cathedral, the Governor's house, and the official buildings, runs a street called Nobility Street. Not a single shop, not a single merchant's house could be seen there. It was embellished by rather low wooden structures, generally with nine little windows, each house standing by itself, the residences of the aristocracy. There the landowning nobility lived exactly as they did during the summer in the country, where their manorial halls were likewise separated from the formal gardens by broad long yards, where the entrance to those gardens was also to be found between stables, sheds, and the cow house, and had to be negotiated among piles of manure and rubbish and puddles of slops. One may judge, from this description, that the gardens were infrequently visited: innocent and peaceful pleasures were still unknown here, no need for fresh air was felt, nature was not yet an object of admiration.

21

By describing the inside of one such house, whether in town or country, I can give an idea of all others, so similar were they. A few stairs usually led to a kind of lean-to, made of boards, half of which, again divided in two, was occupied by two *buen-retiros:* the masters' and the servants'. Holding my nose, I hasten by and enter the vestibule, where I am greeted by another kind of smell. A crowd of servants fills it, all in rags, all moulting; some lie on a bench, others—standing or sitting—chatter foolishly, laugh, or yawn. On a table in a corner a coat or trousers are being cut, sewn, or mended; in another corner boots are being soled or tarred. The smell of onion, garlic, and cabbage mingles with the other emanations of this lazy and frivolous breed. The vestibule is followed by an enfilade of three rooms: a reception room (which also serves as dining room) with four windows, a drawing room with three, and a sofa room or boudoir with two. These make up the front of the house, and here the air is purer. The bedroom, dressing room, and maids' room look out on the yard, and the children's rooms are upstairs. The study, situated beside the pantry, is inferior to the latter in size, but in spite of its humble proportions it still seems too spacious for the master's learned occupations and the keeping of his books.

The decoration of the rooms was also nearly the same everywhere. The reception room was furnished with cane-bottom chairs and folding card tables; the drawing room was adorned with a crystal chandelier and two mirrors between the windows, with stands of painted wood. By the wall, which was merely painted, stood a large settee of the same wood flanked by two smaller ones; in between, armchairs were arranged in orderly fashion. In the sofa room, there was of course a corner sofa. The aspect of the furniture revealed the thrift of the owners, nothing more; the chintz or faded morocco leather upholstery being preserved by thick linen covers. Neither imagination, nor taste, nor money were then expended on interior decoration.

When a formal dinner was given, the men crowded around the set dinner table in the reception room; the ladies, the middle-aged and honored guests, and the card players occupied the drawing room, while the young ladies found a shelter in the gynaeceum or boudoir. Each entering lady had to run the gauntlet of the guests, offering her hand right and left to the standing men and kissing them on the cheek; each man was expected to go to the drawing room and greet all the sitting ladies, kissing each one's hand. At the table several cold dishes followed by several hot ones were served first, then roasts and pies appeared in turn (with the inevitable two white and two red sauces), dividing the dinner in two. A strange custom was the obligation for the servants to call each guest by name as they served food and drink.

On the whole, Penza, like China, though not very courteous, was exceedingly ceremonious; its etiquette was sometimes a torture. The ladies never drove in their equipages or "chariots" without two flunkies behind; the civil servants of field-officer rank jealously cherished the right to drive

22

a four-in-hand, while a state counsellor[2] never drove out with fewer than six nags harnessed in tandem.[3] It sometimes happened, if his gate was situated near his neighbor's, that the first postilion was already in front of the porch of the next house while the master had not yet left his own yard. With Alexander's accession to the throne, ladies everywhere stopped powdering their hair; only in Penza did many of them persevere in this custom. The fair sex in Penza was distinguished neither by elegance of form or costume, nor by attractiveness of features. Only in the first days of my stay, during Carnival, did I glimpse two beauties who appeared like fugitive visions;[4] one, the wife of General Lvov, born Kolokoltseva, was just passing through; the other, Mrs. Beketova, born Opochinina, lived three quarters of the year in her Saratov village, and her demure virtue often resembled austerity.

—Zapiski (Moscow, 1928)

NOTES: [1]Penza was founded in 1666 as a military-administrative center. It became the provincial capital in 1801.

[2]The fifth rank (from the top) of the fourteen in the Table of Ranks instituted by Peter in 1722, corresponding to brigadier in the army. The ranks rose from the fourteenth (collegiate registrar or third lieutenant) through the eighth (collegiate assessor—major), which granted hereditary nobility, to the first and highest (chancellor or field marshal).

[3]Cf. the anecdote told by Vigel about a Moscow lady who asked an English traveler what "chin" (rank) Pitt had. He could not answer. The lady then asked: "How many horses does he harness to his carriage?" "Two, generally." "Well, that's a fine country, in which the Premier is only a captain!"

[4]Allusion to a poem by Pushkin: "I remember that wonderful moment."

■ ■ ■

PENZA IN 1824
Official Report

■ ■ ■ The city of Penza[1] contains:

Churches, 10; monasteries, 2.

Public buildings: (a) 2 official government buildings, a post office; (b) the police station; (c) 3 inns; (d) the City Hall; (e) the Bishop's Palace; (f) the Governor's House; (g) the Nobility Hall; (h) the secondary school; (i) the Seminary; (j) the district school; (k) the Hospital of Public Welfare Administration; (l) the asylum for the insane, with a house for working patients and one for the violent; (m) the storehouse; (n) the prison; (o) the public park; (p) the gardening school.

23

Private buildings: (a) stone houses, 60; (b) wooden houses, 2,257; (c) inns, 2.

Population: male, 3,490; female, 3,652; in the suburbs: male, 1,536; female, 1,829.

Soap and leather manufactures, 7.

Commerce is insignificant, due to the geographical location and the difficulties of shipping. The occupations of the inhabitants consist in the sale of products from the above-mentioned manufactures and in retail trade. The province of Penza has two chief resources: agriculture and alcohol distilleries. The most noteworthy of the industrial enterprises are the crystal works of the landowner Bakhmetev.

—V. S. Nechaeva, *V. G. Belinsky* (Akademiya nauk: 1949), chap. vii

NOTES: [1]This report was written in preparation for the visit to Penza of Alexander I. A report of 1830 gives the male population as 7,562, the female as 6,053, among whom were 676 members of the nobility and administration, 108 merchants, 1,169 artisans, 422 commoners, the others being presumably peasants. The number of stone houses was given as 71, with 2,095 wooden houses.

■ ■ ■

2

**MANNERS
AND
SOCIETY**

Many foreign observers in the sixteenth and seventeenth centuries remarked on the rigorous formality of manners in the Russian official world. The pomp of court etiquette, the strict observance of precedence, impressed even those westerners who were familiar with the elaborate ritual practised in Louis XIV's court. They could not, generally, pursue their observations into the details of address and behavior for which a knowledge of the language and an introduction to the life of the masses would have been necessary. Inevitably their reports are restricted and superficial. However, study of the Russian documents and literature of the same period frequently confirms the travelers' tales. Even this evidence cannot be taken at face value: the sixteenth-century "Household Book," *The Domostroy*, presents an ideal rather than a mirror, and G. K. Kotoshikhin's report in the seventeenth century may have been tainted by prejudice. Indications gleaned from other texts add useful correctives to these official documents. In them, we catch glimpses of individuals and behaviors that seem much nearer western European patterns. The sixteenth-century Moscow "dandy," upbraided by the Metropolitan Daniel for wearing tight red boots, keeping a pack of hounds, wearing silk next to his skin, dousing himself with perfume, shaving his face and using tweezers as if he envied women's looks, sounds familiarly like his English or French-Italianate contemporaries. Spontaneous human feeling may, infrequently, warm the picture. Individual friendships are hinted at in the coupling of names, like the icon painters Rublev and Daniel in the early fifteenth century or, earlier, the saints Sergy of Radonezh and Stefan of Perm; a folk tale tells tenderly of the love between a legendary prince Peter and the girl Fevronia; historical songs, like the song of the Kazan kingdom in the sixteenth century, speak of a widow's grief. No restraint or convention hinders the Archpriest Avvakum's expressions of burning human feeling. But, on the whole, literature, official or otherwise, has not preserved the memory of the softer, more human aspects of Moscow society during those periods. We can only guess at what undoubtedly lay behind the descriptions of ritualized upper-class behavior and the harsh rules proposed to Moscow society as the pattern for human relations.

The spirit of those rules was essentially of Byzantine heritage, interpreted and adapted by Russian churchmen. The Byzantine ideal put strong emphasis on the twin concepts of unity and power: God in his Heaven, the sovereign on his throne, the father in his family. It was natural that Moscow should look for its social code to the country that had given it Christianity. But the course of historical events no doubt fortified the trend. The time when family and societal customs were settling into a fixed pattern was also the time when the unifying and centralizing influence of Moscow was emerging as the overwhelming power in the Russian lands.

27

That relations between members of the family and society should mirror those between state and subjects was perhaps inevitable. Medieval society in the West undoubtedly shared the tendency. But there conflicts between Popes and kings, contacts and minglings between sister civilizations, finally the reciprocal cross-fertilization of feudal and Christian concepts, produced a complex whole in which closely blended elements depended on one another for their mutual development. The social "types" of western society in the Middle Ages and later—knight, clerk, courtly lover, lady, courtier, gentleman—evolved naturally within the frame of society. They were acknowledged in descriptive as well as in didactic literature, were an integral part of the consciousness of the social body, and changed as it did in answer to the demands of both the individual and society. Moscow, however, could not afford either the physical or spiritual leisure to develop such varying social types. Her forces were engrossed in the vital problems of power and unity, and she could accept nothing to distract from those aims. Thus, within the frame of Russian society, the only figure that emerges with distinct traits is that of the Russian and the Christian. Patriotism and faith define an individual in relation to his country and his God, not to his fellow men. Thus we have a vivid impression of the traveler Afanasy Nikitin, the Tver merchant, longing for his native land and disturbed by his lapses from Orthodox practice, but we do not see him as a member of a particular society or concerned with other individual members of that society.

The harsh, puritanical pattern of austerity, obedience, and fear imposed upon family and social relations by church conservatives was not more readily accepted than the concept of the autocratic, absolute power of the sovereign which the same clergy supported. "Foreign" manners repeatedly found their way in, to be repeatedly condemned. But gradually, with the reign of Alexey Mikhailovich, they gained a footing, first in the guise of material relaxation or comfort (toys, western furniture such as mirrors and armchairs) and through illustrated books, before long in more important ways. In 1648, Alexey sent his cities a writ forbidding all songs, dances, and minstrel shows, whether in the houses or out of doors. This was in the spirit of the Church's traditional attitude to all "lay" entertainment. The same Alexey in 1672 attended the *Comedy of Esther*, a play during which dancing and singing were performed on stage. Noblemen of his court had plays acted privately, and one, Matveev, who had married a Scotswoman, invited friends to his house for conversation, not for feasting, his wife remaining present at the gatherings!

28

But it was left to Alexey's son, Peter, to break the old frame. The freedom and ease of manner he forced upon a minority of Russians, both men and women, quickly spread after some initial resistance; and, at the end of the eighteenth century, the "Russian European" was the first social type that could be set beside the western gentleman. As for the Russian lady, emerging formidable from her isolation and obedience, her personality dominates the nineteenth-century Russian scene. Only among the merchants and peasants did the old code of wifely obedience and daughterly subservience survive, often maintained by a puritanical religious dissent or by the necessities of patriarchal and communal living in the village.

At the same time that he liberated Russian manners from the old ritual, Peter unwittingly introduced new patterns of restraint by setting up the Table of Ranks with its all-embracing hierarchy of service. But the climate of society had changed. No religious reference gave substance to the artificial precedence of "chin," and the arrogance of rank soon became food for satire.

29

INTERIOR OF AN IZBA IN THE NINETEENTH CENTURY
Drawing by V. Kiprianoff
From Valérien Kiprianoff, *Histoire pittoresque de l'architecture en Russie* (St. Petersburg, 1864)

THE WEDDING OF THE TSAR AND GRAND-PRINCE, MIKHAIL FEDOROVICH
Illustrated manuscript of the seventeenth century

"And the Tsar went to the Monastery of the Miracle to pray to Michael the Archangel, to the miracle-working Alexey the Metropolitan and to the Ascension of our Lord and the Most Holy Virgin in the Monastery; and the boyars and the lords of the Chamber and the Council and the nobles rode with him."

From *Tri veka*, ed. V. V. Kallash (Moscow, 1912), Vol. I

JOURNEY BEYOND THREE SEAS
Afanasy Nikitin

From Tver the rich,[1] in 1466, a caravan of merchants set off for
Derbent on the Caspian Sea. Various misadventures led one of
them, Afanasy, son of Nikita (we do not know his surname, if
indeed he had one), to Baku and then, by way of Persia and Arabia, to central India. He started back to Tver six years later by
way of the Black Sea, but died before reaching Smolensk.
Nikitin's notes on his wanderings, probably handed by a travel-
ing companion to a Moscow scribe, were later incorporated in
the Chronicles of the Trinity Monastery where, in the early
nineteenth century, they were found by the historian Karamzin.
The work is short, about twenty pages. After a brief relation of
his journey from Tver to Derbent, Afanasy Nikitin describes
what he saw in Persia, and, in more detail, India: its population,
customs, beliefs, resources, and government. The following is
an account of the beginning of his Journey and one of several
passages in which he bewails his solitude and uncertainty during his years in India.

■ ■ ■ For the prayers of our holy Fathers, Lord Jesus Christ, son of
God, have mercy on me, your sinful servant Afanasy, son of Nikita.[2] This
is the relation of my sinful journey beyond three seas: the first, the sea of
Derbent or sea of Khvalin; the second, the Indian sea or sea of Hindustan;
the third, the Black Sea or sea of Stambul.

With God's grace, I left the Holy gold-topped Savior,[3] Prince
Mikhail Borisovich,[4] and my Lord Bishop Gennady of Tver, and I sailed
down the Volga. After I reached Kalyazin, where I was blessed by Abbot
Makary and his brotherhood at the monastery of the holy life-giving
Trinity and the holy martyrs Boris and Gleb,[5] I continued my way to Uglich
and from Uglich to Kostroma, to Prince Alexander. And the Grand-Prince
of all Russia[6] gave me another pass and let me pursue my journey. So I
traveled on without hindrance to Pleso and Nizhny-Novgorod, where are
the Governor Mikhail Kiselev and the tax collector Ivan Saraev.

Vasily Papin[7] had already left, so I waited two more weeks in
Novgorod for Hassan-Bek, the Tatar envoy of the Shah of Shirvan. He was
taking back gerfalcons[8] from the Grand-Prince Ivan, ninety of them. I
traveled with him down the Volga. We went through Kazan, Orda,[9] Uslan,
Saray,[10] Berekezan, without any trouble.

And so we reached the river Buzan.[11] There we met three unclean Tatars who told us falsely that Khan Kassim was lying in wait for merchants on the Buzan, and with him three thousand Tatars. The Shah of

31

Shirvan's envoy, Hassan-Bek, gave them each a coat and a piece of linen so that they would guide us past Astrakhan. The Tatars took the coats, but they passed the news to the Astrakhan tsar. I had left my boat and, with my companions, joined the envoy on his boat. As we sailed by Astrakhan, the moon was shining. The tsar saw us, and the Tatars shouted "Kach'ma" (don't run). And then the tsar set all his horde after us and, for our sins, they caught us at Bugun;[12] they shot one of our men, but we shot two of theirs. Our smaller boat got caught in a fishing trap; they seized it and looted it at once; all my possessions were on that small boat.

We reached the sea in the large boat, but at the mouth of the Volga we were stranded in the shallows. There the Tatars caught us and brought the boat back to the fishing trap. Here they took our large boat and also kept four of the Russians. As for the rest, they let us go, destitute, out to sea. They did not allow us up the river again for fear we should inform against them.

And so we went to Derbent in two boats: in one, Hassan-Bek with Iranians and us Russians—ten of us; and in the other, six Moscow men and six men of Tver. A storm caught us at sea, the small boat broke on the shore, and the Kaytaki[13] captured the people in it.

When we reached Derbent, we found that Vasily had arrived safe, while we had been robbed. I then petitioned Vasily Papin and Hassan-Bek to do something for the people that the Kaytaki had caught off Tarki.[14] And Hassan-Bek did help: he went to Bulat-Bek on the mountain, and he sent a runner to the Shah of Shirvan with the message that a Russian ship was wrecked off Tarki and the goods plundered and the men captured by the Kaytaki. The Shah at once dispatched an envoy to his brother-in-law Halil-Bek, the Kaytak prince, with these words: "My boat was wrecked off Tarki and your people have captured the passengers and plundered the goods; for my sake send me those prisoners and collect their goods, because those people were sent to me. And whatever you require of me, send to me for it and I will do it for you, brother; but just set those people free for my sake." And Halil-Bek at once set all of them free and sent them to Derbent; from there they were sent on to the Shah at his encampment.

We went to the Shah's camp too and prayed him to grant us the wherewithal to get back to Russia. But he did not give us anything, for there were too many of us. And so we wept and went our different ways: if a man had means in Russia, he set off for home, but those who had debts at home just went off at random; others remained in Shemakha,[15] and others again went to work in Baku. For myself, I went to Derbent, and from Derbent to Baku, where burns an inextinguishable fire,[16] and from Baku across the sea to Chapakur.[17]

■ ■ ■

In the month of May I spent the Great Day (Easter) in heathen Bidar,[18] in Hindustan. The heathens had their feast of Bairam[19] in the middle of May; I began my fast on the first day of April. O pious Christians, a man who travels into distant lands falls into many sins, and the Christian faith is denied to him. I, Afanasy the servant of God, have borne much suffering in my faith: four great fasts and four Great Days have already gone by and I, sinner that I am, do not know when the Great Day or the fast comes. I don't know when it is Christmas or another holy day. I know neither Wednesday nor Friday.[20] And I have no books: when I was robbed, my books were taken too. My many misfortunes have brought me to India, for I had nothing to take to Russia, I had no goods left. The first Easter I spent in Kain,[21] the second in Chapakur in the Mazandaran country, the third in Ormuz and the fourth in Bidar in India with the heathens. Here I shed many tears for my Christian faith. . . .

The heathen Malik pressed me to take the heathen faith. I answered him: "Lord, you pray, and so do I; you say five prayers, I say three; I am a foreigner, you are a native." And he replied: "Truly, though you pretend not to be a Moslem, you are no Christian either." And on this I fell into many meditations and said to myself: Woe on me, a sinner, for I have strayed from the true path and know no other, I wander alone.[22] All-sustaining Lord God, Creator of Heaven and Earth, do not turn Thy face from Thy servant in his grief. Lord, comfort and pity me, for I am Thy creature; do not lead me astray, Lord, from the right path, but set me, Lord, on Thy true way, for in my need I have done no virtuous deed for Thee, my Lord, for I have spent my days in evil. Lord my God, Almighty God, protector, merciful, compassionate. Praise be to God! I have spent four Great Days already in the heathen land and have not forsaken Christianity; as for the future, God knows what will be. Lord my God, I trust in Thee, save me, Lord my God.[23]

—*Khozhenie za tri morya Afanasiya Nikitina*, ed. B. D. Grekov and V. P. Adrianova-Peretts (Moscow-Leningrad, 1948)

NOTES: [1]Tver the rich: (now Kalinin) capital of the small Tver principality along the upper Volga (1246-1486). The Tver territory, lying between Novgorod and Muscovite Russia, played an important role as a transit post. In the thirteenth and fourteenth centuries Tver was one of the largest Russian cities. It submitted to Moscow in 1486.

[2]Until the emergence of family names for all classes of the population, a commoner was usually designated by his first name and patronymic. Later, the patronymic frequently became the family name (thus, Petrov syn: son of Peter, becomes Petrov: Peterson).

[3]The cathedral church of Tver.

[4]Prince of Tver from 1461 to 1485.

[5]Sons of Vladimir of Kiev, Boris and Gleb were killed in 1015 at the instigation of their brother Svyatopolk and canonized in 1071. Many churches, monasteries, and cities were named in their honor.

[6]Ivan III of Moscow (1462-1505).

[7]Ambassador of Ivan III to the Shah of Shirvan, who ruled over a territory that included Baku and Derbent.

[8]One of the most common presents to Oriental princelings. Trade exchanges between Russia and the Orient then consisted chiefly of Russian arms, armor, furs, and so forth, in return for Eastern dyes, silks, precious stones, and spices.

[9]Orda (Horde): Mongol name for "encampment."

[10]There were two capitals of the "Golden Horde" bearing the name Saray, both on the lower Volga.

[11]Arm of the Volga just north of its delta and Astrakhan.

[12]Presumably one of the shallows in the Volga delta.

[13]Population of a region in western Daghestan.

[14]A fort on the western shore of the Caspian.

[15]A town in Shirvan (now Azerbaydzhan).

[16]Allusion to the oil wells of the region. Oil was already an object of exportation.

[17]On the southern shore of the Caspian.

[18]Old city in Deccan, conquered by the Moslems at the end of the thirteenth century, and an important trade center in the fifteenth century.

[19]Moslem celebration of Abraham's sacrifice of his son, Ishmael.

[20]See "The Church Against Superstitions," p. 76, note 5.

[21]Kain? Perhaps in Shirvan, or Nain in Iran?

[22]This passage, to the end of the paragraph, is written in Nikitin's Oriental medley, composed of distorted elements of the Turki language mixed with Arabic and Persian terms.

[23]The material in the notes has been gathered chiefly from the commentary in the Soviet edition of *Journey Beyond Three Seas*, ed. B. D. Grekov and V. P. Adrianova-Peretts (Moscow-Leningrad, 1948).

■ ■ ■

CODE OF FAMILY BEHAVIOR IN THE SIXTEENTH CENTURY

The Domostroy

34

The Domostroy or "Household Book," dating from the middle of the sixteenth century, was presumably compiled and in part composed by Sylvester, priest of the Annunciation Church in the Kreml' and adviser to Ivan IV. It is a set of rules, the first chapters of which are concerned with religion and morality, the remainder with everyday behavior in the family. Though it takes its inspiration from Byzantine and other sources and proposes an ideal instead of describing real family relations, its value is great because of its numerous details on life and manners, and because the spirit of *The Domostroy* survived for several centuries in old Russia, especially among the peasants, merchants, and Old Believers.

■ ■ ■ **How to instruct children and save them by fear:**—Punish your son in his early years and he will comfort you in your old age and be the ornament of your soul. Do not spare your child any beating, for the stick will not kill him, but will do him good; when you strike the body, you save the soul from death. . . . If you love your son, punish him often, so that he may later gladden your spirit. Punish your son in his youth, and when he is a man he will be your comfort and you will be praised among the wicked, and your enemies will envy you. Raise your child in fear and you will find peace and blessing in him. Do not smile with him, do not play with him, for having been weak in little things you will suffer in great ones, you will grieve and your teeth will be set on edge. Do not give him his will in his youth, but crush his ribs while he is not grown yet, or else he will harden and cease to obey you, and then there will be grief and vexation for your soul, a loss for your house, a waste of your possessions, blame from the neighbors; your enemies will laugh at you and you will have to pay fines to the authorities and endure bitter affliction.

How to keep your house clean and well-ordered: . . . In a good family, where the wife is careful, the house is always clean and well-arranged; everything is in order, put away in its right place, cleaned and swept. It's like going into paradise. All this is the wife's job; she must instruct the servants and children in friendly manner or in harsh: if words don't help, let blows do the job. But if the husband sees that wife and servants are careless and don't follow the rules set in this manual, he must teach his wife, reason with her and instruct her. If she complies and does everything as it should be done, she deserves love and favor; but if she fails to conform to precepts, to do the work and to teach the servants, let her husband discipline her and scare her in private; and after he should relent and speak kindly. Punishment must be given in love and with judgment. The husband should not be angry with his wife, nor she with him; but they should live in love and openness. Behave likewise with servants and children: punish their offenses, beat them for their faults, then relent. The lady must look after the servants with good judgment; they will then be encouraged. But if wife, son, or daughter pay no heed to word or instruction, if they will not listen, obey, and fear, if they refuse to do what they are told by father or mother, they should be whipped according to their offense. Beat them in private, not in public; punish, then relent and say a loving word. . . . In no circumstance should you beat on the ear or face or in the midriff with your fist or foot, nor strike with a stick or any wooden or metal instrument. Such blows struck in anger or rage may cause great harm: blindness, deafness, dislocation of arm or leg or finger, injury to head or teeth. The whip should be used wisely, in a sensible, painful, frightening, and profitable manner. When the offense is serious and deserving of anger, when there has been great disobedience or carelessness, take off the offender's shirt, hold his hands, and whip him calmly.

—*Russkaya khrestomatiya*, ed. F. Buslaev (Moscow, 1912)

■ ■ ■

RUSSIA IN THE REIGN OF ALEXEY MIKHAILOVICH
G. K. Kotoshikhin

Grigory Karpovich Kotoshikhin (1630?–67) was employed in the Office of Foreign Affairs under Alexey. Little is known about him. The main available facts are to be found in the introduction to the Swedish version of his book, *Russia in the Reign of Alexey Mikhailovich*. This work was written by Kotoshikhin in Sweden, at the instigation of the Swedish Chancellor, though it had probably been begun earlier. Kotoshikhin fled Russia in 1664, after being involved in disagreements with his superiors in Smolensk. He lived successively in Poland, Prussia (where he seems to have become a Lutheran), Lubeck, Narva, and Stockholm. He was beheaded in 1667 for killing his host, the royal translator, during a brawl.

The Swedish version of *Russia in the Reign of Alexey Mikhailovich* was found in Stockholm in 1837. The Russian text was discovered a year later at the University of Upsala by Professor Soloviev, who had also found the first manuscript. Its thirteen chapters deal chiefly with court life, administration, and customs. Though the picture they present seems somewhat prejudiced against the author's native country, it contains many relevant details.

Kotoshikhin writes the language used in government offices, clumsy, repetitious, and lifeless, but free of Slavisms and church usage.

ON THE TSARS, THE TSARITSAS, THE TSAR'S SONS AND DAUGHTERS, AND CELEBRATIONS FOR THE TSAR'S FUNERAL

■ ■ ■ 24. On the tsar's apartments. The tsar and tsaritsa have their separate apartments; the tsaritsa may sometimes be seen by the boyars and lords of the chamber, but rarely by common people. On the Lord's holidays, on Sundays, and during fasts, the tsar and tsaritsa sleep separately; when they are to spend the night together, the tsar sends for the tsaritsa to come to him, or he may wish to go to her himself. After a night together, the next morning, they go separately to the bathchamber or wash themselves

36

with water. Until they have done so, they do not enter a church or kiss the cross, for this is deemed impure and sinful, and is forbidden not only to the tsar and tsaritsa but also to the common people.

25. The tsar's sisters or daughters, the *tsarevny*, have their own private apartments, in which they live like nuns in a hermitage, rarely seeing people or being seen, but spending their days in prayer and fasting, and bathing their faces in tears, since, enjoying princely pleasures, they are deprived of those pleasures granted to man by Almighty God of joining together and procreating. It is not the custom to give them in marriage to princes and boyars of their own land, for these princes and boyars are thralls, signing themselves as such in their petitions,[1] and it is held an eternal disgrace to have a noble lady wed to her slave. Nor can they be married to kings' sons from other lands, for these are not of the same faith, and Russians must not change their faith or let it be put to scorn; also they do not know the language or the politics of other realms, and this would bring shame upon them.

29. The tsar's sons, in their early years, and the tsarevny, young or old, have cloth screens held on both sides of them when they go to church, so that none may look upon them; nor can anyone, save the churchmen, observe them inside the church, for there they are concealed by silk hangings; few persons, except boyars and lords of the chamber, attend church at that time. When they go on pilgrimage to the monasteries, their carriages also are closed with silk curtains. For the winter travel of the tsaritsa and tsarevny, little cabins, lined with red velvet or cloth, are fitted on sleighs; the doors on each side have mica shutters and silk curtains. In summer, they drive in coach-like vehicles, also screened with cloth, and entered by steps. . . .

32. On the demise and interment of tsars and their family: . . . When they arrive at the church, called by the name of Michael the Archangel,[2] where the tsars are interred, near the tsars' court, the deacons and priests remain outside, while the church dignitaries, the tsaritsa and the tsar's sons and daughters, with the boyars and other high lords, enter the church. The tsar's body is laid in the center of the church, near the altar, but not in the sanctuary proper; then the funeral service is sung and the tsar's body laid in the ground under a flagstone. The patriarch then reads a prayer and sprinkles incense over the *kutiya*.[3] This done, he eats three times of the kutiya with a spoon, and then the kutiya is presented to the tsaritsa and her sons and daughters, to the dignitaries and boyars and people of all ranks. After the funeral, all return home, no sermon having been given. During the ceremony, wax candles, plain and twisted, are given to people of all ranks to hold as the tsar is being interred; more than 400 pounds' weight are handed out on that occasion. . . .

For the tsar's funeral, all sorts of criminals are released from prison in Moscow and other cities. Woe to those who are present at the

37

funeral, for it takes place at night, and the city is crowded with people from Moscow itself as well as from other cities and regions. Now, the Muscovites have no fear of God; they rob men and women of their clothes on the streets and kill them; on the day of one tsar's interment, over a hundred people were found stabbed and dead.

When forty days have elapsed after the tsar's death, the dignitaries, the tsaritsa with the tsar's sons, and the boyars come to the same church to hear mass sung for the dead. After mass, a feast is served in the tsar's palace for the dignitaries, the boyars, and the priests; the lords of the chamber feed the monks in the monasteries and give them in alms half the sum they had distributed for the funeral. The money spent for the tsar's funeral in Moscow and in other cities is nearly as much as the government treasury receives in a year.

■ ■ ■

ON THE WAY OF LIFE OF THE BOYARS, LORDS OF THE CHAMBER AND THE COUNCIL, AND OTHER RANKS

■ ■ ■ 1. The boyars and lords of the chamber live in their wooden or stone houses, with few conveniences or comforts; they live in their private apartments with their wives and children. Some of the great boyars, though not many, have their own chapel in their grounds;[4] those who have no private chapel (these are boyars of high or medium rank), but who have permission to have chaplains in their house, have matins, hours, thanksgiving services, and vespers celebrated in their house, but they hear mass in their parish church or in the church of their choice; no mass is ever celebrated in a private house. The boyars and lords of the chamber give their chaplains yearly wages, by agreement, and the married priests receive monthly supplies of food and drink, while the widowers eat at table with the boyars.

2. On the Lord's holidays or other special days such as namedays, birthdays, and christenings, the boyars often feast with guests.

It is the custom to prepare food plainly, without seasoning; using no berries, sugar, pepper or ginger or other spices, and little salt and no vinegar. The food is set on the table one dish at a time; the other dishes being brought from the kitchen and presented by the servants; if any dish needs salt, vinegar or pepper, these are added at the table. There are from fifty to a hundred dishes.

The following custom is observed: the wives come out to greet the guests before dinner. The wives stand in the hall or room,[5] in the place of honor, while the guests stay near the door; the wives bow to the waist and the guests answer with deep bows to the ground. Then the master of the house bows to the guests and begs them to salute his wife: on their

38

entreaty he first kisses her himself; then the guests, one by one, bow deep to the wives of the family and salute them, bowing deep again after withdrawing a few steps, and the wife bows slightly to the guest who has kissed her. Then the host's wife offers each guest a cup of double or triple distilled vodka with herbs;[6] this cup contains about one fourth of a quarter-measure or a little more; then the host bows deep to each guest in turn, begging them to drink the vodka his wife is offering; the guests ask her to drink first, and the host with her; they do so and offer the vodka to the guests, who bow deep both before and after partaking of it. If any person does not drink vodka, he is offered Romanée or Rhenish wine,[7] or some other drink. When all have drunk, the host's wife bows to the company and withdraws to her rooms with her guests' wives. The ladies never have dinner with the men except at weddings, or only if the men are close kin, without any outsiders. In the same manner, during the meal, the hosts and guests drink a cup of vodka, or Romanée or Rhenish, and spiced or plain beers, and various meads, after each dish. When round pasties are brought to the table in the course of the meal, the sons' wives, or the married daughters, or the wives of kinsfolk come into the hall, and the guests arise and leave the table to bow to the ladies; then the husbands bow, begging the guests to kiss their wives and accept some wine from them; this done, the guests resume their seats and the wives go back where they came from. But unmarried daughters are never shown to the guests; they stay in special remote apartments. After the meal, the hosts and guests make merry and drink one another's healths, then they separate and go home. In the same fashion, the ladies dine and drink together, according to rank, in their own rooms; no member of the male sex visits them, only married women and girls.

3. If a boyar or lord of the chamber wishes to marry himself or marry off his son or brother or nephew (or daughter or sister or niece), he finds out who has a marriageable daughter and sends a messenger, male or female, to the girl's father or mother or brother. The messenger asks if they wish to give their daughter in marriage and inquires about the dowry she will receive in clothing, money, land, and servants. And if the father is willing, he answers that he will be glad to give her in marriage but will think it over with his wife and kin and will fix a day later. But if he is unwilling, knowing that the suitor is a drunkard or a wild fellow or has some other shortcoming, he answers that he cannot give her to such a man, or finds some pretext for refusal.

If he decides to accept and his wife and kin agree, he prepares a list of the girl's dowry—money, silver and other vessels, clothing, land, and servants—and sends it to the suitor's messengers; these hand it to the suitor, but the girl is not informed and knows nothing until her marriage. If the dowry is satisfactory, the suitor sends the same messengers back to her parents, asking to see the girl. To this the father or mother answers that

39

they will be glad to show their daughter, only not to the suitor himself, but to his father or mother or sister, or to some woman of the family that he trusts. Then the suitor sends someone to see the bride on the day assigned; and her parents prepare for that day, attiring the girl in good clothes, calling kinsfolk as guests, and seating the girl at the table. Then, when the emissary arrives, she is welcomed and seated beside the bride; and as she sits by her, during the meal, she talks to her about all sorts of things in order to acquaint herself with her mind and speech; she scrutinizes her face, eyes, and features for reporting to the suitor. Then, after staying a shorter or longer period, she goes to him with her information. If the girl did not satisfy the observer, she tells the suitor to give her up, because she has noticed that the girl is stupid, or ugly, or weak in her eyes, or lame, or with some speech defect; and upon this the suitor stops bidding for the girl. But if the observer likes the girl and tells the suitor that she is pleasant and sensible, not wanting in speech or anything else, the suitor sends to her mother and father the previous messengers to say that he is pleased and wishes to come to an agreement with them by signing a contract to have the wedding on an assigned date. Then the girl's parents ask the suitor, through his messengers, to come and see them with a few persons that he trusts, on an appointed day, before or after dinner. On that day, the suitor, with his father or kinsfolk or such friends as he wishes, comes to the bride's house, where the bride's father and kin greet him with due honor. They seat themselves in the reception rooms, according to established order; after a while, the suitor's father or some other relation, speaking for the suitor, says that they have come, as required, for a good understanding, upon which the master of the house answers that he is glad to see them and wishes to settle the matter. Both sides then start to discuss various wedding arrangements and set a wedding date acceptable to all, a week or a month ahead, or half a year, or a year or more. They sign their names in the contract, writing the date agreed on. The contract has a clause stipulating that if the suitor refuses the girl or her father does not give her at the stated time, the offender will pay 1,000 or 5,000 or 10,000 rubles, whatever is written in the article. After eating and drinking, the suitor goes home without having seen his bride or having been seen by her. But during his visit, the mother or a married sister, or some woman of the family, comes to greet him and presents him with a cloth from the bride.

4. It may happen that after this agreement the suitor learns (or another man, wishing to have the girl himself or for his son, will malign her on purpose to the suitor) that his bride is no longer pure, or is deaf, dumb, or crippled, or has some other defect, whether true or rumored. If the suitor then refuses the girl, her father and mother appeal to the Patriarch, saying that he has not taken the girl at the stated time and refuses to marry her, thus shaming her. Or the girl's parents may hear that the suitor is a drunkard, or a gambler, or evil-favored, or has some other failing, and

refuse to give him their daughter, whereupon the suitor appeals to the Patriarch. The latter orders an inquiry, and the offender is made to pay to the claimant the fine stated in the contract. After this, each of them is free to marry whom he or she wishes.

5. If both parties fulfill their obligations, they prepare to have the wedding at the appointed date. The suitor invites kinsfolk and friends to be members of the celebration or honored guests;[8] the same is done on the bride's side. On the wedding day, a feast is set at the bridegroom's and the bride's houses, and the bridegroom is advised when it is time for him to fetch his bride. The wedding procession forms: first the bread-bearers, with loaves on a litter, then the priest with the cross, the boyars, the first groomsman and the bridegroom, all on horseback in summer and in sleighs in winter. They reach the bride's house, enter the rooms, each according to rank, and are welcomed with due honor by the bride's father and his guests. . . . When the time comes to go to the church for the wedding ceremony, the groomsmen ask the bride's parents to give the couple their blessing. This the parents do, both in words and with the icons, after which they take their daughter by the hand and give her to the bridegroom. The wedding procession, with the priest, and the bridegroom and bride hand in hand, then leaves the rooms; the bride's parents and guests accompany them to the gate, where the bridegroom places his bride in a carriage, and he himself on horseback or in a sleigh; with the whole wedding cortege, they make their way to the church for the ceremony. Meanwhile, the parents and guests eat and drink until they hear from the bridegroom: no one accompanies the bride save one of her go-betweens and one of the bridegroom's. After the wedding ceremony, the whole cortege returns to the house of the bridegroom, who sends ahead to inform his father that they were wedded in good health. On their arrival, they are met by the bridegroom's parents, and these, or the wedding sponsors, bless the couple with the icons and offer them bread and salt. Then all sit down at table according to established order and begin to eat. The bride is now unveiled. After the third dish, the groomsmen ask the parents to give the newlyweds permission to go to their chamber. The parents give their blessing, and after taking the couple to their room, all start eating and drinking as before. When the bridegroom and bride are in their chamber, the groomsmen undress the bridegroom and the go-betweens the bride; they put them to bed and go back to the table. After a whole hour has gone by, the parents and best man send a groomsman to inquire about the couple's health. The bridegroom informs them that they are in good health, and the boyars' wives then come to the chamber to congratulate them and drink their health. Meanwhile the best man sends a message to the bride's parents. These welcome the messenger and present him with a cloth for his good news, after which the guests at the bride's house depart. The women in the bridegroom's chamber also leave his apartments, the newlyweds return to their rest, and all the guests leave.

41

6. The next morning, the bridegroom and bride go to the bathhouse. After this the bridegroom and a groomsman call guests to dinner, both his and the bride's friends. At the bride's house, he thanks her parents for having nurtured and brought up his bride; but if the bride came to him without having preserved her purity, he reproaches them privately. When the guests have gathered, the bride presents gifts to the wedding party. Before dinner, the bridegroom and all the cortege go to pay their respects to the tsar. As they enter, they bow deep to the tsar, who receives them seated and hatted. The tsar inquires about the couple's health; then the bridegroom bows to the ground, and the tsar congratulates the couple on their union and blesses them with precious icons.[9] He also makes them each a present of 40 ermines, pieces of velvet, satin and gold brocade for clothes, and pieces of ordinary satin, patterned silk and taffetas, also vessels of silver weighing each one pound and a half, and two other vessels. The bride is not present at this visit. The tsar offers the best man, the bridegroom, and the whole cortege cups of Romanée wine and jugs of cherry mead; when they have drunk they are given leave to go. On arriving home, everybody starts feasting; after the feast, the parents and guests bless the couple with icons and present them with gifts, and then depart. The next day, the couple and guests eat at the bride's house with the bride's parents and guests, who present them with gifts; this is the end of the celebration.[10]

But if the bride had not kept her purity, the bridegroom, after knowing her, will not go to bow to the tsar, for the tsar will be informed already and will refuse to have him admitted to his eyes.

While the bridegroom is with the tsar, the bride sends her own presents to the tsaritsa and her daughters: taffeta kerchiefs, embroidered with gold, silver, and pearls. The tsaritsa and her daughters accept the presents and send a messenger to inquire about the bride's health.

During all the festivities, there are neither girls nor music, except for trumpets and tambourines.

The same ceremonial is observed for the wedding of a widowed daughter, or of a sister or niece.

7. While the preparations for the wedding are taking place, the priest who is to celebrate the wedding receives from the Patriarch and dignitaries a writ to perform the ceremony after making sure that the bridegroom and bride are not related by having been godfather and godmother to the same child, or godson and goddaughter to the same godparents, or go-betweens for the same marriage, and are not kin to the sixth or seventh degree, and that neither has been married three times before.[11] If any of these facts are discovered, the priest is forbidden to perform the wedding. And if, through ignorance or disobedience, he does wed them, he will be unfrocked; moreover, if he was aware of his offense, he will also have to pay a heavy fine and undergo penance for a year. But the bride and bridegroom are merely separated; their marriage is held as a sin and they marry again if they have not been wed three times before.

8. If a widower wishes to marry for the second time, and his bride is a maid, the wedding ceremony follows the same order, but at church the wedding crown is held on the widower's right shoulder, while his bride's is held over her head; if the widower is marrying for the third time, the ceremonies are the same, except that the crown is held over his left shoulder. This is done also in the case of a widow marrying for the second or third time. But if widower and widow marry, there is no ceremony: only a prayer is said, nor are their wedding festivities the same as for other persons.

9. Ceremonies for betrothals and weddings follow the same order as described for the various ranks of boyars and nobility, according to each man's means; except that only lords of the council, chamberlains and their children, and persons of the highest families go to pay their respects to the tsar.

Merchants' and peasants' weddings also follow the same ceremonial in all things; the only difference is in the clothing and behavior, according to their degree and means.

Each man lives in his house, according to his rank and degree, without great comfort. The lowest ranks cannot afford to build fine houses, because this would make people believe that they are very wealthy; and if some government official builds a fine house for himself, he will be slandered to the tsar as being a bribetaker, an evildoer, and a squanderer of the tsar's treasury, or even a thief; much grief and sorrow will be inflicted upon him by these wicked words. Or out of hatred for him, he will be transferred to another government service to do work that he cannot cope with, and instructions impossible to understand will be given him, so that he will be found guilty of some fault and be punished by having his property and lands confiscated for the tsar and sold.[12] If merchants or peasants have fine houses built, they will be taxed more every year. For this reason the people in the Muscovite land live in poorly furnished houses, and the cities and towns are not well built.

10. A father or mother may have two or three marriageable girls, and the first have poor eyes or some defect in leg or arm, or be deaf or dumb, while the others are well-grown, fair, and well-spoken girls, who enjoy perfect health. If then a suitor asks for the girl's hand and sends his mother or sister or any trusted person to look at her, the parents may show, instead of the misfavored girl, the second or third sister, calling her by the eldest's name to the unsuspecting messenger, and the latter, being pleased with her, tells the suitor that she is satisfactory and he may marry her. After this message, the suitor may make an agreement with the girl's parents to marry the girl of that name at an appointed time, and clauses are written in the contract for such fines to be paid as are beyond the suitor's means. At the wedding, the crippled or misfavored daughter, whose name is in the contract, will be given in marriage instead of the one the messenger saw. The bridegroom cannot observe that she is blind or one-eyed or

43

has any other imperfection, nor can he notice that she is deaf or dumb, for at the wedding the bride is veiled and remains silent; likewise, if she is lame or crippled, nobody may note it, since the go-betweens support her on both sides. But if, after the wedding and dinner, in their chamber, he finally sees by candlelight what she is like and that he will have to spend a lifetime of tears and torment with her, then he may decide to force her to become a nun. If she does not submit to his will, he will beat and torture her in every way and not sleep with her, until she consents to take the veil. Sometimes the wife resists all his beatings and torments and complains to her kin. These appeal to the Patriarch or the Church dignitaries, and the neighbors and servants are questioned to find out the truth. If the complaint is founded, the husband is sent to a monastery for penance during half a year or a year, and his wife is left free. When he has finished his penance, or if his wife intercedes for him before his term has expired, he is released and ordered to live with her according to the law; if he does not comply, they are separated and their property divided between them; nor can they marry again until seven years have elapsed. But sometimes a man, seeing his wife crippled or evil-tempered, renounces her and becomes a monk himself; and some husbands or wives do worse and have their spouse poisoned.

11. A man who has been deceived and has received in marriage a girl other than the one shown to his messenger may appeal to the Patriarch and Church authorities. On his complaint, he is made to sign a paper; then the neighbors and servants are questioned confidentially to find out whether his wife is really the girl whose name is written in the contract. If this is the case, the matter will stand according to the contract and evidence, and the messenger's words will not be believed, for a man should not marry without making very sure. But if the witnesses say that the wife is not the girl whose name is in the contract, the couple is separated; moreover a large fine is laid on the guilty party and the husband's expenses are refunded. The offender is beaten with the knout or punished even more severely if the tsar so desires.

12. It also happens that if a father has a girl who is crippled or misfavored in some way, he tricks the suitor by showing in her place a servant girl or widow, calling her by another name and attiring her differently. Or if the girl is too short in stature, she will be set up on a stool, so that she seems well-grown, since nobody notices the deception.

13. Girls who are crippled or advanced in years, and whom nobody wishes to marry, are made to take the veil by their parents.

14. If a suitor wishes to see the girl himself, parents who feel sure that their daughter can be shown in public without disgrace will present her to the suitor. But if the suitor is then dissatisfied and starts to spread evil rumors about the girl, discouraging other suitors, the girl's father or kin complain to the authorities that, after seeing the girl, her

44

suitor is defaming and slandering her and discouraging others; and after inquiry the Patriarch will order the suitor to marry the girl. If he has married another girl before this decision, he will have to pay a fine to the first girl for shaming her.

15. If a man has given his daughter or sister a large dowry in money and lands, and this woman dies after a short time without having borne children (or having borne children who have died before her), the dowry will be taken from the husband and returned to her kin. But if she leaves a son or daughter, her fortune will be left to her husband, for her children.

Discerning reader do not wonder at all this! It is the honest truth that nowhere in the world is such deception practiced about brides as in the state of Muscovy; for there they do not follow the usage of allowing the betrothed couple to see and talk with each other before marriage.

16. The boyars and lords of the council and chamber have up to one, two, three, or five hundred, or even a thousand servants, male and female, in their households, according to their means and rank. They give those servants a yearly salary: from two to ten rubles to married couples, according to their functions, also clothes, bread, and supplies monthly. They live in their own lodgings on the boyar's grounds. The boyars also send reliable married people to live the year around on their estates in the villages and parishes, inspecting the fields and offices and collecting a salary and dues from the peasants, so that they can make a living. The upper servants who are single receive a small salary, while the lower ones are not paid; but they all receive clothing, hats, shirts, boots. The single servants of more importance live in downstairs lodgings at the back of the house and eat from the boyar's kitchen; on holidays they each receive two cups of vodka. The wives and widows live in their husbands' lodgings and receive a yearly salary and supplies every month; some widowed women and unmarried girls live with the ladies of the house; they receive clothes and are fed from the boyar's kitchen. When a girl or widow is of marriageable age, her master, either consulting her choice or against her will, gives her in marriage, with a dowry, to one of his servants. The weddings are celebrated in the boyar's house in the customary way, the food and drink and festive clothes being given by the boyar. Girls and widows are not allowed to wed servants from other houses, for the boyar's servants are bound to him for a term or for life. Offices are set up in the boyars' houses to settle all domestic affairs, manage income and expenses, and judge quarrels among the servants and peasants.

In the same way, persons of other ranks keep servants in their houses, according to their rank and fortune, both for a time or for life. No one is allowed to have servants who are not bound.

45

—0 Rossii v tsarstvovanii Alexeya Mikhailovicha (St. Petersburg, 1840)

NOTES: [1]See Kotoshikhin, chap. viii, items 5, 6: "When the boyars and officials . . . write to the tsar . . . they call themselves 'thy thrall Yanka Cherkaskoy, Ivashko Voro-tynskoy' (or whatever their name is) . . . but do not put down their title or rank; . . . commoners and peasants call themselves 'slaves and orphans.' "

[2]The tsars were crowned in the Church of the Assumption and buried in the Archangel Church, both in the Kreml'.

[3]*Kutiya:* rice or wheat or barley cooked in water sweetened with honey or sugar, with raisins; brought to church for funeral services and served at the funeral meal.

[4]*The Domostroy* recommends that a special room be reserved for icons and divine service.

[5]"*V polate ili v izbe*": *polata* generally refers to a stone house or to a reception room; izba is used for a living room or any heated room.

[6]The text says *vino*, the usual term for vodka; see the distinction made with Romanée and Rhenish.

[7]Romanée and Rhenish were the most popular wines in seventeenth century Russia.

[8]Honored guests: literally, "sitting boyars," guests without any special duties in the wedding ceremonies.

[9]Set in a metal (gold or silver) framework.

[10]As late as the nineteenth century at peasant weddings, the second day's feast was called "the prince's dinner," and the third day's, "the bride's dinner."

[11]The Orthodox Church forbade marrying more than three times.

[12]This had happened to Kotoshikhin's father, whose fortune had been confiscated after he had been accused of squandering the funds of a monastery.

■ ■ ■

ON THE TSAR'S AMUSEMENTS

J. Reitenfels

Jacob Reitenfels, a native of Courland, was an envoy of Rome to Moscow, 1670–73. His *Relation on Muscovy* was published in Padua in 1680. The Latin text was translated into Russian in 1905.

■ ■ ■ Not only remoteness from other lands, but the way of thinking and the rules of society have, up to the present time, prevented the Muscovites' manner of life from becoming similar to that of other nations. For this reason, their sovereigns have not even allowed themselves those relaxations from worries which are accepted in other countries, and in this of course they have set an example to their subjects. Their favorite pleasure is hunting. They will chase wild beasts in the forests merrily, either with beaters or with trained hounds or swift-flying falcons, or lastly with bows or muskets. If Alexey sometimes leaves Moscow in order to refresh his spirit, he prefers to stay in a garden outside the city (he has a huge one which, considering the severe climate, is quite luxuriant) or at some hereditary estate of the tsars.

A few years ago,[1] he allowed the foreigners in Moscow to give him a theatrical performance consisting of dancing and of "The History of Esther" adapted to the stage. True, at first the tsar was reluctant to allow music on the stage; but when it was pointed out to him that it is as impossible to have a chorus without music as for dancers to dance without legs, he left the matter, rather unwillingly, to the actors' discretion.

The tsar saw the performance seated in an armchair before the stage; the tsaritsa and the children sat behind a lattice,[2] or rather they viewed the play through peep-holes in a specially partitioned-off room, while the lords (nobody else was admitted) stood on the stage itself. . . .

On the same day (the Saturday before Lent) the tsar organized on the river Moskva, which was frozen over, a fight between huge dogs of English and other breeds and white bears from the Samoyed country. This was extremely entertaining, since both bears and dogs often slipped and fell on the icy surface.

—*Khrestomatiya po istorii SSSR* (Moscow, 1951), Vol. I

NOTES: [1]1672. The "foreign master," J. G. Gregori, a Lutheran clergyman, was ordered to adapt the Book of Esther to the stage. The first performance was given in German in the tsar's residence of Preobrazhenskoye, not in the Kreml', where traditions and religious scruples were stronger. It is interesting to note that in the first years of his reign Alexey had issued strict decrees against such lay entertainment as singing, dancing, pantomimes, and so forth.

[2]The Russian envoy to France in 1668 was extremely surprised, when he went to the play, to see ladies in the audience.

■ ■ ■

ON CRAFTS AND TRADES IN THE RUSSIAN STATE

J. Reitenfels

■ ■ ■ The number of expert craftsmen, which used to be very small in Muscovy, has greatly increased in our time, and the crafts themselves have improved considerably. In the smiths' art, in the art of preparing powder and weaving cloth, they have already become very knowledge-

47

able. . . . The French and Germans mine iron in the region of Tula,[1] near the source of the Volga, and in other places, also copper near Novgorod; all this with great profit to the state. Recently the Tsar sent some people beyond Kazan, on the way to Siberia (from which a little earlier precious samples had been brought to Moscow) in order to explore in detail the depths of the mountains which contain silver and gold ore. I believe that abundant wealth can be dug out of the depths of the cold Muscovite soil. . . .

In regard to other trades, the Muscovites are traditionally past masters in the art of building elegant wooden houses, of turning wooden utensils, of weaving linen expertly, and in other crafts that require assiduity. I will not speak here of those crafts that call for being constantly seated. Painting with the Muscovites is most particular, concerned with consecrated objects, for, apart from a few flowers and animals, they paint exclusively long-dead saints and follow the Greek patterns.[2] Moreover, it is accounted as not only an impious act but one deserving of punishment if the trader in pictures of blessed heaven-dwellers also displays for sale pictures of lay subjects. If a man wishes to have a picture of a lay person, he asks foreign artists to do the work. These are strictly forbidden, on the other hand, to paint the saints. But the Muscovites, I don't know why, do not care for portraits of people or for any pictures except images of saints.[3]

[On the Red Square] and on other squares constant trade in food and other goods indispensable in everyday life is carried on among a great affluence of people.[4]

This market adjoins another one which spreads in a semicircle of nearly half a Roman mile. There the shops for various goods are set up in such a way that any particular ware is displayed for sale only in its appointed place. Thus, in one place you see silk materials, in another wool, in a third linen; one shows gold and silver objects and precious stones; another perfumes; a third foreign wines (as many as two hundred cellars are situated in a gallery underground); a fourth sells various drinks prepared from honey, cherries, and berries. One glance shows you here expensive furs, there bells, axes, candlesticks, and other metal wares; in a third place skins, mittens, stockings, rugs, curtains, and various materials. Oil, fat, and hams fill one gallery; candles and wax another; various wooden utensils a third. The leather gallery displays leather goods: reins and other harness; the fur gallery has coats and hats. You will find medicinal plants and herbs for sale here; elsewhere locks, keys, nails; farther, silk in threads, silver thread for girls' adornment, bracelets—each in its special place. The same for shoes, greaves, hops, barley, grain, salt fish, hay, oats, not to mention flour, bread, and wares of every sort; cobblers' shops, and the low-ceilinged barbers' shops—all have their own gallery, and everything is handsomely and conveniently displayed so that the buyer can with perfect ease choose the best of all that is gathered here.[5]

The beauty of the market is considerably increased by the fact that there are no living quarters in it, in order to keep the fire that fre-

48

quently rages in this city at the greatest possible distance. For the same reason, the market is carefully guarded by watchmen, and the craftsmen who work with fire live at a distance.

—Khrestomatiya po istorii SSSR (Moscow, 1951), Vol. I

NOTES: [1]Tula is one of the oldest industrial centers in Russia. It had foundries in the seventeenth century, and the Demidov family started an arms factory there in 1695. It is situated nearer the sources of the Oka and the Don than that of the Volga.

[2]"Greek patterns" should be understood as Byzantine traditions, which reached Russia chiefly through the Athos monasteries. See also the Gautier passage on the Troitsa Monastery, "Art and Aesthetics," pp. 145–46.

[3]The Moscow court then attracted, or brought forcibly, both Russian artists from the northern towns (Ustyug, Vologda, Kostroma, and others) lying on the trade route with Europe, and foreign artists, who were generally better paid than the natives.

[4]The following description of the old Merchant Court and Trading Galleries remained accurate until the early nineteenth century.

[5]Actually there was some mingling of wares of various categories in each gallery. A leather goods dealer might, for instance, buy a vacant booth in the wool row.

■ ■ ■

INTRODUCTION OF THE NEW CALENDAR
Peter the Great

■ ■ ■ His Majesty has ordered the following to be proclaimed: It is known to His Majesty that not only many European Christian lands, but also Slavic nations which are in total accord with our Eastern Orthodox Church, such as Vallachians, Moldavians, Serbs, Dalmatians, Bulgarians, and his Majesty's own subjects the Circassians, and all the Greeks, from whom we have received our faith—all those nations agree to count their years from the eighth day after the birth of Christ, that is from the first day of January, and not from the creation of the world,[1] because of the many difficulties and discrepancies of this reckoning. It is now the year 1699 from the birth of Christ, and from the first of January will begin both the new year 1700 and a new century; and so His Majesty has ordered, as a good and useful measure, that from now on time will be reckoned in government offices and dates be noted on documents and property deeds, starting from the first of January 1700. And to celebrate this good undertaking and the new century, the following is ordered: in the sovereign city of Moscow, after due thanks and praise to God in the churches, or, as the case may be, at home, let the reputable citizens arrange decorations of

49

pine, fir, and juniper trees and boughs along the busiest main streets and by the houses of eminent church and lay persons of rank. These decorations may follow the pattern of those set up in the Merchant Court[2] or near the Lower Pharmacy,[3] or they may be disposed in the way most convenient and fitting to the various places and gates. Poorer persons should place at least one shrub or bough on their gates or on their house. All this should be made ready by the first of January, and remain in place until the seventh of January of the year 1700. Also, on the first day of January, as a sign of rejoicing, wishes for the new year and century will be exchanged, and the following will be organized: when fireworks are lit and guns fired on the great Red Square, let the boyars, the Lords of the Palace, of the Chamber, and the Council, and the eminent personages of Court, Army, and Merchant ranks, each in his own grounds, fire three times from small guns, if they have any, or from muskets and other small arms, and shoot some rockets into the air.

—"Decree of December 20, 1699," *Khrestomatiya po istorii SSSR* (Moscow, 1953), Vol. II

NOTES: [1]Before January 1, 1700, the Russian calendar started from the date of the creation of the world, which was reckoned as 5508 B.C. The year began on September 1.

[2]In Kitay-Gorod.

[3]The first pharmacy in Russia had been set up in 1581 for the tsar and his family. A new one had been installed in 1672 in the Merchant Court, and, presumably, others were in existence by the end of the century. They were under the control of the government's "Pharmacy Office."

■ ■ ■

THE FIRST RUSSIAN NEWSPAPER
Vedomosti

A decree of December 16, 1702, called for the printing of newspapers to inform the public of events outside and inside the country. The first number of *Vedomosti* (News), from which the following passages are taken, appeared on January 2, 1703. It was an official gazette to which Peter himself was a contributor. Published in Moscow and later in St. Petersburg also, it was printed in the Church Slavic alphabet until the introduction of the new simplified script in 1710. After 1727, it was replaced by the Academy of Sciences' publication, *The St. Petersburg News.*

■ ■ ■ Four hundred bronze cannon, howitzers, and mortars have recently been cast in Moscow. The guns shoot shells of twenty-four, eighteen,
and twelve pounds. The howitzers are for bombs of forty and twenty
pounds; the mortars for three hundred and sixty—one hundred and twenty—
eighty-pound bombs, and less. There are also many more big and medium
molds ready for the casting of cannon, howitzers, and mortars. More
than forty thousand puds[1] of bronze are stored at the Arsenal for further
casting.

By order of His Majesty, Moscow schools are multiplying, and
forty-five students are studying philosophy, having completed dialectics.

Over three hundred students are attending the Mathematics and
Navigation School[2] and are doing well in their work.

Between the twenty-fourth of November and the twenty-fourth
of December, there have been three hundred and eighty-six births, male
and female, in Moscow.

News from Persia.—The Indian Tsar has presented our great
Sovereign with an elephant and a number of other gifts. The elephant has
been sent by land from the city of Shemakha to Astrakhan.

From Kazan.—A quantity of oil and copper ore has been found
by the river Oka. A good amount of copper has been smelted from this ore
and much profit is expected from this for the Muscovite State.

From Siberia.—The Jesuits are excessively unpopular in the
Chinese state by reason of their cunning, and a certain number have been
executed.

From Olonets.[3]—The priest Ivan Okulov, of the city of Olonets,
has assembled about a thousand of our volunteers and crossed the Swedish
border. He has defeated Swedish posts. . . . A great number of Swedes
have been killed and a cavalry flag, drums, and swords, with a quantity of
muskets and horses are in our hands. He distributed to his soldiers the
stores and effects seized, and what he could not take with him, in grain
and other effects, he burned. He also burned the Solovsky manor and many
other manors around, with about a thousand village houses. According to
the prisoners' reports, fifty men of the Swedish cavalry were killed and
four hundred of the infantry. Fifty horsemen and a hundred foot soldiers
escaped. Of the priest's men, only two were wounded.

From Nien (Nienshantz in Ingermanland), **October 16.**—Life is
difficult for us here, since Muscovy acts very harshly in this region; and for
this reason many people are leaving in fear, going to Vyborg and Finland
and taking the best of their belongings with them.

The Fort of Oreshek (Schlusselburg) is high, surrounded with
deep water on all sides; it is forty versts distant from here. The Muscovite
troops are laying vigorous siege to it, and more than four volleys from
twenty guns have already been fired and more than fifteen hundred bombs
thrown. However the damage so far is small, and they will have considerable trouble in seizing this fort.

From Narva, October 13.—On September 26, Muscovite troops, ten thousand strong, advanced on this side of the Neva near Notenburg, between the Russian and Ingermanland borders, and started to dig trenches five hundred steps from the fort on this side of the river. Our troops under General Koniort are standing on the other side of the river between Notenburg and the Muscovites. They prevent the Russian troops from crossing the Neva when these attempt to do so. The Muscovites intend to shell the fort, but it is all built of stone and has a strong garrison. Four hundred soldiers were brought in recently as reinforcement, so for the present there is no danger.

From Amsterdam, November 10.—We hear from the city of Arkhangelsk, on September 20, that after His Imperial Majesty had sent his troops on several ships to the White Sea, he himself proceeded further and sent the vessels back to Arkhangelsk, where there are fifteen thousand soldiers, of which six thousand work daily at building a new fort on the river Dvinka.

> —"Moscow, 1703, On the Second Day of January," *Khresto-matiya po istorii russkogo yazyka*, ed. S. P. Obnorsky and S. G. Barkhudarov (Moscow, 1949)

NOTES: [1]Forty Russian pounds, or 16 kg. 380.
[2]The Navigation School was officially founded in Moscow in 1701. It was under the direction of a British professor from Edinburgh University, with Russian helpers. After 1715 it became the Naval Academy, which in spite of its name prepared engineers rather than sailors.
[3]After Peter's defeat by Charles XII at Narva (1700), the Russians gradually became more successful. In 1701 they conquered—and kept—Livonia and Ingria (Ingermanland).

■ ■ ■

PETER'S ASSEMBLIES
La Vie and F. V. Bergholz

"*Assembly* is a French term, which cannot be expressed by any single Russian word; to explain it thoroughly, it is a free gathering in a house which takes place not only for pleasure but for business also, since there people can meet and talk about all sorts of necessary affairs, likewise hear what is going on; entertainment is also provided."—Decree on Assemblies, 1718.

DESCRIPTION OF ONE OF THE FIRST ASSEMBLIES

La Vie

■ ■ ■ Yesterday I had the honor of attending the assembly which took place at the residence of Vice-Admiral Kruis and at which were present His Majesty the Tsar with the Tsaritsa his spouse and a great number of persons of quality; the envoys of Prussia, Denmark, and the resident of His Britannic Majesty from his electorate of Brunswick-Luneburg were also there. . . . These assemblies are held three times a week, at the residence of each of the court dignitaries in turn; some guests play chess and cards, others smoke, drink, discuss the news, and even talk of trade, since the chief merchants are also admitted. If, as the Tsar walks about in the rooms, anyone stands up to show his respect, he is fined, that is, compelled to drink a large glass of wine. The assemblies begin at four and end at ten. The ladies sit in a separate apartment to which, from time to time, the Ministers and other lords are summoned in order to dance with them.

—"Dispatch of La Vie, French Consul, January 1719," *Materialy imperatorskago russkago istoricheskago obshchestva* (St. Petersburg, 1884), Vol. XL

■ ■ ■

ASSEMBLIES IN MOSCOW

F. V. Bergholz

■ ■ ■ I will now say briefly what these assemblies are and what rules are observed there. They are organized on the pattern of the Petersburg assemblies which, on the Emperor's personal order, are held in that city regularly every winter.

First, they are distributed among all the dignitaries, but regardless of any particular order or sequence. The military governor of Moscow either inquires of His Majesty the Emperor (when he is here) at whose house the next assembly is to take place, or he asks the lords themselves when it is more convenient for them; and then, at the close of an assembly, he informs the guests before they leave of the next meeting place. In Petersburg this is generally done by the General-in-chief of the police.[1] Everyone has the right to come to an assembly. Secondly, the host must not leave the rooms to greet or accompany any guest, not even the Emperor. Thirdly, in the room where dancing takes place, if it is large enough, or in the next one, the following must be prepared: a table with pipes, tobacco, and matchwood (which is used here instead of paper spills), and a few other tables for chess and checkers; but cards are neither provided nor

53

allowed. Fourth, the host, hostess, or one of the household opens the dancing, after which one or two couples may dance the minuet, the "anglaise," or the "polonaise," as they wish. . . . If the dancers desire, after the minuet, to dance the anglaise or polonaise, they say so, and then the gentlemen who wish to take part in the dance choose their ladies, but the ladies do not choose their partners; they leave this to the men. Fifth, each may do as he pleases, that is, dance or smoke or play or talk or look on; likewise everyone may ask for wine, beer, vodka, tea, coffee, and he immediately gets it; but the host need not and indeed dare not insist that his guests drink or eat. He can only say what refreshments are available and then allow his guests entire freedom. Sixth and last, these gatherings begin around five o'clock and break up no later than ten, when everybody must go home.

What I don't like in those assemblies is this: first, in the room where the ladies are and where dancing goes on, people smoke and play checkers, as a result of which there is a bad smell and a clatter, which are not fitting in the presence of ladies or while music is played; secondly, the ladies always sit apart from the men, so that not only is any conversation impossible, but you can hardly exchange a single word with them: when they are not dancing, they sit tongue-tied and stare at each other.

—*Diary of F. V. Bergholz*[2] (1722), *Khrestomatiya po istorii SSSR* (Moscow, 1953), Vol. II

NOTES: [1]The chief of police's duty was also to attend the assemblies and take down the list of the guests.

[2]Bergholz' diary covers the years from 1721 to 1725. Though he was in the service of the Duke of Holstein, he had spent his youth in Russia and returned there later.

■ ■ ■

THE TRUE MIRROR OF YOUTH—1719
Anonymous

This very popular compilation of rules for behavior in society was first published in 1717 and was frequently reprinted. The first part consists of religious instructions, the second of practical advice for everyday behavior, compiled from various sources, Russian and foreign.

54

■ ■ ■ 22. A youth should always be considerate and polite, both in words and deeds, not quarrelsome or hasty with his hands; if you chance to meet an acquaintance, greet him at three steps' distance, taking your hat off pleasantly, and not after you have already passed him, turning your head back. For it is no disadvantage to hold one's hat in one's hand, but it deserves praise, and it is better when people say of a man: "he is polite; he is a gentle fellow and a gallant," than if they say that he is an arrogant ass. . . .

27. Young people should always use foreign languages when talking together, for practice: and specially when they happen to mention something secret, so that the servants will not obtain knowledge of it, and also in order not to be confused with ignorant asses: for each merchant sells his wares as he can, by praising them. . . .

55. Again, if you happen to stand in a group of people talking, or if you are sitting at table, or are conversing together, or are dancing with someone, it is not seemly to spit rudely right in the middle of the group; turn aside instead. And if you are in a room with many people, use your handkerchief for your spittle. Don't spit on the floor of a room or in a church in a manner disgusting to others; walk a few steps apart, taking care not to be noticed, and afterwards rub the floor as clean as possible with your feet. . . .

59. It is not seemly either when a man cleans his nose with his handkerchief or his finger, as if he was rubbing some sort of grease in, this especially in the presence of other honorable persons.

How a youth should behave when in conversation with other persons.—When you are at table with other persons, behave according to these rules: First, trim your nails, so that they will not seem to be lined with velvet. Wash your hands and take your seat in a mannerly way; sit straight, and don't grab first at the dish; don't gorge like a pig; don't blow into the soup to make it splash in all directions; don't snort while eating. Don't be the first to drink; be temperate and avoid drunkenness; drink and eat what you need; be last to help yourself. When you are offered anything, take part of what you are offered and give back the rest with thanks. Don't leave your hands in your plate too long; don't swing your legs; when preparing to drink, don't wipe your lips with your hand, but use a napkin; don't drink until you have swallowed the food in your mouth. Don't lick your fingers, and don't gnaw at bones, but use a knife. Don't clean your teeth with a knife, use a toothpick, and while doing so cover your mouth with one hand. Don't hold bread to your chest while cutting it. Eat what is in front of you and don't grab elsewhere. If you wish to proffer food to somebody, don't take it with your hands as is the custom with some nations. Don't champ on your food like a pig; don't scratch your head; don't talk with your mouth full—those are all peasant manners. It is not seemly to sneeze, blow one's nose, and cough too frequently. When you eat an egg,

55

cut a piece of bread first, and be careful not to let the egg dribble; don't dawdle over it and don't break the shell to bits; while you're eating the egg, abstain from drinking; don't dirty the tablecloth, and don't lick your fingers. Don't build a barrier of bones, crusts, and other things beside your plate. When you have finished eating, give thanks to God, wash your hands and face, and rinse your mouth.[1]

—*Khrestomatiya po istorii* SSSR (Moscow, 1953), Vol. II

NOTES: [1]Cf. the Italian guide of manners *Galateo* (sixteenth century), which enjoyed tremendous success, not only in its native country, but in others. In France, it was published sometimes as a bilingual text, so that it could also serve as a manual for the study of Italian. The *Galateo*, like the *Mirror*, recommends eating cleanly, frowns upon coughing immoderately, spitting or sneezing at table, or having one's hands perpetually in the dishes.

■ ■ ■

THE OFFICIAL CREATION OF THE RUSSIAN THEATER
Elizabeth I

In the middle of the eighteenth century, plays in the Russian language were given in Russia only by private theaters of amateur or semi-amateur status. The court theaters chiefly performed Italian or French plays, operas, and ballets. However, the students of the Cadet Academy, founded in 1732, had, in the late forties, started acting both French and Russian plays—the latter composed by the dramatist A. P. Sumarokov, himself a former cadet. The performances in Yaroslavl by the troupe of the young merchant F. G. Volkov attracted the attention of the Empress Elizabeth who summoned the amateur actors to Petersburg. Though their acting did not meet with great success at the court, it was decided some time later to establish a permanent Russian theater in Petersburg.

DECREE OF AUGUST 30, 1756

On the Establishment of a Russian Theater for the Representation of Tragedies and Comedies.

■ ■ ■ We have this day ordered the creation of a Russian theater for the representation of tragedies and comedies; it will be established in the Golovin house on Vasilevsky Island, near the Cadet Academy. Actors and actresses will be engaged for this purpose: the actors to be taken from among the singers and Yaroslavl students[1] in the Cadet Academy, as many as necessary, and, to complete their number, actors chosen from other per-

56

sons not in government service, also a suitable number of actresses. Starting from this day, an annual sum of 5,000 rubles is assigned by this our decree for the upkeep of the theater.[2] This sum will be allocated by the Treasury at the beginning of each year following the signing of our decree. Alexey Dyakonov, scribe in the bodyguard company, to whom we now grant the rank of second lieutenant in the army, is appointed overseer of the theater with the annual salary of 250 rubles. The theater building will be placed under adequate guard. The direction of the theater is entrusted to Brigadier General Alexander Sumarokov,[3] who, over and above his military pay, will receive an allowance of 1,000 rubles a year from the sum assigned for the theater. This allowance will be added to the pay due to him from the date of his appointment as brigadier, supplementing his former pay as colonel. From now on he will also receive the full pay of a brigadier and will not be struck from the army lists. He will be responsible for distributing the wages to the actors, actresses, and other theater personnel, according to the register delivered to him. This our decree is to be enforced by our Senate.[4]

—Khrestomatiya po istorii SSSR (Moscow, 1953), Vol. II

NOTES: [1]A number of actors from the Yaroslavl troupe were then studying, on the Empress' orders, at the Cadet Academy.
    [2]The French troupe at the Court received 20,000 rubles in 1742; the Italian opera and ballet troupe, 22,500.—*Volkov and the Russian Theater of His Time* (Moscow, 1953).
    [3]A. P. Sumarokov (1718–77) wrote tragedies on Russian subjects in the French classic manner (*Khorev*, 1749; *Sinav and Truvor*, 1750). He resigned his post in 1761.
    [4]The present-day Pushkin Theater in Leningrad is considered the direct heir to the Russian theater founded in 1756. Before the Revolution it was called the Alexandra Imperial Theater.

■ ■ ■

THE HERMITAGE UNDER CATHERINE II

A. I. Somov

A. I. Somov, a Russian art historian (1830–1909), was curator of the Hermitage Museum. He wrote on several Russian painters.

■ ■ ■ The Empress Catherine II wished to have a comfortable refuge where she could relax during her leisure hours in a small company of intelligent, talented, and well-informed people. At first a group of such persons gathered at the Empress' invitation in the reception rooms of the Winter

Palace; but later, shortly after 1765, the French architect Vallin de la Mothe[1] constructed beside the Palace, fronting the Neva, a special building for those gatherings. This was called the Hermitage. Here Catherine appeared as merely a friendly hostess, a sociable woman, who charmed her guests by her personal qualities rather than by the prestige of rank.

Here she laid aside the demands of etiquette as she conversed with Grimm, Orlov, Diderot, Potemkin, Zavadovsky,[2] the Prince de Ligne, Bezborodko,[3] Ségur,[4] and others. Here she listened to the comedies of Fonvizin and the poetry of Derzhavin,[5] played cards, or looked on as amateurs performed on the stage, or was entertained by dancing and other diversions. At the Hermitage parties, Russians were expected to converse together in Russian only; when the Empress came in or when she addressed any of the guests, these were forbidden to rise. Rules of behavior, written by Catherine herself, were posted at the entrance to the Hermitage. This is what she proposed:

1. Leave all rank outside, likewise hats and especially swords.

2. Quarrels of precedence, arrogance, and all such things must be left at the door.

3. Let gaiety reign; however, do not damage or break anything; abstain from munching.

4. Sit, stand, walk, as suits you, no matter who is present.

5. Talk moderately and not too loudly; spare people's ears and heads.

6. Argue without anger or heat.

7. Do not sigh or yawn; bore or embarrass no one.

8. Eat with enjoyment, drink in moderation—everyone should be able to find his legs on leaving.

9. Do not wash dirty linen in public.

10. Let what came in at one ear go out by the other before you leave.

These articles were followed by this warning: "If anyone breaks one of the above rules, he will have, on testimony of two witnesses, to drink a glass of cold water for each offense—ladies are not excepted—and read a page of the *Telemachide*.[6] Whoever breaks three rules in the course of an evening will have to memorize six lines of the *Telemachide*. Anyone guilty of breaking the tenth rule will not be invited in future."

Another notice, in French, hung on the door to the drawing room. This was also written by the Empress: "Sit if you please and where you please, without having to be asked a hundred times. The hostess here hates all formalities, they vex her; and everyone is master in his house."

—*Rossiya i russkie*, ed. S. Yablonovsky and V. Boutchik (Paris, 1930)

NOTES: [1]This French architect was in Russia from 1759 to 1775. He came to Petersburg as professor in the newly founded Academy of Arts.

[2]1739–1812; a favorite of Catherine's.

[3]1747–99; diplomat and politician.

[4]Louis Philippe de Ségur (1753–1830) was French plenipotentiary to Russia and a man of letters.

[5]Denis Ivanovich Fonvizin (1745–92) was the author of satirical plays, the most famous of which are *The Brigadier* and *The Minor*.

Gavrila Romanovich Derzhavin (1743–1816) was the greatest Russian poet of the eighteenth century, a master both of the grand style and of lyrical intimacy.

[6]The *Telemachide*, by Tredyakovsky (1703–69), was a Russian adaptation of Fénelon's work. It was written in heavy and archaic hexameters and was subjected to much ridicule at the time.

■ ■ ■

SATIRICAL NEWS

N. I. Novikov

Nikolay Ivanovich Novikov (1744–1818) was one of the most active "enlighteners" of his time. In his various journals he engaged in polemics with Catherine II, ridiculed the foibles and harshness of Russian society, and pleaded for better education and more humane laws. As a printer and publisher, he tried to bring knowledge to literate commoners. He was arrested by Catherine in 1792 and freed by Paul in 1796.

■ ■ ■ **From Kronstadt.**—The following ships have recently arrived in our port: 1. "Trompeur" from Rouen,[1] in eighteen days; 2. "Vétilles" from Marseilles,[2] in twenty-three days. They have brought us the following necessary goods: French swords of various kinds, snuff boxes made of tortoise shell, papier-mâché, and lacquer; laces, blonde lace, fringes, cuffs, ribbons, stockings, buckles, hats, cuff links and all sorts of so-called haberdashery wares; Dutch quills, in bundles, sharpened and not sharpened; pins of various kinds, and other fashionable petty goods. The ships will load various Russian trifles in Petersburg, namely hemp, iron, Russian leather, tallow, candles, linen, and so forth. Many of our young nobles laugh at the stupidity of the French, who sail so far to exchange their fashionable wares for our inconsequential trifles.

Information.—A young Russian sucking pig, having traveled in foreign lands for the enlightenment of his mind and having profited by his journey, has returned a full-grown pig and can be seen gratis in many streets of this city.

For Sale.—A recently appointed Governor is leaving for the province entrusted to him and, in order to travel lighter, is selling his conscience; prospective buyers may find him in this city.

59

From Kronstadt.—A ship from Bordeaux has recently arrived in our port; in addition to fashionable goods, it brings twenty-four French-men who say that they are all barons, knights, marquesses, or counts and that, having met with misfortune in their country in various affairs concerning their honor, they have been reduced to the extremity of having to come to Russia in quest of gold instead of going to America. They lie very little in their stories; for according to trustworthy sources they are all indeed native Frenchmen who were engaged in various trades and practices of the third estate. Many of them lived in great disagreement with the Paris police, and the latter, moved by extreme hatred for them, sent them a message which they received with little favor. The message proposed that they should decamp immediately from Paris unless they wished to dine, sup, and sleep in the Bastille. Though this message was most sincere, the French gentlemen did not find it to their liking and consequently they have come here, intending to become teachers and court masters to young people of the nobility. They will soon leave for Petersburg. Dear fellow citizens, lose no time in engaging these foreigners as educators for your children! Entrust the future pillars of the state immediately to these vagabonds, and consider that you have fulfilled your parental duty by engaging Frenchmen as tutors, without inquiring about their learning or morality.

—*The Painter* (1772), *Izbrannye sochineniya* (Moscow-Leningrad, 1951)

NOTES: [1]*Trompeur:* Deceiver.
[2]*Vétilles:* Trifles.

■ ■ ■

SERF THEATERS IN PENZA IN THE EARLY NINETEENTH CENTURY[1]

F. F. Vigel

■ ■ ■ Who would believe it? At the time[2] there were three theaters and three troupes of actors in Penza. This miracle requires an explanation. Such is the way we have done things since the times of Peter the Great: the roof is put on before the foundations are even laid; we already had universities, academies, secondary schools, when we still lacked teachers and students; there were theaters everywhere before we had any plays or actors of value. Really, it's a pity that, forgetting the proverb "Nothing funnier than a hurrier," we have exhausted ourselves in our scramble after Europe. And so, there were three theaters in Penza, for the reason that the semi-lordly whims already forgotten in Petersburg[3] could still be found here and there in Moscow and continued to reign with all the force of tradition in the provinces.

The troupe of Mr. Gorikhvostov was devoted entirely to the acting of operas and exclusively to Italian music; a certain Arinushka was its most famous member. This troupe played for the entertainment of the worthy public that gathered at the worthy Mr. Gorikhvostov's. Not belonging to this society, I have never heard the singers and I regret it exceedingly: as an example of the ludicrous, it must have been perfect.

Grigory Vasilevich Gladkov, a most ugly, immoral, and cruel person, but a man of some parts and education, had a passion for the stage. Near his home, on the city square, he had built a small stone theater-house which was furnished with all the requisites: parterre, boxes, and stage. He drove all his servants onto that stage—from the major-domo to the stable-groom and from the chambermaid to the washerwoman. His taste inclined him to tragedies and dramas, but now and again, for a change, he would have comedies. These went worse, if only anything could be worse, than the tragedies. All the actors were lamentable figures; there was an echo of blows in the air and some people asserted that under the red and white of the make-up blue bruises could sometimes be discerned. I saw these performances, but what could I say about them? The memory arouses pity and revulsion. This wretched troupe played in the winter for money which of course went into their master's pocket. The audience did not belong to the highest walks of life.

A nobleman of the ancient stamp, the big-nosed, fat-paunched Vasily Ivanovich Kozhin, without any special penchant for this pursuit, in a spirit of imitation or simply to while away the time, had also started a "comedy" of his own; and surprisingly he was more successful than others. But let me put off discussing his troupe and now touch a more entertaining topic: his private life. He had been a bachelor until the age of sixty, rarely leaving his village, when there suddenly appeared in the neighborhood an old princely couple who had dilapidated their fortunes on pomades, perfumes, and silk laces. Prince Vasily Sergeevich and Princess Nastasya Ivanovna Dolgorukov, close kin to all the most illustrious families, with sons who had reached the rank of generals, had been compelled to settle for their declining years in the Penza village that remained their property. With them lived their daughter, Katerina Vasilevna, a maiden of forty years. I do not know whether in Moscow she had been difficult to please, but in the backwater where she now found herself she was only too glad to marry—Vasily Ivanovich; kind neighbors somehow arranged the match. She had been educated in Smolny Monastery,[4] could not draw a single breath without the French language, in which, however, not a word could be exchanged with the families of the vicinity. A whole life to be spent with an old bear, quiet and tame, true, but in his lair! This was frightful. Her mind was made up; she bought a large decrepit wooden house in

61

Penza and transferred her husband with all his theatrical appurtenances to this new residence. . . .

The troupe of such good-hearted masters could not be anything but merry and most original. The Kozhins had managed to engage somewhere the free actor Gruzinov, who knew his job excellently. Besides, one of their own maidservants, Dunyasha, unexpectedly revealed some native talent. Katerina Vasilevna, remembering how in Smolny Madame Laffont herself had taught her to play Athalie, passed on her precepts, though in this case, to my thinking, they were useless; her actors could play only comedies, with or without singing. This troupe was called the Governor's, since my father was indeed its patron and had persuaded the Marshals of the Nobility to lend for its performances their large Assembly Hall which, save at election time, was always empty.

It became the fashion for the best society, irrespective of political opinions, to attend these performances. . . . On the other hand, the parterre at Gladkov's was filled exclusively by the lower orders, while in the boxes yawned the most fanatic opposition, though Gladkov himself in no wise belonged to it.

—*Zapiski* (Moscow, 1928)

NOTES: [1]The vogue for serf actors lasted from the second half of the eighteenth century to the middle of the nineteenth. It was one of the most curious episodes in the history of the Russian theater. Moscow set the example of privately-owned serf troupes; Petersburg and the provinces followed.

[2]In 1803.

[3]However, there were still over a score of serf theaters in Petersburg at the beginning of the nineteenth century.

[4]The Smolny Institute for girls of the nobility was founded by Catherine II in 1764, on the model of the French school of Saint-Cyr. The first headmistress was Madame Laffont.

■ ■ ■

THE BRIDES' FAIR[1]

F. F. Vigel

62 ■ ■ ■ During that winter I also attended Moscow balls; I went twice to the Nobility Assembly Hall.[2] This building is situated near the Kreml', in the very middle of Moscow, which itself is considered as the center of our country. Not only the Moscow nobility, but the gentry from nearly all

the Great-Russian provinces flocked here every winter to entertain their wives and daughters. In the huge hall, as if in a magnificent temple in the heart of Russia, was set up the image of Catherine, which no jealousy of her memory had been able to cast out.[3] A three-tiered columned hall, all white, flaming with the fire of dazzling lights, crowded with thousands of visitors of both sexes in their best attire, thunderous with the music of its galleries—and at one end, slightly raised above it all, the marble visage of Catherine, smiling at the general gaiety as in the days of her life and of our felicity! I was impressed and enraptured by this marvelous sight. When my first wonder had passed, I began to examine more carefully the numerous company in whose midst I found myself; what a number of fair countenances, important figures, and brilliant costumes! But even more, what a number of odd features and accoutrements!

The landowners of the neighboring provinces deemed it an obligation to leave their villages in December of each year with their whole family, driving to Moscow in their own equipages and arriving about Christmas; they returned to the country in the first week of Lent. These trips were not expensive. The travelers were generally preceded by long convoys drawn by the peasants' horses and loaded with frozen sucking pigs, geese and chickens, groats, flour, and butter, and all the necessary provender. Every squire had his own wooden house in the city, plainly furnished, with a wide yard and a pathless garden overgrown with nettles, but in which you could find a dozen crab apple trees and a hundred or so raspberry and currant bushes.

The whole district south of the Moscow river was crowded with these gentry houses.[4] During the owners' short stay in Moscow, they had no time to make new acquaintances; they lived among themselves in the society of their country neighbors: each province had its own circle. But on Thursdays they all gathered in the large circle of the Nobility Assembly. There they could see the court ladies in waiting with the Empress' portrait, the court maids of honor with the Empress' monogram,[5] and such ribbons, such crosses, such rich dresses and diamonds! There would be plenty to tell about in the country during the next nine months, with wonder, but with no envy: they admired these unattainable heights of aristocracy as a traveler gazes upon the glittering summit of Elbruz.[6]

But the petty glory of spending evenings with the highest representatives of the Russian nobility was not the only thing that drew them to the Assembly. There is scarcely a Russian family that is not blessed with half-a-dozen daughters. And, who knows—perhaps Dunyasha or Parasha would catch a good man's eye. But what if the good man knew none of their acquaintances? There was a remedy for that too. In the old times (and perhaps in our days too) Moscow had a whole class of marriage-brokers. They were supplied with a list of the marriageable girls: age, dowry, conditions for the marriage contract. One could apply to them directly, and they would give the parents all the additional information

63

that the suitor's glances at their daughter had been unable to convey. Let others laugh; for myself I find something touching in the simplicity of our grandfathers' ways.

Curious observers found much to interest them in those assemblies; it was easy to note the preoccupied mothers, arm in arm with their daughters, and to read in their eyes the uneasy thought that this very minute would perhaps decide their fate. The merry bonhomie of the provincial visitors clearly distinguished them from the Moscow residents.

—*Zapiski* (Moscow, 1928)

NOTES: [1]From Pushkin's *Eugene Onegin*, canto 7, 26.

[2]The Assembly Hall of the Nobility, now Union Hall, is famed for its Column Room, the work of the Moscow architect, M. F. Kazakov, in 1784.

[3]This is an allusion to Paul's hatred of his mother's memory. See also Vigel's text on Petersburg monuments, "Art and Aesthetics," pp. 137–39.

[4]Later in the nineteenth century the "Zamoskvoreche" district lost its gentry character, and many merchants settled in it.

[5]The Smolny students, on completion of their studies, received this monogram, which was also the emblem of the court maids of honor.

[6]The highest peak in the Caucasus.

■ ■ ■

PARISH PRIESTS AND VILLAGE LIFE

A. N. Engelhardt

A. N. Engelhardt (1832–93), artillery officer, professor of chemistry at the Agronomical Institute in Petersburg from 1866 to 1869, was assigned to forced residence in his family estate of Batishchevo, in the Smolensk province, in 1871. He lived there until his death. His "Letters from the Village," published in the journal *Annals of the Fatherland* from 1872 to 1887, enjoyed considerable success. Marx and later Lenin greatly admired them.

■ ■ ■ Every month I receive the "popes'" visit. By "popes" I don't mean "a pope" in the plural. The word "popes" designates all those who belong to the ecclesiastical calling, all those who wear long hair and clerical garb of a special cut: this goes for priest and deacon and sacristan and bell ringer, active or retired, and all the churchpeople in the parish. During Easter Week or at Christmas, wherever traditions are kept, a whole troop of such "popish" folk follows the priest as he goes about the parish. The

64

word "popes," then, is used in the same way as the word "crows" for raven, rook, crow, jackdaw, magpie—all that feathered tribe which is lumped under the term "crows."

I like it when the popes come. They visit me every month, to bless the water in the cattle yard. This is an ancient custom. Every first of the month or so, the popes—priest, deacon, two or three sacristans—bless the water in the cattle yard, farmyard, shed or izba, and walk around the yard singing "Save Thy people, Lord," as the priest enters each shed to sprinkle holy water. If I am at home, I generally attend the ceremony, and when it is over, I invite them in for refreshment. We eat, drink tea, and talk. I like to talk with the popes and I find their conversation useful and enlightening. In the first place, nobody knows the life of the common people in all its details as they do; whoever wishes to obtain a genuine knowledge of the people's way of life, circumstances, customs, manners, philosophy, their bad and good points; whoever wishes to discover the nature of that unknown and unexplained creature called "muzhik"[1] should not remain satisfied with what he can observe by himself, but seek for the necessary information among the popes; in any particular area, the popes are invaluable in that respect because they know the exact circumstances of each peasant in their parish. In the second place, no one, except the peasants themselves, knows local farming conditions as the popes do. The priests are our best farmers—they are even superior to the peasants in that respect—and much can be gained from their experience. Farming, in fact, is the popes' most important source of income. What indeed could a sacristan or even a deacon live on, how could he bring up his children, of which he always has a considerable number, if he was not a good farmer? Of course,

> There's meat in the pope's pirog,
> There's butter in the pope's kasha,
> There's fish in Lent in the pope's shchi.[2]

But this is true only for the parish priest himself, not for the lesser fry among the clerics, who live from hand to mouth.

I don't know about other regions, but in our area the churches are many, the parishes small, the peasants poor, and the priests' income is insignificant. How small their resources are can be seen by the low fees they receive for the services. For the monthly blessing of the water I pay three rubles a year, which means twenty-five kopeks a visit. These twenty-five kopeks are divided into nine shares of about two kopeks three-quarters each (one quarter of a kopek being left over every month). The parish priest gets four shares or about eleven kopeks, the deacon two shares or five and a half kopeks, the three sacristans each one share. So a sacristan who comes from the village seven versts[3] away gets a mere two kopeks and three quarters for his trouble. Say that in a day the popes can visit three landowners and perform three blessings—which means twenty-five versts on the road; in the best of circumstances the sacristan will earn eight kopeks and a quarter, the deacon sixteen and a half, and the priest himself thirty-three.

65

I have given these figures to show how insignificant the popes' income is in our region. Of course they get more from the peasants. These don't have services every month, but two or three times a year the popes make the rounds of all the homesteads. For instance, during Easter Week, they sing one, two, four services in each house and get, according to the peasant's means, a ruble, seven grivny (seventy kopeks), half-a-ruble, twenty kopeks—this last from the very poorest peasants. . . . Payment is made immediately, or in the fall if the peasant has no ready money. In this respect our local clergy is good-natured and they do not press the peasants for payment. Of course, apart from money, the popes are given eggs and are fed the whole week as they go from hamlet to hamlet. Since the services are short, they can easily visit seven houses in one morning (this counts as a good-sized hamlet in our area), and their daily earnings during Easter Week are reasonable; but still the take in cash is miserable. So it's clear that with such meager resources the popes depend chiefly on their farming, thus, if a sacristan, for example, is not good at farming, he's bound to go under.

—"Letters from the Village," Letter 2, *Iz derevni* (Moscow, 1937)

NOTES: [1]Allusion to the Populists' and Slavophils' belief in the peculiar depth of wisdom of the Russian peasant. See the Korolenko text on "Populism in the Seventies," pp. 202–6.

[2]*Pirog*: meat or vegetable or fruit pie. *Kasha*: buckwheat groats. *Shchi*: cabbage soup.

[3]A *versta* (pre-revolution) was slightly longer than a kilometer, about two-thirds of a mile.

■ ■ ■

3

POPULAR
BELIEFS
AND
TRADITIONS

In the early sixties of the nineteenth century, Dostoevsky and a few other writers, such as Apollon Grigoriev and Nikolay Strakhov, were sometimes referred to as "pochvenniki," from the word "pochva," soil. For those writers Russian life was, more closely than in other countries, organically related to the forces of the earth. Although the Slavophils also spoke of Russian culture as "native," they emphasized its religious traits or the essential strength and goodness in the Russian man. The pochvenniki, on the other hand, stressed some sacramental element in Mother Earth herself, a mystic link between her dark, life-giving warmth and Russian destiny. Whatever value is given to this interpretation of Russian life, it is true that the Russian people, overwhelmingly composed of peasants for most of Russia's historical life (90 per cent in the eighteenth century, over 75 per cent at the 1897 census), have remained closer to primitive nature and more attuned to her mysteries than most of their Western neighbors. Amidst the migrations and oppressions that marked the passing centuries, the earth, the tilling of the soil, represented the only permanence of life. As he changed his habitation, fleeing Tatar conquerors or his own lords, the Russian peasant did not have to change his mode of life in any essentials: climate, land, and forest remained much the same, the rhythm of seasons unaltered, the isolation undiminished. Whatever memories endured were linked with the earth. The native civilization that emerged was that of an earth-bound and earth-loving peasant tradition.

Much in that tradition is pre-Christian. It has often been remarked that Christianity, as it spread in Russia, met with relatively little resistance. Sporadic "sorcerers' uprisings" are noted in the chronicles, but the process of evangelization required few, if any, martyrs. The new faith was accepted easily. However, the Christianized peasant felt no antagonism between old and new, and the old deities lived on, side by side with the new saints, both equally identifying themselves with peasant life and modes of thought. As elsewhere, the Church assimilated what it could and fought what it must. The cattle-god Volos became Vlasy, the saint, whom icons show accompanied by an ox. Ilya, the severe saint who brings thunder, replaced the fire-god Perun. But priests were few at first, and the peasant world soon absorbed them; the elaborate ritual of the Church often served merely as a new language for ancient fears and aspirations. As time went by, the Church fought more strongly against the "double faith," its puritanism increasing as it suspected everywhere a mingling of immorality or social unrest with traces of pagan worship. It was easier to attack such manifestations than to understand the uncertainties and weaknesses in the Church that they revealed. But the attacks were futile. Although bear shows, which delighted the Russian peasants, were forbidden repeatedly by the Church—

the bear was considered an unclean, devilish beast, and the shows were frequently bawdy or satirical—they were still popular in the nineteenth century. From earliest times the Church feared and denounced wandering minstrels, who took part in heathen dances and songs and also jested against clergy and lords. But the minstrels disappeared only when Europeanized entertainments such as the theater took their place.

Thus, in its generic, elemental aspects, the force of tradition defied the efforts of "imported" cultures. The pilgrims and wandering monks who roamed over the land as late as the nineteenth century spread legend, myth, or tale from south to north, west to east. The old memories stretched from past to present as endlessly as the Russian roads trodden by the wanderers. These memories united the inarticulate peasant masses by the only consciousness they could recognize as their own: that of the eternity of the land and their own belonging to that eternity.

As the peasant clung to the instinctive, timeless memories that were the image of his ancestral being, so did he create in turn his own ideal image from the fragments of the past that came down to him in the form of epic songs. Beside the warrior and the prince, he set up the peasant hero, stronger and better than they: half myth, half man, Mikula Selyaninovich, the ploughman of heroic dimensions who alone can lift from the soil the plough that has resisted the efforts of all the warriors; Svyatogor, with the strength of Mother Earth herself, hardly to be distinguished from her; and the most popular of all the semihistorical figures, Ilya of Murom, the peasant's son, who in one version of a bylina proclaims that he serves "the Christian faith, the Russian land, the capital city of Kiev, the widows, the orphans, and the poor people." Ilya of Murom is still proposed nowadays to Soviet youth as the embodiment of the generic virtues of the Russian people.

Russian popular traditions and beliefs remained part of the national heritage until the seventeenth century. The break in social customs that occurred with Peter's reign reduced the peasant tradition, for a time, to the level of "folklore," isolating and to a certain degree sterilizing it. Ignorance and disdain of this folklore among the Russian elite lasted until the end of the eighteenth century, when interest in popular culture revived, fostered at first by the burgeoning literary taste for simplicity and sentiment. From the first collection of songs by Chulkov in 1770 and the first Russian opera on peasant life, *Aniuta*, in 1772, the study of folklore steadily broadened and deepened. The Romanticists, the Slavophils, the Nationalists reintroduced its wealth and beauty into the national consciousness. Thus, even though the civilization it expressed may no longer exist, it lives on in such works as Pushkin's *Tales*, Rimsky-Korsakov's *Sadko* or *Snegurochka*, or the painter Vasnetsov's "Three Bogatyrs."

70

POPULAR PASTIMES IN THE SEVENTEENTH CENTURY
Olearius' "Voyages and Travels"

"A Dancing-Bear, a Puppet-Show, a Gusli-Player"
From *Istoriya Moskvy* (Moscow, 1952), Vol. I

FOLK MYTHOLOGY
I. E. Zabelin

■ ■ ■ The "domovoy"[1] embodied the life of the house, the sum total of mysterious and unfathomable happenings around the homestead. Why did the cattle grow fat, why did they suddenly grow lean, why did a panic arise among cattle and fowl, why did certain breeds of cattle always sicken and die in spite of all possible care? These and numberless other occurrences all pointed to the same fact: a mysterious force, an unknown will was behind it all. On the other hand, the domovoy also embodied the wishes, aspirations, and efforts of the master of the house for the welfare of his household. As we know, the hearth or the stove is the foundation and heart of the house. It contains the essential well-being of the home, giving heat in cold weather, preparing food at all times, able to transform any substance into something useful or pleasant for man. Fire was a living being, a little god. So, in a sense, the domovoy was this domestic fire itself, the hearth. When moving into a new izba, the master of the house took the fire with him, in the form of burning coals, from the old stove into the new, with the words: "Welcome, old one, to your new home."

The domovoy generally lives behind the stove, where domestic offerings, such as little loaves, are left for him. He is fed like a human: bread, kasha, pirogi, flat cakes; at night supper is set out for him. But his favorite present is a rooster. This offering appeases him completely if anything has vexed him. The sorcerer kills the bird at midnight, lets the blood drip on a little broom, and sweeps out all the corners of izba and farmyard with suitable incantations. . . .

The domovoy is a good fellow and the most careful keeper of the household. Newly bought horses and cows are entrusted to him with the words: "Love them, make them eat and drink, keep their coats smooth, don't play tricks yourself, keep my wife in check and the children quiet." The rope with which the animal has been brought to the farm is then hung by the stove.

The domovoy loves only his own home, and he has been known to steal fodder for his charges from other haylofts and grain bins. He notices every detail, is tirelessly busy putting everything in good order and readiness, giving a hand here and setting things to rights elsewhere. At night you can hear him tapping as he works at various chores. If the house suits him, he looks after the whole place and cares for the property better than the owner himself; he keeps an eye on the horses, cows, pigs, sheep, and goats; minds the poultry, with a special care for the chickens; and watches over the drying shed, kitchen garden, stables, cow house, and barn. . . .

It is apparent that this image of the domestic spirit is in fact the embodiment of the happiness and prosperity of the household. The domovoy is the guardian of the house. His physical appearance is in keeping with

72

this notion, for he is covered with thick shaggy wool and soft down. Even the soles of his feet and the palms of his hands are hairy. At night he strokes sleepy human beings with the palms of his hands: if the hands are warm and soft, it's a good omen, but if they're cold and prickly, it's a bad sign. At night the domovoy sometimes chokes sleepy people, but only for a joke, just as he plays tricks in the farmyard; he doesn't mean any harm. The domovoy is evil only outside his own realm, so any real hurt is the work of a domovoy from another house.

The concept of domestic labor, happiness, wealth, and prosperity links the domovoy to the cult of dead parents and ancestors, since nobody can desire the happiness of the family more strongly than departed kinsfolk. For this reason he is called "grandfather," not only as being a ruling spirit, but as a real forefather. This may explain why the domovoy sometimes takes human shape and appears now as a boy, now as an old man. Thus the concept of the domovoy contains all the notions about the life of the homestead, its past and future, happiness and misfortune, worries and labors. It represents the whole life of people in the limits of their house and yard.

A similar process created the image of the "leshy." The leshy embodies the life of the forest and all that confused and perplexed man in it. The leshy disappeared in the fall to come back in spring: this means that he represented the living forest, clad in greenery, singing with the voice of birds, swarming with beasts, whistling with the sinister hiss of the mysterious *Div.*[2] The leshy is as tall as the tallest tree, as small as the smallest blade of grass. He is the forest itself, not seen as a number of trees, but as the living fullness of the forest kingdom, as one complete unique being. The leshy's hair and beard are long, tangled, and green. His head is narrow and shaggy. He likes to hang from trees, rocking on branches as in a cradle or swing. He whistles and roars with laughter that can be heard forty versts away, claps his hands, neighs like a horse, bellows like a cow, barks like a dog, mews like a cat, cries like a child, moans like a dying man, and rumbles like a torrent. Sometimes he leads the traveler into impassable thickets and swamps and then plays with him: he turns into familiar landmarks such as a tree, a stump, or a track, confusing his victim while he himself shouts with laughter. He can change into a wolf or owl; or else, in the shape of an old man dressed in furs or a peasant with a pack on his shoulder, he stops the traveler, starts to talk with him, asks for a pirog, or begs for a ride to the village, and then disappears, leaving the traveler in a swamp, in a gully, or on the edge of a precipice. Having fooled his man, he starts tickling him and may tickle him to death. He carries off children, who sometimes return home after several years. The leshy is also fond of the fair sex. This is why children and women gathering mushrooms and berries sometimes disappear for several days, if not forever. To avoid such a misfortune, one should wear one's clothes inside out.

73

Nevertheless, the leshy is a kindhearted and grateful spirit if he is mellowed with offerings. The herdsman must sacrifice a cow to him, then he willingly looks after the herd. Huntsmen always honor him with a gift of bread and salt, a pancake, and a pirog which they leave on a tree stump. Or they may present him with their first kill. On Erofey's day (October 4) the leshy disappears: he starts raging and chasing the beasts of the forest, and then he vanishes into the earth. The forest dies until spring.

The life of the water—river, lake, swamp—is similarly reflected in the image of the "vodianoy," who represents all the unaccountable manifestations of that element. The vodianoy lives in a deep water hole, in an eddy, and particularly near a water mill, that cunning structure whose master the miller is himself always a sorcerer and a friend of the vodianoy.

The vodianoy is a naked old man with a big swollen belly and puffy face—like a drowned man. His hair and beard are long and green. Sometimes he is covered with slime. He wears a tall hat of waterweeds and a grass belt. All sorts of water grasses make up his costume, his skin. But he may also take the appearance of an ordinary peasant. Then it is easy to recognize him: the skirts of his caftan[3] are always wet, water drips from the left side, and wherever he sits he leaves a wet stain. He has a fine time in his water hole: he lives in a stone palace and has herds of horses, cows, sheep, and pigs (all drowned). He marries a *rusalka*.[4] He can drive a quantity of fish into the fishing nets. He rides a large fish which he loves tenderly. By day he sits deep in the water; his active life begins at sunset: then it's dangerous to bathe or even to drink there—you might catch the dropsy, the water sickness. During moonlit nights he slaps the water with the flat of his hand and you see the water suddenly foam and swirl— that's the vodianoy. It's only in summer that he's awake: in winter he sleeps. After his hibernation he wakes up on Nikita's day, the third of April. The spring ice breaks and pushes down the stream, the water bubbles and rages— that means old man Vodianoy is waking up, the river is coming to life. He will quiet down if you sacrifice a horse to him. Fishermen pour oil as an offering, butchers bring him a fattened black pig. In the fall, when the life of the river comes to its end, a goose is presented to him as a farewell gift.

—*Istoricheskaya khrestomatiya*, ed. Ya. G. Gurevich
(St. Petersburg, 1904), Vol. I

NOTES: [1]Other names for the domovoy are: grandfather, master, neighbor.
        [2]Presumably a forest spirit: the name occurs in the "Lay of the Host of Igor" (twelfth century).
        [3]The caftan is traditionally a double-breasted long coat.
        [4]The "rusalka" or water nymph is generally a girl who has drowned. The rusalka legends are linked with the cult of the dead.

■ ■ ■

THE CHURCH AGAINST SUPERSTITIONS

Council of the Hundred Chapters

"In the year 7059, on the twenty-third day of February, these numerous questions concerning various church matters and rules were asked in the ruling city of Moscow, in the Tsar's palace, by the piously-crowned Orthodox Lord Tsar and Prince Ivan Vasilevich, autocrat of the Russian land, of the very holy Makary, consecrated Metropolitan of Moscow and all the Russian land, and of all the holy council, in the eighteenth year of the Tsar's reign, in the twenty-first of his birth, Makary, consecrated Metropolitan of Moscow and all the Russian land, being in the tenth year of his prelacy."

The Council of the Hundred Chapters, or Stoglavy Sobor, convened in 1551 to correct church rites and reform corrupted customs. The sessions, attended by archbishops, bishops, hegumens, archimandrites, and high-ranking boyars, were opened with a speech by the Tsar. The decisions of the Council were presented in the form of questions and answers.

■ ■ ■ **Question XVI:** At the weddings of lay persons, clowns, jews'-harp players, pranksters, gusli-players[1] make merry and sing devilish songs; when the wedding procession proceeds toward the church, the priest accompanies it bearing the cross, and ahead are those gambollers with all their devilish tricks; the priests allow this, and it behoves them to forbid it.

Question XVII: Our Orthodox Christians are addicted to quarrels; some practice disloyalty, and having accused falsely they kiss the cross or the holy icons; they fight in duels[2] and shed blood. And then wizards and sorcerers give them devilish assistance: they work spells, consult the *Aristotle Gates* and the "Rafli,"[3] and study the stars and planets, the days and hours; by such devilish tricks they seduce and cut off from God. And relying on those charms, the slanderer and defamer refuses to make peace; he kisses the cross, fights on the field, and kills the man he has slandered.

Question XIX: Minstrels[4] travel to distant lands in bands of sixty, seventy, a hundred men; they stop in villages, at the peasants' houses, drink and eat their fill, steal the goods that are kept in closets, and rob passengers on the road.

Question XXI: In the parishes, villages, and districts travel false prophets, men and women, both young and old, half-naked and barefoot, with long hair streaming; they shake and rave to exhaustion. And they say that Holy Pyatnitsa[5] and Holy Anastasya appear to them and order them to urge Christians to promise services in their honor. Also they urge Christians not to do any work with their hands on Wednesdays and Fridays; they tell women not to spin or wash clothes or light the stove. . . .

Question XXIII: On the Saturday before Trinity, men and women gather in the villages and parishes, go to the common burial grounds and weep on the graves with loud cries. Then, when minstrels and rebec-players begin to make merry, they stop weeping and start to jump and dance and clap their hands and sing satanic songs; there are also charlatans and thieves in those burial grounds.

Question XXIV: At the Rusaliya on St. John's Eve, on Christmas Eve, and on Twelfth Night Eve,[6] men and women and girls gather for night revels, for shameful talk and devilish songs, with dancing, jumping, and acts hateful to God. . . . When night is at its end, they go to the river with loud shouting, like demons, and wash in the water. And when matins are rung, they go home and fall down as if dead after their great excitement.

Question XXVI: On Good Thursday, early in the morning, straw is burnt and the dead are called on; some ignorant priests put salt under the altar on that day and keep it there until the seventh Thursday after the Great Easter Day, and then they give that salt for the cure of sick people and cattle.

—Russkaya khrestomatiya, ed. F. Buslaev (Moscow, 1912)

NOTES: [1]The gusli, which was the minstrels' favorite instrument, was a stringed instrument (the number of strings was variable), generally in the form of a trapeze, plucked by hand and played on the minstrel's knees.

[2]These were judiciary duels.

[3]The *Aristotle Gates* was a medieval work often called "The Secret of Secrets," containing instructions supposedly written by Aristotle to Alexander the Great. The chapters were called "gates," hence the name. "Rafli": old fortunetelling books.

[4]This refers to the "skomorokhi," wandering minstrels, jesters, and actors, who were extremely popular with both peasants and boyars in spite of all Church denunciations.

[5]Or Paraskeva: Friday. Wednesday and Friday were popularly deemed to be holy days.

[6]This describes the pagan rites on Midsummer Night and during the Christmas season. The Rusaliya proper, linked to the rites of spring and the cult of the dead, was generally celebrated during the seventh week after Easter or just before Whitsunday—"Semik," or Rusaliya week.

FOLK SINGERS AND RECITERS

V. N. Kharuzina

> With her brother Nikolay, Vera Nikolaevna Kharuzina studied the ethnography and folklore of northern Russia in the last decades of the nineteenth century.

■ ■ ■ There was a singer of *byliny*[1] in Burakovo, Nikifor Prokhorov, nicknamed Utka (Duck).

"He sings the old songs really well," we were told, "and if he gets a drink or two for the voice, he will be at his best."

"Here comes Utka, here he comes!" they shouted joyfully, pointing to a boat which came dipping on the grey waves of the lake. Our hosts were looking forward, no less than we were, to the pleasure of hearing the singing of the byliny.

"Wouldn't it be possible to come and listen in your room?" an elder asked my brother in the name of the other peasants who had gathered on hearing of the singer's arrival. It was a Sunday, and the village was crowded. The room soon filled up. However, there were few young lads; mostly older men sat on the benches and on the bed or huddled in the doorway.

Utka came in; he was an old man, short, squat, and broad-shouldered. His grey hair, short and curly, framed his high forehead; a sparse goatee covered his chin. His face was wrinkled, with a good-humored, rather playful mouth and large blue eyes. There was something naïve and childishly helpless in his whole expression.

The audience encouraged him to take a drink "for the voice," and he accepted after some fuss.

"What old song shall I sing for you?" he asked, taking off his warm coat and throwing his head back slightly. "Are you going to write it down?" The old man had already sung byliny for Hilferding.[2]

. . .Utka cleared his throat—and everybody fell silent at once. He threw his head back, glanced round with a smile and, noticing the general impatient expectation, cleared his throat again and began to sing. His expression changed gradually, until no trace was left of naïveté or playfulness. Now his face was alive with inspiration: his blue eyes widened and glowed; two bright tears glistened in them; a flush came out on his tanned cheeks and now and again his neck twitched convulsively.

He was sharing his beloved *bogatyrs'*[3] adventures; he was moved to tears of pity for helpless Ilya Muromets,[4] when he "sat and sat" for thirty years; with Ilya he triumphed after his victory over Nightingale the Robber.[5] At times he would break off and put in remarks of his own.

And all his listeners, too, lived with the hero of the bylina.

77

Bylina on Volga and Mikula, noted by Mussorgsky and used by him
in his opera "Boris Godunov" (Song of Varlaam and Misail).

Жил Свя-то-слав де-вя -нос-то лет, жил Святослав да пере-ставил-ся, о -ста-

ва-лось от не-го ча -до ма-ло -е мо-ло-дой Вольга Свято -сла-во-вич

The first ride of Ilya Muromets.

За -ле - га-ла до - рош -ка пря- мо - ех-ха- я

Пря -мо - ех- ха до - рош-ка пе- шо - ход-на- я

Bylina on Dobrynya Nikitich.

Как во столь-нем бы-ло го-ро- де во Ки- е-ве да и у

ла - ско -ва да кня-зя у Вла- ди -ми- ра

THREE BYLINA TUNES
From: (1) *Istoriya russkoy muzyki*, ed. M. S. Pekelis (Moscow, 1940); (2) M. Shtokmar,
Issledovaniya v oblasti russkogo narodnogo stikhoslozheniya (Moscow, 1952); (3) A. M.
Astakhova, *Byliny severa* (Moscow, 1951)

At times an exclamation would break out, at times a bursting roar of laughter. Some eyes were moist with tears, furtively wiped off. All sat with their gaze fixed on the singer; they caught every single sound of the motive he sang, as it flowed on monotonously, but quietly and beautifully.

Utka ended and looked round triumphantly. There was a moment's silence, then everybody burst into speech.

"Good for the old one! What a singer! He's cheered us, he has. That drink wasn't wasted!" Utka smiled: his face had assumed its former everyday expression.

"Maybe it's just a story," remarked a peasant doubtfully.

All the others set on him.

"What do you mean, just a story? . . . Didn't you hear, it's about the old times . . . It happened under the good prince, under Vladimir."[6]

"But I just thought: who'd be strong enough? Look what he did to the other. . . ."

A chorus of explanations arose:

"That's because he was a bogatyr. What do you think? Not like us—a bogatyr! We couldn't do it, but it's easy for him."

"What's the use of talking? Old man, better give us another one."

Everybody fell silent; a minute later the characteristic music was sounding again.

. . . My brother was told: "A reciter has come from Melentevo— could we hear him?"

The reciter was an old man, tall and thin, with long snow-white hair and an intelligent friendly face. He bore himself calmly and decorously. Being an Old Believer, he refused the vodka with restraint and dignity.

Utka's greetings to him were rather tense: he knew that now a contest was inevitable between them for the listeners' appreciation. The old man from Melentevo shook his head, sat down on the bench and, leaning back, began his tale.

A reciter knows the same byliny as the singer of "old songs," but he has no voice, no talent for singing, and so he relates them. Now the story of Dobrynya[7] and his wife Nastasya Mikulishna flowed in the measured even tones of the byliny style from the reciter's lips. He never broke off; he never hesitated for a word that might have slipped his memory. His clear old eyes gazed calmly on the audience. Utka was uneasy, though he tried to hide his nervousness. He kept his hands on his knees as he looked round the room in pretended tranquillity.

The peasants gave Utka their preference.

"The reciter speaks well, you can't deny it," they said in his praise; "but the old tales are better sung."

And triumphant Utka was asked to sing again.

—In the North (1890), Russky folklor, ed. N. P. Andreev (Moscow-Leningrad, 1938)

NOTES: ¹*Byliny* or *stariny* (old songs) are epic songs that originated between the eleventh and the sixteenth centuries. They have been preserved chiefly in the provinces of northern Russia.

²Hilferding collected byliny in the Onega region around 1873. He was the first to classify the songs by reciters and not by subjects.

³The *bogatyrs* are the heroes of the byliny.

⁴Ilya Muromets is the most popular byliny hero. After sitting helpless and paralyzed for thirty years, he rose in overwhelming strength and engaged in a number of adventures. Over the centuries, Ilya "the peasant's son" or "the old Cossack" has become an idealized figure of the Russian people, peaceful though quick-tempered, the defender of the weak and a great fighter for his country.

⁵One of Ilya's fabled enemies, half monster, half man; he killed travelers on the road to Kiev, but was finally caught by Ilya, taken to Kiev, and executed.

⁶Vladimir the "Fair-Sun," who reigned in Kiev from 980 to 1015. The byliny Vladimir also has traits of Vladimir Monomakh, Prince of Kiev in the twelfth century.

⁷Another bogatyr, noble and magnanimous, who often had adventures with women.

■ ■ ■

4

**FAITH
AND
THE
CHURCH**

In his *Essays on Russian Culture*, Milyukov writes that the question "Are Muscovites Christians?" was the subject of a dissertation presented before the Upsala Academy in 1620. Only three decades later, Paul of Aleppo, deacon to the Antioch Patriarch during the latter's journey to Muscovy, exclaimed in wonder, exhaustion, and exasperation at the lengthy church services and rigorous fasting practiced by the Russians: "All Russians will undoubtedly become saints: they outdo even the desert hermits in piety."

The Swede's doubts and the Syrian's amazement were probably both justified, even though they seem to proceed from directly opposite observations. In both cases, the source of their perplexity or admiration is the all-important place of the ritual form in Russian religion. (Similarly, foreigners observed the all-important place of ritual form in Russian society.) Russian tradition—flattering, as traditions are, to national pride—attributes Vladimir's choice of Byzantine Christianity in the tenth century to the admiration he felt for the beauty of its rites. Both austere and splendid, the forms of the Orthodox Church are indeed impressive esthetically. Spiritually, they carry a high symbolic value, which, however, may not always be perceived and therefore may be demoted into meaningless convention. Seen as an empty shell, the formal religion of the Russian has often been denied any value; considered as symbol-bearing, we find it dignified by the epithet "platonic." Since the question of the relations between form and content can hardly be settled for any people or period in their entirety, it does not seem either possible or profitable for a modern observer to do more than describe the forms that were so important to the Russian religious life and trace the problems and conflicts they engendered.

The general features of Russian Orthodoxy are well known. Christianity came to Russia from Byzantium during one of the great periods of Byzantine culture, carrying all the weight of Byzantine prestige. From Byzantium, Russia took its canon law; its artistic modes; the traditions of the Greek Fathers, their monastic rules, and the division of churchmen into "black and white" (regular and secular) clergy, the monks being the bearers of culture and power. But it evolved its own liturgical language—Church Slavonic—and was thus deprived of a language of communication with its mother church. Likewise, it did not participate in the disputes on dogma or religious concepts that stirred thought in the West nor did it really define its own dogma. Few heresies arose, and these chiefly through its open door to the West, Novgorod. A fifteenth-century attempt to "free" the Church from the State and material power failed. Inside the Church itself, the monks, from whose ranks alone the ecclesiastical hierarchy could be recruited, remained an amorphous mass that never separated into various orders. The Basilian rule, applied with more or less severity, dominates the whole history of Russian monasticism. In the West, Benedictines (with their widely different branches of Clunisian and Cistercian), Franciscans, Dominicans, Jesuits, to mention only the most important, have each contributed their material achievements and philosophies to the development of European culture. The history of Russian monasticism, as has often been remarked, is reduced to the history of the great monasteries: The Caves for Kievan Russia, The Trinity for Muscovy, Solovki for the Schism. Though the monks' contribution to Russian culture, as settlers in new lands, chronicle writers, icon painters, translators, copiers and correctors of sacred books, is immense, it is varied more in the record of their activities than in spirit.

In everyday Russian life, the liveliest activities of priests and monks were directed against the remnants of pagan beliefs known in Russian as "double faith," and against the lay entertainments in which they often suspected either those same pagan traditions or the heretic influences of the West. These were specially dangerous, since the West also represented a threat against the integrity of the Russian state. The adjectives "Russian" and "Orthodox" were for a long time synonymous. Russia's position between the heathen Asiatic menace and the peril of the "Latin" West so strengthened the normal tie between nationality and faith that one became unthinkable without the other. The law expressed this confusion when it forbade a Russian Orthodox to change his faith, and when it labelled as "foreign" all the other religions in the land.

Religious nationalism, added to the already-mentioned "platonism" of the Russian faith, partially explains the schism of the seventeenth century. When, after the Time of Troubles, the lowering and loosening of religious standards called renewed attention to the need for spiritual, intellectual, and moral reform, the best representatives of the clergy were united in their efforts to improve understanding and practice of the faith by both priests and parishioners. But suspicion of heresy or corruption tainted all foreign sources of intellectual reform: the Greeks were under Turkish rule; the Ukrainians, then scholastically far more active than the Muscovites, had fallen under Jesuit influence. Books published in Kiev were submitted to Moscow censorship when they were not forbidden outright. Thus a Gospel published in Kiev in 1619 was banned in Moscow in 1625. When Patriarch Nikon adopted Greek revisions of the holy books and rites, all his hatred of Western innovations did not save him from the accusation of betraying the true faith.

The schism, then, was born of a passionate impulse toward purity and of a fierce and unreasoning belief in the purity of the national tradition. The first had been shared by all the reformers. The second bred dissent. Subsequently this dissent evolved into a strong peasant and merchant-

84

class movement, identified sometimes, as some Western reformed sects were identified, with a desperate rebellion against the cruelty of the State's power. But, unlike some Protestant movements, the Russian dissent lacked intellectual substance; it settled early into formalized rules of behavior—no smoking, no shaving, no drinking—or dissolved into blind feeling. It is ironical that the *Domostroy* spirit, which embodied the coldest and deadest of the official Church's attitudes, came later to be identified with the Old-Believers' mode of life.

"Our Church," says Dostoevsky, "has been paralyzed since Peter the Great." It had been maimed spiritually by the schism; it was reduced to an administrative, state-serving body by Peter; and the deep kinship with the sovereign power that in the past had justified its nationalism, was lost. When, in the nineteenth century, Russian national consciousness awoke to the need of analyzing itself, the role of faith and the Church in the country's life was re-examined. The Slavophils based their whole concept of Russian destiny on the purity and depth of the Russian faith. But the critic Belinsky, in his famous 1847 letter to Gogol, asserted that the Russian peasant was "deeply atheistic by nature." In his turn, Dostoevsky, calling the Russian people "God-bearing," sanctified the very nature of the Russian mass. Thus nineteenth-century Russian thinkers, still wondering whether Russia had not only a culture but also a religion, found themselves as much at variance in their conclusions as had the Swedish theologian and the Syrian deacon in the seventeenth century.

HOW CHRISTIANS SHOULD RESTORE THEIR HEALTH
The Domostroy

■ ■ ■ If God sends anyone sickness or pain, he should restore his health through the grace of God with tears, prayers, fasting, alms-giving, and sincere penance. He should thank the Lord, beg His forgiveness, show humanity and true charity to one and all. We should ask our spiritual directors to pray God, sing church services, consecrate water with the venerable cross and with the holy relics and icons of miracle-working saints; we should anoint ourselves with holy oil, make vows in the holy places where miracles occur, pray with a pure conscience. Thus does one obtain from God the healing of all possible ills; by the renunciation of all sins, by the resolve to abstain from evil, by heeding the commandments of our spiritual directors and complying with the penance laid upon us. Thus are we cleansed from sin; thus is sickness of body and soul healed; thus is divine mercy obtained.

A man cannot be healed if he is insolent and disorderly; does not fear God or comply with His will; does not keep Christian law and the tradition of the Fathers on the Church and on Church singing, on reading from the holy books before communion, on prayer; if he is not concerned with praising God; if he eats and drinks to excess and fills himself with food and wine when it is not fitting to do so; does not honor Sunday, Wednesday, and Friday, the holy days, the great Lent, the Lent of the Mother of God;[1] if he fornicates with no restraint, at improper times; if, against nature and the law, he commits adultery or sodomy; if he commits shameful and sacrilegious deeds, indulges in debauchery, obscenity, indecency; sings devil-inspired songs; plays the tambourine, the trumpet, the pipe;[2] keeps bears,[3] birds, hounds, goes horse-racing; enjoys devilish pleasures and indulges in scandal and impudence; if moreover he practices spellbinding, sorcery, magic knots, astrology, has recourse, in order to foresee the future, to almanacs, black magic, divination, the Seraph;[4] if he uses thunder arrows, hatchets,[5] plays the two-stone game, the magic bones; uses herbs and roots for all sorts of devilish purposes, feeds his victims to kill them or make them his accomplices in witchcraft or, through demoniac words and spells, causes men to do evil under all its forms, and adultery; if he calls upon the holy name of God to support a lie, or if he slanders a friend.[6]

—Chapter xxiii, *Russkaya khrestomatiya*, ed. F. Buslaev (Moscow, 1912)

NOTES: [1]From the first to the fifteenth of August.
[2]The Stoglav, Council of the Hundred Chapters, also forbids these instruments.

[3]See Avvakum on bears, too, p. 91. The Stoglav also forbids keeping bears. The bear was an unclean animal, and in early times Russian priests hesitated to wear coats made of its fur.

4The Shestokryl or "Seraph" consisted of a short text and astrological tables composed in the fourteenth century by an Italian Jew, Bar-Jacob.

5The thunder arrows and hatchets seem to refer to the "Lucidarius," a mystical work of uncertain origin and date. (Twelfth century?)

6For a commentary on *The Domostroy*, see E. Duchesne, *Le Domostroï, ménagier russe du XVIè siècle* (Paris, 1910).

■ ■ ■

THE FINDING OF AN ICON

Alexey Mikhailovich

> The tsar's writ to Matvey Spiridonov, governor of Tsarev-Kokshaysk,[1] concerned the bringing to Moscow of the miraculous image of the Holy Myrrh-Bearing Women and the building of a church of their name at the place of their apparition.

■ ■ ■ From the Tsar and Great-Prince of all Russia, Alexey Mikhailovich, to our Governor Matvey Mikiforovich Spiridonov, in Tsarev-Kokshaysk. In this year 7155,[2] on the twenty-fifth day of June, you wrote us that on May the first the peasant's son Ondryushka Ivanov, surnamed Zholnin, of our personal village Kuznetsova, district of Tsarev-Kokshaysk, brought to the cathedral church of the Resurrection of Our Lord in Tsarev-Kokshaysk an image of the Holy Myrrh-Bearing Women, set in silver, engraved on slate, of the Greek pattern; when questioned, the peasant Ondryushka related the following:

He was ploughing in the Cheremis[3] country, in the Manansk county, together with the Cheremis Aytuganko Pedeshev of the same county, when a light appeared on the field, upon seeing which he fell to the ground and started to cross himself, and then the wonder-working image of the Holy Women appeared to him. Aytuganko the Cheremis then began to laugh, and he lost his sight; but on the same day it was restored after he had prayed and wept.

The Cheremis Aytuganko Pedeshev, being questioned, has given the same story as the peasant Ondryushka.

You have placed this icon in the cathedral church of the Resurrection of Our Lord and a solemn service was sung on this occasion; and you have sent us a memoir of the cures worked by this icon; you have ordered a chapel to be erected at the place where the image was found; and

THE HOLY WOMEN   Icon by an unknown master, fifteenth century
From *Istoriya Moskvy* (Moscow, 1952), Vol. I

the garrison and townsmen of Tsarev-Kokshaysk, and the people of all ranks in the district, both Russian and newly baptized, beg us to allow them to have a church built on the place where the image of the Holy Women appeared.

When this writ reaches you, have a copy made of this wonder-working image to remain in Tsarev-Kokshaysk, and have the image itself brought to us in Moscow by a reputable noble or boyar-son;[4] also have the icon accompanied to Moscow by the priest and deacon of the cathedral church, by the peasant Ondryushka and the Cheremis Aytuganko Pedeshev; give them transportation to Moscow when they are ready to start. Send off the wonder-working icon with great honors: have it accompanied by priests and deacons with holy images, candles, censers, and the ringing of bells; and you yourself, with all the people of the city and district, go with the wonder-working icon out of the city, as far as you think fit.

Also order the noble or boyar-son to do this: when he is ten versts or more from Moscow, have him give notice of his arrival to the Office of the Kazan Palace,[5] and then await our orders in a village or borough, at his convenience. Write us also informing us of the date when you have sent the miraculous icon to Moscow and with whom, by name, and of the miracles worked by the icon since your previous report; sign the list with your own hand and have the priest sign too and send it to the Office of the Kazan Palace, to our boyar Prince Alexey Nikitich Trubetskoy, and to our secretaries Larion Lopukhin, Pyaty[6] Spiridonov, and Tomila[7] Porfirev. And let the garrison and townspeople of the city and the people of all ranks in the district build a church, according to their promise, on the place where the miraculous icon appeared, and dedicate it to the Holy Myrrh-Bearing Women.

Written in Moscow, in the year 7155, on the sixth day of July.

—*Akty istoricheskie* (St. Petersburg, 1842)

NOTES: [1] Tsarev-Kokshaysk (now Yoshkar-Ola) was founded in 1578 in the newly-acquired Kazan province.

[2] 1647.

[3] Now the Mari tribe. See note 2, "Beyond the Volga," p. 12.

[4] Name given to the descendant of a boyar family no longer entitled to this rank.

[5] The Office of the Kazan Palace had been created to administer the newly-conquered Kazan region.

[6] Pyaty: "Quintus"; the habit of numbering children in large families was still common in the seventeenth century. Cf., in English, "Septimus."

[7] Or Tomilo. Beside the Christian first name, given at baptism, Russians kept a Slavic first name, frequently descriptive. Tomila comes from "tomit," to weary.

89

■ ■ ■

THE LIFE OF ARCHPRIEST AVVAKUM

Avvakum

Avvakum (1621–82), son of Peter, a village priest, is one of the most fascinating figures of old Russia. His aspirations for moral and religious reform coincided with those of "The Friends of God," the group of priests who, in the first years of Alexey's reign (1645–52), were intent on making Russia worthy of their high Christian ideals. However, after Nikon's elevation to the patriarchate (1652), the drastic and often unconsidered changes that, under Greek influence, he imposed on the Church ritual shocked the religious nationalism of many reformers, whose leader Avvakum became. With the defeat of those who came to be known as "Old Believers," Avvakum was banished, imprisoned, exiled to the North, and finally burned at the stake in Pustozersk, on Good Friday of the year 1682.

His *Life*, composed in his Northern prison about 1672–73, was first revealed to the public in 1861. It is outwardly composed on the model of the traditional Saints' Lives: preface, relation, miracles. But the language, which combines Church Slavonic phrases and quotations with the familiar, racy Russian speech of the period, makes it a unique linguistic and literary document. It is also valuable as a description of Russian life and manners.

■ ■ ■ **Preface.**—With the blessing of my Father, the Elder Epiphanes,[1] I, Archpriest Avvakum, have written this with my sinful hand. If aught in it is expressed in homely words, I beg of you for the Lord's sake, you who read or hear, do not despise our common speech.[2] I love my Russian mother tongue and I am not used to embellish my speech with learned verse,[3] for fine words are not what God hearkens—He will have our deeds. And Paul writes: "Though I speak with the tongues of men and angels and have not charity, I am nothing."[4] But why long arguments? It is not phrases in Latin or Greek or Hebrew or any other language that God awaits from us, but charity and the other virtues; for this reason I have no concern with fine speech and do not humiliate my Russian language. Forgive me then, a sinner, and may God forgive and bless you all, servants of Christ.   Amen.

The Beginning.—I was born in the region of Nizhny-Novgorod, beyond the river Kudma, in the borough of Grigorovo. My father was the priest Peter, my mother's name was Mary—Martha in religion. My father indulged in strong drink; my mother fasted and prayed and ever instructed me in the fear of God. And once, at a neighbor's, I saw a cow that had died; that night I rose and before the icon I wept abundantly for my soul, thinking of death, for I would die too. And since then it has been my custom to pray every night. Some time later my mother became a widow;[5] I found myself, still a child, an orphan; and my kinsfolk drove me out in exile.

My mother wished to see me married. I begged the Most Holy Mother of God to give me a wife who would help me in my salvation. Now, in the same borough, there was a girl, also an orphan, who attended church diligently: her name was Anastasia. Her father had been a smith, Mark by name, and wealthy, but after his death all his fortune had gone. So she was poor and prayed God to unite her to me in wedlock; and by His grace this came about.

Shortly after, my mother returned to God in great advancement of soul. And I, being driven away, went to another place.

I was ordained a deacon at twenty-one and received the priesthood two years later; I remained a parish priest for eight years and then was made archpriest by the Orthodox bishops—twenty years ago, that is. So I have been in holy orders for thirty years. As a priest I have had penitents in great numbers, five or six hundred by now. I, a sinner, have toiled without respite in the churches, in the houses, at crossroads, in cities and villages, and also in the sovereign city and in the Siberian land, preaching and teaching the word of God: this for about twenty-five years now. . . .

As a Parish Priest in Lopatishchi.—A short time after, as it is written, "Lo, the sorrows of death compassed me, the pains of hell got hold upon me, I found trouble and sorrow."[6] An officer stole her daughter from a widow; I begged him to return the orphan to her mother, but, scorning our prayers, he raised a storm against me, and coming to the church with a troop, they crushed me nearly to death. I lay dead half an hour or more, and came to life by the divine will. He then, in fear, gave up the girl. But later the devil urged him: he came into the church and dragged me along the floor by my feet, in my vestments; and while he did this I prayed.

Another time, an officer became furious against me; he rushed into my house, beat me, and bit my fingers like a dog with his teeth. And when his throat was full of blood he let go my hand and went off to his house. Then, thanking God, I bound up my hand and went to vespers. But on my way the same man jumped at me with two pistols; he fired one at me, but by God's grace the powder kindled on the pan and the weapon misfired. Then he threw it down and shot with the other; through God's will it misfired again. As for me, I prayed God ardently as I walked, blessing my assailant with my hand and bowing to him. He barked at me, but I said: "Grace be on your lips, Ivan Rodionovich!" He was angry with me because of the Church services (he wanted them to be brief, but I sang without haste, as the rules prescribe; this it was that vexed him).[7] Later he took my house from me and drove me out, robbing me of everything, with no bread even for the road. . . .

There came to my parish some dancing bears, with tambourines and guitars: I, a sinner, in my zeal for Christ, drove them away, broke masks and tambourines, alone on the common among the crowd. I took away two big bears; one I knocked down, it came to life again; the other I sent off into the fields. For this, Vasily Petrovich Sheremetev,[8] who was sailing down the Volga to Kazan to be governor, had me brought to his boat and upbraided me. Then he bade me bless his son Matvey, a shaven face. This I did not, but cursed him by the Holy Writ on seeing his lecherous mien.[9] The boyar, in great anger, ordered his men to throw me into the Volga. And after many torments I was thrown out. But later they were good to me; in the Tsar's palace they made their peace with me, and my younger brother even had Vasily's lady as a penitent. So does God lead his people!

In Yurevets.— . . . Shortly after, others drove me a second time from that place. Then I made my way to Moscow, and, by God's will, the Tsar ordered me to be archpriest in Yurevets[10] on the Volga. But I did not stay long there either, only eight weeks: the devil spurred the priests and peasants and women; they came to the patriarchal office where I was busy with spiritual affairs; they dragged me out of the office all together—a thousand or fifteen hundred of them perhaps!—and they whacked at me with sticks and tramped me underfoot; the women used their pokers too! For my sins they left me for dead and threw me in the corner of an izba. The governor rode up with the gunners; they picked me up, carried me off on horseback, and brought me to my house, and the governor posted gunners at the doors. But the people now came toward the house and there was a great rumor in the town. The priests and women especially, whom I prevented from fornicating, were howling: " Kill the robber! The dirty hound, we'll throw his body into the moat for the dogs!" . . . .

Arrest in Moscow.— . . . And I, too, as I was celebrating vespers, was arrested by Boris Neledinsky and his streltsy; they seized about sixty men with me. They were taken to prison, but me they chained that night in the Patriarch's mansion. At dawn on Sunday they put me in a cart and drove me, with my arms outstretched, from the Patriarch's mansion to the Andronicus Monastery.[11] There they put chains on me and threw me into a dark room underground. I remained there three days with nothing to eat or drink. As I sat in my chains, I made my obeisances to the Lord, not knowing whether I bowed east or west.[12] Nobody came to me except mice or blackbeetles; the crickets chirped, and there were many fleas. . . .

In Siberia.[13]—When we reached the Shaman rapids, we met other navigators and with them two widows, one about sixty, the other older still; they were going to a convent to take the veil. But Pashkov wanted to turn them back and give them husbands.[14] I told him: "The rules forbid marrying for these women." But instead of listening to me and releasing the widows he took it into his head to torment me in his rage. At the next rapid, the Long rapid, he tried to drive me off the barge: "It's because of you the barge won't make headway! You heretic! Go off into the mountains, don't stay with the Cossacks!" O the grief of it! High mountains, impassable thickets, a stone spur standing like a wall—your head breaks just to look at it! Big snakes live in those mountains; geese and ducks with red feathers fly there, black ravens, grey jackdaws, eagles and hawks and gerfalcons, and Indian hens and pelicans and swans and other wild birds of all kinds in great multitudes. And many wild beasts roam there too: goats and deer, buffalo, moose and boars, wolves, wild rams—all there under our eyes, but there's no catching them! That's where Pashkov wanted to send me, to live with the beasts and snakes and birds. . . .

Then I was brought to the Buriats fort[15] and thrown into prison, with some straw to lie on. I lay in a cold tower until Advent; it's winter there in that season, but God kept me warm without a coat! I lay in the straw like a dog, and sometimes I would be fed, and sometimes not. There were many mice; I used to hit at them with my skullcap—the fools wouldn't give me even a stick! I lay on my belly all the time: my back was all sores. Fleas and lice were plentiful. I wanted to cry to Pashkov, "Have pity!" but God's strength stopped me; it was my fate to bear all. I was then transferred to a heated izba and I lived there with the hostages[16] and dogs, chained, all winter.

My wife and the children had been sent twenty versts away. The woman Xenya tormented her all winter, yelling at her and scolding. My son Ivan—he was quite small—came to see me after Christmas, but Pashkov had him thrown into the cold prison where I had been kept; the poor dear stayed the night and nearly froze. The next morning he was told to go back to his mother. I didn't even see him. He trudged back to his mother, with hands and feet near frozen. . . .

Return to Russia.—So we returned to Russia from the river Nercha. We drove five weeks in our sleighs on the bare ice. We had two nags for the children and for our belongings; as for myself and my wife, we trudged on foot, stumbling painfully on the ice. It's a barbarian country, the natives are hostile, we didn't dare to lag behind and yet, tired and hungry as we were, we couldn't manage to keep up with the horses. My poor wife would tramp on and on and suddenly fall—it was so slippery! Once, as she was stumbling on, she tripped and another man, as worn out as she was, came up and fell on top of her. Both lay there exclaiming, but unable to get up. The man cried out: "Forgive me, matushka, good lady!" and my wife shouted: "What are you crushing me for, old man?" I came up, and the poor woman started reproaching me, saying: "When will this torment end, Protopope?" And I said: "Markovna, not until death!" And then she answered with a sigh: "All right, Petrovich,[17] we'll go on some more!" . . .

Fedor the Fool for Christ.[18]— . . . There [in the monastery where he was held] my dear Fedor, my poor hanged fellow, used to come secretly, with my children, to consult me: "How should I live? Should I go on

93

wearing just a shirt, or should I put on other clothes? For the heretics are looking for me and seek my death. . . . I was in Ryazan for penance, in the archbishop's mansion, and he, Ilarion, tormented me sorely; few days went by without a whipping; he held me in chains to compel me to receive the new sacrament of Antichrist. At last I could bear no more. One night, weeping and praying, I said: 'Lord! if you don't help me, they will defile me and I will perish. What will you do with me then?' " And he continued with many tears: "But suddenly my chains clatter down, the door is unbolted and opens by itself. I prostrate myself before God and walk out. I reach the gate: the gate is open too. And so on the high road straight to Moscow! At break of day horsemen pursue me. Three men ride by without noticing me. I put my hope in Christ and trudge on. Shortly after, back they come, swearing: 'He's made off, the dirty dog; where shall we find him now?' And again they went by without seeing me. And now I have come to ask you: should I return there to suffer new torments or wear ordinary clothes and live in Moscow?"

I, a sinner, bade him wear clothes. Yet he did not escape heretic hands; they strangled him on the Mezen, hanging from the gallows. Eternal memory to him and to Luka Lavrentevich! My dear children, they have suffered for Christ! Glory to God in their persons!

Fedor's feat was a strong one indeed: by day he would be the fool for Christ, and all night he spent in prayers and weeping. I know many good people, but such an ascetic I have not seen! He spent six months with me in Moscow; I was still sick then, we were both in a back room; he used to rest an hour or two, no more, and then was up again. He would make a thousand obeisances and then sit on the floor or else stand weeping during three hours. Meanwhile I lay, now asleep, now ill. When he had wept his fill, he would come near me, saying: "Hey, archpriest! are you going to lie there much longer? Remember, you're a priest; aren't you ashamed?" I had no strength, but he would help me to my feet and say: "Come, up, dear Father, manage somehow, just try!" And so he set me going. . . . He made me say my prayers sitting while he performed the obeisances for me. He was my heart's friend indeed! He was ill, the dear man, with exhaustion: once five arshins[19] of his bowels came out. . . . He was barely alive, but he measured them, while I didn't know whether to laugh or cry. At Ustyug, for five years on end, he bore the cold, wandering barefoot in his shirt: that I saw myself. It was there he became my penitent, on my return from Siberia. At the church, in a little room where he came to pray, he would tell me: "It's when you come in from the cold, Father, that it's hard," and then he would make the brick floor ring with his feet; they were as hard as cabbage-stumps. But in the morning the pain would be gone. He had one of the new psalters in his cell—he didn't know much yet about the new stuff. I told him in detail about the new books; and, seizing his, he at once threw it into the stove and cursed all new things. His faith in Christ was indeed a burning one! . . .

Before the Council.[20]— . . . I will say something more about my misfortunes. When I had been brought from the monastery of St. Paphnuty to Moscow and confined in the bursary, they dragged me time and again to Chudov[21] and brought me before the oecumenical patriarchs; ours too sat there, like foxes. I spoke much from the Scriptures to the patriarchs; God opened my sinful lips, Christ confounded my enemies! Then they spoke these final words to me: "Why are you stubborn? All our Palestinians, and Serbs, and Albanians, and Wallachians, and Romans, and Poles, all make the three-fingered sign of the cross; you alone stand in your stubbornness and cross yourself with five fingers![22] This is unseemly!" I answered this before Christ: "Oecumenical Masters! Rome fell long ago and lies prone ever since, and the Poles perished with her, being forever the enemies of Christians. Among you too Orthodoxy has become spotty from the oppression of Turkish Mahmet. There's nothing to admire in you; you've become impotent. In the future, as before, come and learn from us; by the grace of God, we have our autocracy. Before Nikon the Apostate, Orthodoxy was pure and immaculate and the Church in our Russia was undisturbed under the pious princes and tsars. The wolf Nikon, with the devil, ordered the three-fingered sign of the cross; but our first pastors, as they themselves used five fingers for the sign of the cross, likewise blessed with five fingers in the tradition of our Holy Fathers. . . . Under Tsar Ivan, the Moscow Council also ordered the sign of the cross to be made with fingers joined, as earlier the Holy Fathers had instructed. At the Council, during Tsar Ivan's reign, were the Kazan thaumaturgists, and Philip the abbot of Solovki, among our Russian saints."

And the patriarchs fell into thought; but our men, jumping up like wolf cubs, started to howl and vomit on their Fathers, saying: "Our Russian saints were stupid and empty-headed; they were not learned men. Why believe them? They could not read!" O holy Lord! How could you bear such derision of your saints? It was bitter hearing for me, poor wretch, but what could I do? I upbraided them as I could and said a final word: "I am pure, and I shake the dust from my feet before you, as it is written, Better one who does the will of God than clouds of impious ones!" Then they shouted more loudly at me: "Take him! He has blackened us all!" And they started to hit and beat me. The patriarchs themselves set upon me—there must have been forty of them. Strong was the army of Antichrist![23]

—*Zhitie protopopa Avvakuma* (Paris, 1951)

95

NOTES: 1 The Elder Epiphanes was a monk in the Solovki Monastery and later a hermit. The council of 1667 sentenced him to have his tongue cut off. He was banished to Pustozersk with Avvakum and became his spiritual director. They died together at the stake.

2 Cf. Avvakum's letter to the tsar: "Say in Russian: Lord, have pity on me, a sinner! and forget those Kyrie Eleison; that's the way Hellenes speak, to the devil with them! You're a Russian, Mikhailovich, not a Greek. Speak your native tongue, don't shame it in church or at home or in your common speech. God gave us no less than the Greeks: didn't he give us our writing in our own language through Cyril and Methodius? Why should we wish for anything better? The speech of angels? No, that we shall not receive—not until the great Resurrection."

3 Syllabic verse, rhymed, had been introduced in Russia at the beginning of the seventeenth century.

4 I Cor. 13:1.

5 Avvakum's father died about 1632.

6 Ps. 116: 3-4.

7 This was one of the reforms that the Friends of God insisted on. It made the services more dignified, but exceedingly long.

8 Sheremetev was governor of Nizhny-Novgorod from 1634 to 1639.

9 The Stoglav had forbidden shaving. But shaving had become popular under Boris Godunov. Under the reformers' influence, however, it was again frowned upon. Old Believers did not shave and despised "the scraped snouts."

10 Yurevets is about ninety miles north of Nizhny-Novgorod.

11 The Andronicus Monastery was more than two miles from the Patriarch's mansion in the Kreml'. Rublev is buried there, and it is now the Rublev Museum.

12 Prayers were to be made to the east.

13 This concerns the years 1656 and 1657.

14 Women were rare in Siberia in that pioneer age, so, in spite of their age, Pashkov wanted to get them for the settlers.

15 The Buriats fort was founded in 1631.

16 The hostages were held to guarantee tribute.

17 Markovna: daughter of Mark; Petrovich: son of Peter—a respectful and affectionate form of address. See note 2, above, Avvakum's letter to the tsar.

18 The fools for Christ, or *iurodivy*, were religious and ascetic counterparts of the Western court "fools." Their supposed madness and total detachment from all worldly interests made them, in people's eyes, the vessels of God's wisdom. The Church of Vasily the Blessed in Moscow commemorates the name of a Fool for Christ. There is also a iurodivy in *Boris Godunov*. They were especially numerous in the troubled times of the sixteenth and seventeenth centuries.

19 Twenty-eight inches.

20 The Council of 1667 deposed Nikon and anathematized the Old Believers.

21 Monastery of St. Paphnuty: about a hundred miles south of Moscow; Chudov, or Monastery of the Miracle: the chief monastery in the Kreml'.

22 On the sign of the cross, Avvakum wrote: "Join the tips of thumb and little finger and the finger next to the little finger: this is the image of the Divinity in three substances, Father, Son, and Holy Ghost; now the index and middle finger should be joined together and the middle finger bent slightly: this represents the mystery of divinity and humanity in Christ."

23 The best work on Avvakum is *Avvakum et les débuts du Raskol* by Pierre Pascal (Paris, 1931). The notes in his translation of the *Life* are extremely valuable and have been used extensively in these notes.

96

PETITION ON THE FAITH

Monks of Solovetsky Monastery

The Solovetsky Monastery was founded in the fifteenth century on an island off the shore of the White Sea. It became for northern Russia what the Monastery of the Caves was to Kiev and the Troitse-Sergieva Lavra was to Muscovy. The monks of Solovki refused to accept Nikon's reforms, and the monastery became a center of resistance. Open rebellion began in 1667. Besieged for several years, the monastery fell to the tsar's troops in 1676. Tradition has it that the tsar fell ill on that very day, to die a week later. The petition that is quoted here was composed in 1667 and was the third the monks had sent to the tsar.

■ ■ ■ Tsar Lord and Prince Alexey Mikhailovich, Autocrat of Great, Little, and White Russia, your servants in God from the Solovetsky Monastery, Azarey the cellarer, Gerontey the treasurer, the priests, deacons, and monks, with all the rank and file of the brotherhood and hospital workers and lay brothers and novices, petition you. In this year 1667, on the fifteenth day of September, according to your decree, great Tsar, and with the blessing and letters patent of the most holy Iosaph, Patriarch of Moscow and all Russia, and of the most reverend Pitirim, Metropolitan of Novgorod and Velikolutsk, the monk Joseph, who had taken his vows in our monastery, was sent to us as archimandrite instead of our archimandrite Bartholomew. He has been ordered to officiate here with the new Church books. But we, your servants in the Lord, dare in no way alter the tradition of the Apostles and Holy Fathers, since we stand in awe of the King of Kings and His terrible interdict. We wish to end our days in that old faith in which, following the Lord's will, your sovereign father and other pious tsars and princes spent theirs: for, Tsar, that old Christian faith of ours is known to all of us as being agreeable to the Lord; it has pleased God and the saints, and the patriarchs Jeremy and Theophanes and other Palestinian elders have never found anything to condemn in our Russian books and our Orthodox faith; rather did they praise it always. With their testimony we hope that on the Day of Judgment we shall not stand condemned before our Lord God, but will enjoy His clemency.

Merciful Sovereign, we implore your pious power and pray you with tears: spare us, your orphans and servants in the Lord. Do not command our traditions and the rites of the blessed elders Zosima and Savvaty[1] to be altered; let us, Tsar, continue in that old faith in which the Tsar your father and all the pious tsars and princes have died, and in which the blessed elders Zosima and Savvaty and German, and Philip the Metropolitan, and all the Holy Fathers have found grace in God's eyes.

Great Sovereign, Anointed of the Lord, if you deign not to allow us to remain in the faith that has been transmitted to us by the Holy Fathers, if you command the books to be altered, we beg this mercy of you: Spare us, Sovereign, do not send us any more teachers in vain; for we will not change our Orthodox faith. But send us, Tsar, your sovereign sword, and dispatch us from this troubled life to peaceful eternity. We are not rebels against you, great Tsar; in very truth, Tsar, we beg of you this mercy with all our hearts, and in readiness to take upon ourselves the high angelic estate, we await in repentance this hour of death. Great Tsar, our Sovereign, have pity, grant us your favor.

—*Khrestomatiya po istorii* SSSR (Moscow, 1951), Vol. I

NOTES: ¹Founders of the monastery.

■ ■ ■

SPRING PILGRIMAGE OF A TSARITSA IN THE SEVENTEENTH CENTURY
Painting by V. G. Schwartz, 1868
From an album of reproductions of paintings in the Tretyakov gallery, Moscow

5

92401

**BOOK LEARNING
AND
EDUCATION**

There is a widespread opinion that until the contemporary period education in Russia remained at a very low level. This opinion is generally supported by statistics on literacy at the end of the nineteenth and the beginning of the twentieth century. Going back to the Muscovite period, we find numerous echoes of the same realization. Obviously statistics are not available, but ecclesiastical authorities repeatedly voiced concern. Their preoccupation, however, was not with the lack of learning among the lay population, but with the ignorance of the clergy, especially the parish priests, who were the natural teachers of the people. Thus, as early as the fifteenth century the problem was posed in the same terms that confronted Peter the Great three centuries later: the lack of cadres.

Actually western Europe faced many of the same problems as Russia. If at the end of the fifteenth century, Archbishop Gennady was appalled at the ignorance of Novgorod priests, so, in France, in the sixteenth century swarmed a mass of parish priests among whom only one out of ten could read, if we believe Protestant evidence, and who, to rely upon a Catholic witness, "explain their disregard of daily services by their ignorance or lack of skill in reading." In addition to this common problem, Russia had difficulties peculiar to herself: the lack of a language of culture to communicate with the scholars of the Western world; the distrust with which any "Latin" work was viewed as the possible bearer of religious and political infection; the hardships, isolation, and instability engendered by Russia's own geographical and historical circumstances; the heritage of the Byzantine eschatological teaching, often altered and degraded by the necessities of Russian life. To the student of Muscovite education, such factors explain the glaring differences from Western developments. He finds no schools in the Western sense, certainly no universities; no "modern" method of teaching, such as the scholastics of the thirteenth century; no centers of learning to attract an international concourse of students who, in their turn, would carry back to their native environment both information and critical views on society. He finds little penetration of the Greek scientific knowledge through Arabic or Jewish scholars. Instead, what does he find?

At the elementary level, the picture is familiar enough: the parish schools, under a deacon or precentor, may provide a minority of the village or town boys with a knowledge of reading in the Church Slavonic script. The primer which they memorize and which, with a Psalter and Prayer Book, makes up the sum of the school texts, contains—besides the alphabet—moral formulas, the elements of scripture, and notions of arithmetic. Their Western contemporaries will have been offered an equivalent learning opportunity, since until the eighteenth century the difference lies

101

in the number of boys who can receive knowledge rather than the quality or extent of the knowledge. At a higher level, the situation changes.

In the fifteenth century and earlier, the merchant city of Novgorod was Muscovy's gate to the West. Small groups there studied Latin and translated Latin texts into Slavonic, and something similar to the episcopal schools of western Europe had developed. But Novgorod was crushed by Moscow. In the sixteenth and seventeenth centuries the center of culture had shifted to the Trinity Monastery near Moscow, where Greek and Slavic scholars were engaged in a study of Greek texts comparable to that of the early European humanists, though more limited in scope. The prevailing view, however, was still the one that we find expressed in the works of Krizhanich, a Croatian priest who lived in Russia in the seventeenth century. While he held high views of Russian possibilities, Krizhanich was distressed by Russian ignorance. But his complaints to Muscovite churchmen brought forth the answer that since heresies arise among learned people, learning should not be pursued. Thus, even among the professionally educated clergy, the study of philosophy and theology was discouraged and other branches of knowledge were slow to develop. Prior to the eighteenth century, arithmetic was hampered by the use of letters instead of Arabic numerals. Though medicinal herbalism was practiced, there were no medical schools until the early eighteenth century. History alone flourished, in the form of chronicles written in Russian from the earliest times and collected by Moscow authorities in the fifteenth century to support their policy of centralization. To a lesser degree, geographical information, long dependent on translations from Byzantine semi-fantastic tales of India and elsewhere, was gathered by the practice of having returning pilgrims and merchants submit or dictate their travel reports to the central government offices in Moscow.

By the sixteenth century, a new group of "educated" persons arose: government office scribes, interpreters, and translators who, through the necessities of their functions, contributed both to the penetration of foreign learning and to the development and simplification of the written Russian language. What chroniclers, copyists, and translators of sacred books did in their monasteries, the scribes continued until, under Peter, they eliminated their monastic predecessors. However, those scribes and civil servants never emerged as a powerful cultured class like the clerks and government officers in western Europe.

102

What Novgorod had been in the Middle Ages on the borders of Muscovy, Lithuania was in the sixteenth century and Kiev in the seventeenth century: the teachers of Moscow, spiritually and linguistically akin, but open to Western thought. Jesuit methods of education had come to the Ukraine with the Catholic Poles, and reunion with Moscow in the seventeenth century brought to the capital a flood of Ukrainian scholars and political thinkers who were admired, mistrusted, and reluctantly followed. As in thirteenth-century France, the Southern culture ceased to exist independently and impregnated the Northern. The Moscow printing press, which had started production in 1564 but had fallen under Church suspicion in the late sixteenth century, now became extremely active, printing new (often revised) translations of missals, Psalters, and primers. A school in the Western sense finally appeared in Moscow in 1687: the Slavonic-Greco-Latin Academy, whose name combined the native and foreign cultures symbolic of the past and present.

The semi-medieval, semi-Jesuitical spirit of that Academy was to be preserved in the seminaries of the eighteenth and early nineteenth centuries which finally brought to Russia the methods of scholasticism, and from whose walls were later to emerge the doctors, teachers, and journalists who would form the radical rationalistic intelligentsia of the mid-nineteenth century.

Meanwhile Peter had imposed on a reluctant minority his purely civilian, practically-oriented schools. His eighteenth-century successors turned their efforts to a more humanistic education. Russian emerged as a language of culture, and the late seventeenth-century grammarian's dictum, "One should talk in Russian, but write in Slavonic," ceased to be true. In the nineteenth century, though a respectable number of specialized schools and new universities were founded and elementary education was expanded rapidly under Alexander II, the government out of caution or suspicion frequently resorted to measures intended to limit both the numbers of students and the scope of their education. In regard to the mass of the Russian people, Nicholas I essentially subscribed to the seventeenth-century conservative view that "heresies arise among the learned and therefore learning should not be pursued," though now the heresies were political. In a country now provided with at least the frame of public education, however, such an attitude was bound to defeat its purpose. Although to many young Russians of the nineteenth century, higher education was no longer an end in itself, but a means to serve the suffering masses better—as teachers, midwives, doctors—for a considerable number the University was merely the milieu for liberal or radical propaganda. Thus did the word *student* become synonymous with the word *revolutionary*.

103

PAGE FROM A 1692 PRIMER ILLUSTRATING THE LETTER "B"
From *Istoriya Moskvy* (Moscow, 1952), Vol. I

THE CHURCH ON SCHOOLS AND BOOKS
Council of the Hundred Chapters

The low level of culture among the parish priests had long been
a matter of concern to the ecclesiastical authorities. The Stoglav
Council (1551) attempted to remedy the situation by recom-
mending that schools be established and by stressing the need
for correct manuscript copies. However, the first recommenda-
tion was not enforced, and the second was soon to lose its importance with the introduction of printing.

On learned schools in all cities[1]

■ ■ ■ Following the councils of the church, our assembly has decided
that in the sovereign city of Moscow and in all cities, the archpriests, the
elder priests, with all the priests and deacons, each in his city, with the
blessing of their prelate, will choose good priests, deacons, and sacristans,
married and pious, having the fear of God in their hearts, who are capable
of instructing others and who are skilled in reading and writing. Schools
will be established in the houses of these priests, deacons, and sacristans,
and to those schools the priests and deacons and all Orthodox Christians in
each city can send their children to be taught to read and write, and copy
from books, and sing in church, and read at the lectern. These chosen priests,
deacons, and sacristans will teach their students to have the fear of God,
to read, write, and sing, and will give them all religious instruction.[2]

On the holy icons and the correction of books

The archpriests, the elder priests, the chosen priests, all the
priests in each city are to inspect in all the holy churches the holy icons and
the sacred vessels and all that is used in church worship, the holy antiminses[3]
on the altar, the sacred books, Holy Gospels and Apostles, and other holy
books accepted by the universal Church. If any icons have suffered from
time, let them be restored by painters; those that are not sufficiently varnished with oil must be varnished again. If in any churches are found holy
books, Gospels, Epistles, Psalters, and others, which are faulty and ill-
written, work together to correct those holy books by means of good copies;
for the holy rules forbid faulty books and prohibit their introduction into
church or their use for singing.

On book copyists

The manuscript copyists in the cities should be ordered to copy
from good originals, to correct their completed manuscripts, and then only
to sell them. If a copyist sells his book without correcting it, he should be

105

forbidden to do this and severely punished. The man who buys such an uncorrected book should be punished in the same way, so that neither will repeat his offense; and if buyer and seller are caught in such a practice again, let the books be taken from them with no compensation, without any qualms; once corrected, the books will be given to churches that are poor in books and in this manner your diligence will inspire others with fear.[4]

—*Russkaya khrestomatiya*, ed. F. Buslaev (Moscow, 1912)

NOTES: [1]About a half century earlier, Gennady, Bishop of Novgorod, complained: "They bring me a man who wants to become a priest or deacon. I order him to read from the Apostles and he can't even begin; I give him the Psalter, and all he can do is to stumble along."

[2]A seventeenth-century satirical poem "Pope Savva" describes one such school. The priest Savva, who serves in a prosperous parish of Moscow, spends so much of his time looking for students that he is hardly ever in church. He makes the students work in his garden, keeps them only as long as they have money, and so on. He is finally arrested and chained in the Patriarch's barn to sift flour, a common punishment then for erring priests.

[3]An antimins was a consecrated altar cloth on which were represented the instruments of the Lord's Passion and His entombment.

[4]Correction of books, either by comparison with Greek originals or earlier Russian translations, or by new translations, had been going on during the earlier part of the century, especially at the Troitsa Monastery under the direction of Maxim the Greek.

■ ■ ■

THE BEGINNING OF BOOK PRINTING IN THE RUSSIAN STATE

It is generally assumed that the first book printed in Russia proper was the *Acts of the Apostles* (1564). Slavonic books had been printed earlier in Cracow (1491) and Venice (early sixteenth century), but the fear of heresy and the existence of a great number of book copyists had delayed the introduction of printing in Muscovy. However, manuscript copies were often faulty (see page 105). Moreover, territorial gains (Kazan) and cultural developments made more books necessary and encouraged the establishment of a printing press in Moscow. The text that follows is the Postface to the *Acts of the Apostles*, the first book known to be printed in Moscow.

106

■ ■ ■ By the grace of the Father and the assistance of the Son and the achievement of the Holy Ghost, according to the command of the Orthodox Tsar and Prince Ivan Vasilevich, Autocrat of all Russia, with the blessing of

Makary, Metropolitan of all Russia,[1] many holy churches have been erected in the sovereign city of Moscow, in its vicinity, and in all the cities of the realm, especially in the newly-consecrated place in the city of Kazan and in the limits thereof.[2] The Orthodox Tsar has adorned all these holy temples with venerable icons and holy books, vessels, vestments, and other church appurtenances, according to the tradition and rule of the Holy Apostles and God-bearing Fathers, and following the precepts of the Orthodox Greek tsars that ruled in Tsargrad,[3] the great Constantine and Justinian, Michael and Theodora, and other Orthodox tsars who lived in their own time. And the Orthodox Tsar and Prince Ivan Vasilevich of all Russia commanded holy books to be bought on the markets, and Psalters, Gospels, Acts of the Apostles, and other holy books to be placed in the churches. But few fitting texts were found; all the others were corrupted by the ignorance and lack of skill of the scribes or their failure to correct mistakes.[4] This news reached the Tsar; he began to reflect on the making of printed books, as is done in Greece and Venice and Italy and among other nations, in order that the holy books might be set forth more truly in future. He then expressed his thought to Makary, Metropolitan of all Russia; the latter rejoiced greatly and, having given thanks to God, told the Tsar that he had received this inspiration as a gift from Heaven.

Thus, by the command of the Orthodox Tsar and Prince Ivan Vasilevich of all Russia, and with the blessing of the most holy Metropolitan Makary, the art of book printing began to be studied, in the sixty-first year of the eighth millenium. In the thirtieth year of his reign, the Orthodox Tsar ordered a house to be fitted out from his own funds to set up the printing shop;[5] he gave liberally of his treasures to the deacon Ivan Fedorov[6] and to Petr Timofeev of Mstislavl, both of the church of Nicholas the Wonder-Worker,[7] entrusting them with the undertaking and maintaining them until it was carried out. The first books to be printed were the Acts of the Apostles, with the Epistles of the Councils and the Epistles of St. Paul. They were begun in the year seventy-one, on April 14, on the day dedicated to the Blessed Father Ivan Palevret, and completed in the year seventy-two, on the first day of March, the archbishop Afanasy being Metropolitan of all Russia, in the first year of his office, to the glory of the almighty life-giving Trinity of the Father and the Son and the Holy Ghost. Amen.

—*Khrestomatiya po istorii* SSSR (Moscow, 1951), Vol. I

NOTES: [1]Metropolitan of Moscow from 1542 to his death in 1563. He was active in the so-called nationalization of saints, by which process local saints were promoted to the status of national ones, their relics and icons being brought to Moscow, thus heightening the capital's spiritual significance. He presided over the Stoglav meetings. All cultural innovations had to be blessed by the tsar and the Metropolitan, since a suspicion of heresy or sorcery was often attached to them.

[2]Kazan was conquered in 1552.

[3]Constantinople.

[4]See the passage on faulty book copies, pp. 105-6.

[5]The press was instituted in 1553 (7061); the printing shop itself was built in 1563. This reading follows the interpretation given in "At the Sources of Russian Printing," *U istokov russkogo knigopechataniya* (Moscow, 1959).

[6]Ivan Fedorov (?-1583) left Moscow about 1565, for reasons unknown, and the press was inactive for a number of years. He went on printing in Lithuania.

[7]A church in the Kreml'—no longer in existence.

■ ■ ■

FOUNDATION OF THE ACADEMY OF SCIENCES
Peter the Great

The foundation of an Academy of Sciences was the last of Peter's educational innovations. The decree instituting it was issued on December 28, 1724, a year before Peter's death, and the Academy opened in 1725. The following are extracts from Peter's decree.

■ ■ ■ [The Emperor has ordered] an Academy to be instituted for the study of languages, likewise of other sciences and notable arts, and for the translation of books[1]. . . . It will be maintained by the money collected from the customs and licenses in the cities of Narva, Derpt, Pernov, and Arensburg,[2] namely 24,912 rubles. . . .

The growth of arts and sciences is generally furthered by means of two different systems: one being called University, the other Academy or Society of Arts and Sciences. . . .

Since at present a system for the cultivation of arts and sciences has yet to be set up in Russia, it is impossible to follow here the pattern accepted in other countries; but it is fitting, in accordance with the state of our Empire, and in the interests of both teachers and students, to institute a system through which our Empire shall gain glory in our time by the progress of science, and one that will also, in the future, bring profit to our people through the acquisition and increase of knowledge.

The institution of a mere Academy of Sciences would not fulfill this double purpose; though the progress and propagation of arts and sciences in themselves would be furthered, these would not fructify fast enough among the people. On the other hand, the organization of a University would avail us still less, since the lack of ordinary schools, gimnazii,[3] and seminaries in which young people could learn the elements and later obtain the higher degrees of knowledge to make themselves fully capable makes it impossible for a University to be of any help in this situation.

108

And so it would be most desirable for us to initiate a society composed of the most learned persons who are capable (1) of advancing and perfecting science, moreover (2) of teaching young people in public, and (3) of instructing in private a few persons who in turn could teach young people the elements of all sciences.

In this manner one single institution would, at little expense, give the great profit that is obtained in other countries by three different bodies.

—*Khrestomatiya po istorii SSSR* (Moscow, 1953), Vol. II

NOTES: [1]Translation was promoted during Peter's reign. A decree of 1724 points out the necessity of instructing in translating techniques those who knew a language, and of instructing in the languages those who already knew the techniques. About 400 translations were printed between 1708 and 1724, many of them by an Amsterdam printing house. The first printing house in Petersburg was set up in 1711.

[2]Narva, on the Baltic, was conquered by Peter in 1704. Derpt (Dorpat, Iuriev), now Tartu, in Estonia, was occupied by Russian troops in 1704. Pernov, now Pärnu, is a port on the Baltic. Arensburg, now Kingisepp, is located on Sarema Island in the Baltic.

[3]Secondary schools. A gimnazia was organized at the Academy, but did not prosper. Students, chiefly commoners, sometimes had to be recruited by force. In 1731, the foundation of the Cadet Academy finally diverted students who were of the nobility away from the Academy gimnazia.

■ ■ ■

ON THE RUSSIAN LANGUAGE

M. V. Lomonosov

"He created our first university, or rather he *was* our first university." Pushkin's famous words on Lomonosov (1711–65) express the general feeling of Russians about this universally-gifted and active man, who has left his mark on physics, geology, astronomy, geography, mosaics, history, grammar, poetry, drama, etc. In his definition of the Russian language, which he undertook to describe in his *Rhetoric* and his *Grammar*, he "opens the road," to quote his own words, and orients the development of linguistic studies in Russia.

109

■ ■ ■ The language used in the Russian Empire to command over a considerable part of the world has received from nature a wealth, a beauty, and a strength that correspond to the might of Russia and make it the equal

MIKHAILO VASILEVICH LOMONOSOV (1711–65)

Portrait by an unknown eighteenth-century artist

From *Istoriya Moskvy* (Moscow, 1953), Vol. II

of any of the European languages. And for this reason there is no doubt that Russian can attain the perfection which we admire in other languages. —From dedication of *The Brief Handbook of Eloquence,* 2nd version (1748).

Sovereign among many, the Russian language is greater than all others in Europe, not only because of the extent of the regions over which it rules, but by virtue of its own scope and abundance. This will seem incredible to foreigners and to some native Russians who have applied their labors to other languages rather than to their own. But whoever, without being prejudiced by high opinions of other languages, will direct his mind to it and study it diligently will agree with me. Charles the Fifth, Roman Emperor, was wont to say that one should address God in Spanish, one's friends in French, one's enemies in German, and the ladies in Italian. But had he been familiar with Russian, he would certainly have added that our language could well serve in each of these cases. For in Russian he would have found the magnificence of Spanish, the vivacity of French, the vigor of German, the tenderness of Italian; and moreover the wealth and energetic brevity of Greek and Latin.[1]—From the dedication of *The Russian Grammar*[2] (1755).

The Russian language can be divided into three main dialects: the Moscow dialect, the Northern, and the Little-Russian. The first is the chief one, used at court and among the nobility, especially in the cities situated not far from Moscow. The second is slightly closer to Slavonic and it spreads over a great area of Russia.[3] The third shows the greatest differences and is mixed with Polish.—From materials for *The Russian Grammar.*

The speech of Moscow is rightly preferred to others, not only because of the importance of the capital city, but by reason of its own eminent beauty; in particular the pronunciation of the unaccented *o* as *a* is much pleasanter to the ear.[4]—From *The Russian Grammar.*

—*Polnoe sobranie sochinenii* (Moscow, 1952)

NOTES: [1]This passage is inspired by a similar one in a French work by Bonhours (*Entretiens d'Ariste et d'Eugène,* 1671), in which, however, Charles V is reported as saying that one should speak German to one's horse. Since the *Grammar* was dedicated to Prince Paul Petrovich, who bore the title of Duke of Schleswig-Holstein, no doubt Lomonosov saw fit to substitute enemies for a horse.—Note in *Polnoe sobranie sochinenii.*
      [2]This is the first real grammar of Russian in Russian. Former works had been in Latin (Ludolf's *Grammatica Russica,* Oxford, 1696) or in Slavonic (Smotritsky, 1619). The latter had been reprinted or imitated several times in the seventeenth century and

had been used as textbook by Lomonosov himself. Lomonosov's *Grammar,* which had a normative purpose, served as reference book for several generations of grammarians.

[3]Lomonosov himself was from the Archangelsk region.

[4]Elsewhere Lomonosov says: "Great Moscow is so delicate in her speech that she bids us pronounce *o* as *a.*" This is the speech habit known as "*akane,*" as opposed to the "*okane*" of the north and northeast regions.

■ ■ ■

PROPOSAL FOR THE ESTABLISHMENT OF MOSCOW UNIVERSITY
Ivan Shuvalov

The Academy of Sciences had been intended to serve also as a university and school, but it was not very successful in these roles. Talk of founding an independent university was in the air. The Russian scholar and scientist M. V. Lomonosov (1711–65) first suggested the main points for establishing a university in Moscow. These points form the basis of the following proposal by Shuvalov[1] (July 1754), which was approved and confirmed in January 1755. The statutes were in force till the early nineteenth century.

■ ■ ■ 1. A sum of ten thousand rubles a year will suffice for the needs of the university and the gimnazia attached to it.[2]

2. It is considered most necessary for the encouragement of sciences:

(a) That Her Imperial Majesty take the newly established university under her most high personal protection and that she condescend, as is the custom in other states, to appoint as curators of the university one or two distinguished personages who will be in charge of the whole institution and will report on its needs to Her Imperial Majesty.[3]

(b) That this institution be independent of all official administration except the Senate, and take no orders from any.

(c) That the professors and teachers, as all others under the protection of the university, be brought before no court of justice except that of the university without the permission of the university curators and directors.

(d) That all the members of the university be exempted in their private residences from all billeting and police obligations and likewise from deductions from their salary and all other contributions.

3. A special director will be appointed, to be responsible for the welfare of the university according to the instructions given to him and

112

to administer its revenue, to organize the curriculum at the university and the courses at the gimnazia in agreement with the professors, to correspond on the affairs of the university with government offices, to report on all the aforesaid to the curators and obtain their approval.

4. Though all universities, beside the sciences of Philosophy and Law, should also offer courses in Theology, however it is fitting to entrust the care of Theology to the Most Holy Synod.

5. There will be ten professors in the three schools of the university.

In Law School

(a) A professor of general jurisprudence, who must teach natural and national law and the codes of the Roman empires, old and new.

(b) A professor of Russian jurisprudence, who in addition to the above must know and teach especially the Russian State laws.[4]

(c) A professor of politics, who must instruct in the reciprocal relations, alliances, and actions of states and rulers, as they were in past centuries and as they are in our days.

In Medical School

(a) A doctor and professor of chemistry to teach especially physical and pharmaceutic chemistry.

(b) A doctor and professor of natural history to instruct in the various kinds of minerals, plants, and animals.

(c) A doctor and professor of anatomy to teach and show concretely the system of the human body in the anatomy theater and to instruct the students in the medical practice.

In Philosophy School

(a) A professor of philosophy to teach logic, metaphysics, and morals.

(b) A professor of physics to teach experimental and theoretical physics.

(c) A professor of eloquence to teach oratory and versification.

(d) A professor of history to instruct in universal and Russian history, likewise antiquities and heraldry.

6. Each professor must lecture on his subject at least two hours a day, excluding Sundays, prescribed holidays, and Saturdays, in the university building, without demanding special pay from his auditors; moreover, he may, for a moderate fee, tutor privately whom he will, provided his public lectures suffer no hindrance or interruption.[5]

7. Once a week, on Saturday mornings, all the professors will meet in the presence of the director to consider and discuss all possible dispositions and regulations concerning the best advancement of learning; at that time each professor will report to the director about what he considers to be necessary or in need of improvement in his specialty. At those meet-

113

ings all affairs concerning students will be decided, likewise the fines to be inflicted on any student guilty of insubordination or insolence.

8. No professor may of his own free will choose a system or an author and present his course accordingly, but he should conform to the order and authors prescribed by the faculty and curators.

9. All public lectures will be given either in Latin or Russian, depending on the subject and also on the nationality of the professor, whether he is a foreigner or a native Russian.

■ ■ ■

21. Those students who have graduated from the university and whose talents and zeal have entitled them to rewards, besides having conducted themselves in praiseworthy manner, will receive diplomas signed by the director and faculty. These diplomas will serve to appoint those who so desire to civil service, according to their nature and knowledge, and to advance them for the encouragement of other students.

22. Each student will study three years at the university, during which time he can successfully cover all the subjects offered there or at least those that may serve him in his future career. Before the expiration of that period, he is not to be taken away from his studies and forced to serve against his wishes.[6] Moreover, it is suggested to Her Majesty that she deign to maintain twenty students on a salary, with a view to appointing from their number teachers to the lower grades in the gimnazia.

23. Every candidate to higher education at the university is to present himself to the director who will ask the professors to examine him, and if he is deemed capable of taking the courses he will be registered, given a course program suitable to his inclinations and future condition, then sent with a written statement to the professors whose courses he is to attend. It is suggested that students might be allowed to wear a sword, as is the custom in other lands.

24. The students of the university will be responsible to no jurisdiction except that of the university; if they are discovered in any misdeed, no finger may be put on them, but they will be brought immediately to the director, who will fine them according to their offense or send them to the appropriate court.[7]

25. The conduct of students at the university and under its direction will be prescribed, as in all other universities, by special rules to be printed, one copy being given to each student entering the university. He will then be requested to sign his name and his agreement to obey the said laws in the university register; any transgressor will be fined regardless of person, according to the powers given to the university body.

26. Since learning cannot be under restraint and is rightly reckoned among the noblest occupations of humanity, for this reason no

114

serf may enter the university or gimnazia; however, if a noble observes a particular sharpness of mind in the son of one of his serfs and wishes to have him instructed in the liberal arts, he must first declare him free and, renouncing all his former rights and power over him, give him a letter of discharge signed by himself and witnesses. Moreover, he must undertake, both for himself and his heirs, to give the student a sufficient stipend during his years at the university until his graduation, nor can he cancel this agreement under any pretext.[8]

27. On admission of such a student to the university or gimnazia, the letter of discharge will be required of him and kept at the university; on his leaving after graduation, for appointment to the service of the State or for private employment, he will receive the said letter and his freedom, so that in no circumstances may he be reduced to serfdom. But if he abuses his liberty and commits offenses, he will be excluded and given up to his master with the letter of discharge.

28. Any one who wishes to attend courses at the university must previously master languages and the elements of sciences, but since Moscow has no well-established free schools in which young people could be suitably prepared for higher education, it is suggested that Her Imperial Majesty deign to command that two gimnazii be established at the university and under its responsibility: one for the nobility, the other for commoners, serfs excepted.

29. Four schools are to be established in each gimnazia, with three grades in each.

First: a Russian school, with the following curriculum: grammar, and purity of style in the lower grade, versification in the intermediate, oratory in the higher.[9]

Second: a Latin school: the elements of Latin, vocabulary and conversation in the lower grade, explanation of easy Latin authors and translation from Latin to Russian and Russian to Latin in the intermediate, and explanation of more elevated authors, with composition in prose and verse, in the higher.

Third: a preparatory school: arithmetic in the lower grade, geometry and geography in the intermediate, a survey of philosophy in the higher.

Fourth: a Language school for the most illustrious European languages: the elements, conversation, and vocabulary of German and French to be taught in the two lower grades, purity of style in the two higher.[10]

■ ■ ■

39. To distinguish the nobility from the commoners, they will study in different gimnazii; but when they become students at the university,

nobles and commoners will study together, in order to give the greater encouragement to diligent study.

■ ■ ■

42. All professors, teachers and other personnel should reside in the vicinity of the university and gimnazii, to prevent waste of time in going to and fro.

■ ■ ■

45. In due time, as the university grows, I do not doubt that the ruling Senate will approve other useful developments, the revenues of which may take the place of Her Majesty's Treasury grant.[11]

Likewise, it is considered necessary to teach the Greek language. Oriental languages may also be taught in due time, when the university revenues are sufficient and capable instructors are found.

—*Osnovanie Moskovskogo universiteta*,[12] ed. N. A. Penchko (Moscow, 1953)

NOTES: [1]Ivan Shuvalov (1727–97): a favorite of Elizabeth; patron of arts, letters, and sciences. He also inspired the creation of the Academy of Fine Arts in Petersburg (1758) and protected artists, such as the sculptor Shubin and the painter Losenko. He commissioned Voltaire's *History of Russia*.

[2]Fifteen thousand rubles were assigned, plus extras and private subsidies.

[3]The "protection" was intended to make the university more independent of petty authorities. The medieval universities in Europe had likewise found it desirable to place themselves under the direct authority of the Pope rather than of the local church powers.

[4]The teaching of Russian law was a novelty. However, the chair remained empty for some time.

[5]Professors at the Academy of Sciences were not exact in this respect.

[6]This had often been the case at the Academy of Sciences.

[7]This, with article 2, p. 112, formed part of the program of academic privileges by which Lomonosov and Shuvalov hoped to give dignity to learning and to create a cultured class, independent of traditional social conditions.

[8]In spite of this regulation, non-freed serfs were sometimes enrolled, though not formally registered, at the university.

[9]The systematic study of the native language was an innovation.

[10]In the early nineteenth century the gimnazia for the nobility was an excellent establishment (until Nicholas I deprived it of its privileges in 1830). Zhukovsky, Griboedov, Chaadaev, and Lermontov were among its students.

[11]The Moscow University Press was founded in 1756.

[12]The documents and commentary to be found in this book have been used in the notes.

■ ■ ■

ON THE PRINTING AND SELLING OF BOOKS
N. I. Novikov

> In 1773, Novikov founded the Society for the Advancement of Book Printing. Though this society was dissolved in 1775 because of lack of funds, Novikov renewed his activities in 1779 when he was allowed the use of the Moscow University Press. He printed and distributed a great variety of books: primers and textbooks, popular books on religion, children's books, and translations from the French essayists and philosophers. The following "exchange" from the columns of *The Painter*, Novikov's journal,[1] explains and advertises his reasons for setting up the society.

Mr. Painter:

■ ■ ■ Since I am aware that you never fail, in your praiseworthy sheets, to reveal to the world all that deserves its scorn in order thus to rouse in the hearts of our fellow citizens due aversion for evil, you will not, I trust, disregard the opportunity to inform all thinking Russians (since it is for them only, I think, that you write) of the most deserving and useful undertaking that private persons may conceive. By this I mean the recently formed Society for the Advancement of Printing. The statutes of this Society may be familiar to you, a man who moves about in the world, but, as I read them and noted their deserving purpose and the advantage that all Russian people may derive from this undertaking, I was so enraptured that I cannot refrain from wishing to inform the whole world about them. Though I will later attempt to tell you about all the articles of the Society, I intend now to speak of its usefulness both for public education and in relation to commerce.[2]

An unquestionable rule of government policy is to strive for the flourishing of commerce. This I hold true for large countries, for insomuch as commerce is useful in them, insomuch, and more, is it harmful in a state limited to one city or a few. What, if not exchange, brings money, the sign that measures national fortune, into circulation, thus providing the population with a subsistence? To say nothing of the fact that through exchanges rich men get rid of their superfluous wealth, which would lie dead, so to speak, in their coffers if luxury, breeding new needs, did not incite them to purchase the works of artists which give equal satisfaction to their magnificence, vanity, and sensibility—how many people commerce supports, people whose daily occupation consists in furnishing the artists with materials from which their skilled hands extract the inventions of art! What would factories, manufactures, etc., do without trade? Public commerce is the more profitable for a state as, being able to initiate greater undertakings, it gives subsistence to a greater number of people. But though the foundation of the Society for the Advancement of Printing does not apparently come under this rule, it is useful in that it provides a model of how to set up commercial enterprises, how to achieve this without embarrassment, how to prevent the drawbacks which lead to their ruin. I will not hesitate to say that this Society puts to shame the greater part of our merchant class, who are ignorant of the very principles of commerce. May this association be their teacher! God grant that, enlightening all minds, the example of this Society may also enlighten the minds of our merchants and reveal their real advantage to them! They would be richer themselves, and the State would be mightier and happier.

As to the advantage of this Society for the enlightenment of minds, who is not sensible of it? The printing of books, bringing centuries and lands closer together, providing everyone with information on discoveries and events, is the greatest of all inventions accessible to the mind of man.[3] What, if not the printing of books, can better cause to fructify a single truth, otherwise destined to oblivion, and breed, so to speak, as many heads able to think rightly, like the inventor of that truth, as there are readers? Printing respects all truths in the best manner, communicates them to the greatest number of people, and through this cleanses society from ever-harmful errors and prejudice (for I am not of the opinion that these can sometimes be beneficent: their usefulness is ever brief, but the harm they cause is regurgitated, if I may say so, for whole centuries).

This is what I had to say about the most useful undertaking of private persons in our country. Please insert this letter in your paper: for information about this Society may incite others to organize a similar one, far more useful than our clubs, assemblies, and other gatherings of the kind. Continue on your way, friends of truth. Russia will be in your debt.

Your obedient servant,
Wisdomlover
1773, February 28, Yaroslavl

■ ■ ■

Mr. Wisdomlover:

■ ■ ■ I am pleased to insert your letter in my paper, knowing that it will be of no little encouragement to the founders of the Society for the Advancement of Printing. And though the plan of this organization is not known to me, I agree with you that this project is most useful to our fellow citizens. The commerce of books, by its nature, deserves to be better understood and to have more energy applied to its development in our country than has been the case up to our time. But in my opinion, Sir, it is not

118

enough to print books as, I understand, is your purpose from the name of your Society; we should also concern ourselves with selling them.[4] Petersburg and Moscow have means to buy books, to set up bookstores and make use of them for their own advantage, if they only desire to do so. But allow me to say that Petersburg and Moscow citizens enjoy many pleasures; they have various shows, entertainments, and gatherings; consequently very few people have time left for reading; moreover, our enlightened education or, rather, our blind passion for French books prevents us from buying Russian works. What is published by the Russian printing press is rarely considered by our coxcombs as passable, and hardly ever as good. On the contrary, the nobles and merchants who live in remote provinces are deprived of the means of buying books and using them for their advantage. A book printed in Petersburg will reach Little-Russia,[5] for example, through three or four hands; each go-between sets himself an excessive profit, because he operates with extremely small funds: thus a book sold in Petersburg for one ruble sells there for three or even more. Therefore, the number of prospective buyers decreases, fewer books circulate, and the publishers often sustain a loss instead of being rewarded for their labors. Such, Sir, is the aim which this Society should pursue; and if it can bring the book-trade to a flourishing condition, it will deserve just praise. . . .

The most illustrious Empress, our most gracious Mother and Sovereign, has used every means available to a ruler for the enlightenment of her subjects, for the cleansing of their minds and hearts, and for the uprooting of all repulsive vices and prejudices; it remains to us, her faithful subjects, to speed her purpose and accomplish her will for our own felicity. And what more worthy offering can we return this great Sovereign for her innumerable favors to us than the real fulfillment of her desires? Her Imperial Majesty has founded the Society for the Translation of Foreign Books into the Russian Language; she has assigned five thousand rubles annually to pay the translators for their labors. By itself this action has been most advantageous: the translators have thus gained an honorable and satisfactory income, and this in turn encourages them, far more than a set salary, to apply themselves to learning: where obligation is, there also is constraint, but learning loves freedom and develops better where thought is free. How much good has derived from the books translated under the sponsorship of this Society? Impartial and patriotic reader, you know this. But how much more can be expected from those books when commerce will enable them to reach our nobility and commoners in the remote provinces? But the propagation of commerce is not the business of the Sovereign; it is that of private individuals.

This, Sir, is my sincere opinion on the subject concerning which you wrote me in your letter!

119

—*Izbrannye sochineniya* (Moscow-Leningrad, 1951)

NOTES: [1]*The Painter*, a weekly journal, lasted from 1772 to 1773.

[2]The importance of commerce was frequently discussed in the eighteenth century. See, as early as 1721–24, Pososhkov's book, *On Poverty and Wealth*, in which the author, an economist, insists on the necessity for developing Russian commerce and industry.

[3]Cf. Novikov's phrase, in the true spirit of the eighteenth century: "The reason for all human errors is ignorance, while perfections are bred from knowledge."

[4]In the early seventeen-fifties, apparently, there were no bookstores in Moscow. Books were sold in the open markets, as had been the custom for manuscript copies in the sixteenth century. According to the historian Karamzin, two bookstores existed in Moscow in 1775.

[5]Novikov was especially concerned with reaching the commoners in the provinces. He attempted to create a collection of useful and easy outline-type books to serve as small household encyclopedias in chemistry, natural history, husbandry, and so forth.

■ ■ ■

DECREE ON EDUCATION FOR SERFS—OCTOBER 1827
Nicholas I

> In spite of government regulations, serfs were sometimes enrolled in the secondary schools (gimnazii) and the universities. This situation attracted the attention of Tsar Nicholas I, and he attempted to put a stop to it by allowing serfs to enroll in vocational schools and especially by making more stringent rules concerning secondary and higher education, thus fulfilling his program of "education according to condition in life." The following is part of a decree on this question. Admiral Shishkov[1] was then Minister of Public Education.

■ ■ ■ It has come to my knowledge that serfs, both house-servants and villagers, are frequently enrolled in the gimnazii and other institutions of higher education. This is doubly harmful: in the first place, these young people, having received their first education from their squires or from careless parents, mostly enter the gimnazia with bad habits which infect their fellow students or cause prudent fathers to abstain from placing their own children in such establishments; secondly, the most proficient among them become used to a way of life, to a manner of thinking, and to notions that are not fitting to their situation in life. The inevitable hardships of this situation become unbearable to them, and this frequently causes them to indulge in pernicious dreams or low passions.[2] In order to prevent such consequences, at least in the future, I find it necessary to order:

(1) The universities and other institutions of higher education, official or private, under the supervision or control of the Ministry of Public

Education, also the gimnazii and similar establishments, may accept in their classes and admit to their lessons only students of free condition, including freed serfs who will present satisfactory documents to that effect, even if they have not yet registered as merchants or city-commoners and have no other status.

(2) The serfs of the landed gentry, villagers or servants, may, as formerly, study freely in the parish and county schools and in private establishments, the curriculum of which does not extend beyond the courses taught in county schools.[3]

(3) They may also be accepted in special establishments which already exist or will be set up in the future by the government or by private individuals for the study of rural economy, horticulture, and the arts and crafts necessary for the advancement and propagation of agriculture, crafts, and all other industries; but these schools will teach those sciences which are not useful or essential for the crafts and trades only in the same measure as the county schools.

—*Khrestomatiya po istorii* SSSR (Moscow, 1953), Vol. II

NOTES:　[1]Admiral Shishkov, Minister of Education from 1824 to 1828, is famous for his position in the language controversy that, in the early nineteenth century, opposed innovators and conservatives.　Shishkov belonged to the latter camp, advocating recourse to Slavonic for the enrichment of Russian as a literary language.

　　[2]The Manifest of July 13, 1826, which made public the sentences passed on the Dekabrists (Decembrists), also spoke of "the fatal luxury of half-knowledge, the impulse to dream-born extremes."

　　[3]The county schools, which had been intended chiefly for commoners, had a strong minority of students of the nobility, thus partially defeating Nicholas' purpose of class education.

■　■　■

MOSCOW UNIVERSITY IN THE 1830's

A. I. Herzen

Alexandr Herzen (1812–70), the son of a Russian nobleman and a German governess, is perhaps the last great "Russian European." He received his education first at home, with tutors, and later at Moscow University. After several brushes with the authorities, who banished him to Vyatka and later to Novgorod, he left Russia in 1847, never to return. The faith he placed in western Europe did not survive close contact with European

121

realities and his Western-style socialism took a tinge of Slavophil communitarianism. In 1857, in London, he founded the Russian-language monthly, *The Bell,* which, though illegal in Russia, was widely read and had considerable influence on public opinion. Herzen's *My Past and Thoughts* is not only an autobiography, it is also a vivid picture of Russian social and intellectual life from the eighteen-thirties to the eighteen-fifties.

■ ■ ■ Moscow University and the Tsarskoe Selo Lyceum[1] play a considerable role in the history of Russian education and in the life of the last two generations.

Moscow University grew in significance, as Moscow did, after 1812. Retrograded by the Emperor Peter from the rank of tsars' capital, Moscow was promoted by the Emperor Napoleon (more in spite of himself than intentionally) to the rank of people's capital. The grief the people felt on hearing that Moscow had fallen to the enemy made them aware of their blood ties with the city. A new era then began for Moscow. Its university became increasingly the focal point of Russian culture. All the conditions for its development were assembled: historical significance, geographical position, and the absence of the tsar.

The intellectual activity that, after Paul's death, had been strongly stimulated in Petersburg gloomily ended with the Fourteenth of December. Nicholas came on the scene, with five gallows, with penal servitude, with the white police strap and the blue Benkendorf.[2]

Everything shrank into itself; the blood rushed to the heart; activity, outwardly concealed, stirred in secret. Moscow University stood firm and was the first to emerge from the all-pervading fog. Ever since the Polezhaev affair,[3] the Emperor had hated it. He sent A. Pisarev,[4] the major general of the Kaluga evenings, to be curator; he ordered the students to wear uniforms, ordered them to wear swords, then forbade the wearing of swords. He had Polezhaev sent to the army as a private for his poetry, did the same to Kostenetsky and his friends because of his prose; he destroyed the Kritsky brothers[5] because of a bust, sent us to banishment for Saint-Simonism; then he appointed Prince Sergey Golitsyn as curator and from then on ignored that "nursing-ground of corruption," piously advising the young men who had completed their studies at the Lyceum or in the School of Jurisprudence not to enroll at the university.

Golitsyn was an amazing man: he could not get used to the irregularity of having a lecture cancelled when a professor was ill; he thought that the next in line should substitute, in which case Father Ternovsky would sometimes have had to lecture in the clinic on women's diseases and the obstetrician Richter to discuss the Immaculate Conception.

But though the university was out of favor, it grew in influence: the youthful strength of Russia streamed to it from all regions, from all

132

classes, as into a common reservoir; in its halls they discarded the prejudices imbibed in their homes, mingled on a common level, fraternized together, and again streamed out to all the regions of Russia and among all its classes.

Before 1848 the organization of our universities was democratic. Their doors were open to all those who could pass the entrance examination and were neither serfs nor peasants still bound to their community. Nicholas spoiled all this; he limited the enrollment, raised the fees, and allowed exemptions only for poor noblemen. All this belongs to the number of crazy measures which will disappear, together with the law on passports and religious intolerance, with the last breath of the man who drags on the Russian wheel.

The motley youth that came from high and low, north and south, rapidly merged into one compact mass of comradeship. Social distinctions did not then have for us that insulting importance that we see in English schools and barracks. I do not speak of English universities, for these exist only for the aristocrats and the wealthy. A Russian student who took it into his head to boast of his blue blood or his wealth would have been ostracized and his life made altogether miserable.[6]

The external differences between the students did not go very deep and arose from other causes. Thus, for example, the medical school, which was located on the other side of the garden, was not so closely bound to us as the other schools; besides, most of its students were ex-seminarists or Germans. The Germans stood somewhat aloof and were imbued with the petty bourgeois spirit of the West. The whole education of the seminarists, their ideas, were totally different from ours—we had no common language; brought up under the yoke of monastic despotism, oppressed by rhetoric and theology, they envied our casual ease, while we were vexed by their Christian humility.

I entered the school of physics and mathematics, in spite of the fact that I had neither great ability nor great liking for mathematics. Nick[7] and I had studied them under a teacher whom we liked for his anecdotes and stories; but with all his liveliness, he could hardly have inspired any special passion for his subject. He knew mathematics as far as conic sections inclusively, that is, just enough to prepare students for the university; a genuine philosopher, he had never had the curiosity to glance beyond, into the "university parts" of mathematics. What is particularly remarkable is that he read one book only, and that constantly for ten years: this was Francoeur's course; but being of a moderate temper and disliking excess, he never went beyond a certain page.

I had chosen the school of physics and mathematics because the natural sciences, for which I had developed a strong passion, were also taught there. . . .

And so, at last, the seclusion of my parental home was over. I was *au large*;[8] instead of solitude in our small room, instead of quiet and

123

half-clandestine meetings with Ogarev only, I found myself surrounded by a boisterous family of seven hundred persons. In two weeks I felt more at home with them than I ever did in the parental home where I was born.

But my parental home pursued me even at the university, in the form of a manservant that my father ordered to accompany me, especially when I was on foot. For a whole semester I tried to get rid of him and managed to do so officially with the greatest difficulty. I say "officially" because Petr Fedorovich, my valet, to whom this duty was assigned, understood very quickly that I disliked being escorted and that he would enjoy himself far better in various places of entertainment than in the vestibule of the school of physics and mathematics, where his only pleasures consisted in conversing with the two porters and in exchanging gifts of tobacco.

Why was an escort provided for me? Could Petr, who from his youth had been given to drinking for several days at a time, really stop me from doing anything I wanted to do? I suppose that my father did not really think so, but for his own peace of mind he took measures, even though they were inefficient, as people fast though they are not believers. This is a typical trait of our old gentry education. Until I was seven, I was not allowed up the stairs, which were rather steep, without being led by the hand; Vera Artamonovna washed me in a wooden tub until I was eleven; so that it was perfectly logical that a servant should escort me and that, until the age of twenty-one, I should not have permission to stay out after half past ten. Actually, it was only in banishment that I found myself free and independent; if I had not been exiled, the same regime would probably have been applied until I was twenty-five—or thirty-five. . . .

The boys in my class were remarkable. That was the time when theoretical interests grew stronger in us. Seminary discipline and aristocratic indolence alike were disappearing, without yet being replaced by the German utilitarianism which enriches minds with knowledge, as fields with manure, for better harvests. A good number of students no longer considered learning as a necessary but boring shortcut to reach the rank of collegiate assessor[9] more rapidly. The questions that arose among us did not concern the Table of Ranks. On the other hand, interest in learning had not yet degenerated into doctrinarianism; learning did not cut us off from the life and suffering that surrounded us. The sympathy they roused in us raised the students' social conscience to a high level. We and our friends expressed openly in the lecture halls whatever came into our heads; copies of forbidden verse circulated, prohibited books were read and discussed, and yet I cannot remember a single case of talebearing, or one betrayal. Some timid young people kept apart or turned away, but they too were silent. . . .

The rector then was Dvigubsky, one of the remaining specimens of the professors in the pre-Flood, or rather pre-Fire period, that is before 1812. They are now extinct; the curatorship of Prince Obolensky marked

124

the end of Moscow University's patriarchal age. In those times, the authorities took no interest in the university, the professors lectured or not, the students attended or not, and when they did, they did not wear uniform tunics *à l'instar*[10] of the light cavalry, but all sorts of wildly eccentric costumes, with tiny caps perched on top of their virgin locks. The professors formed two camps or clans, engaged in placid detestation of each other: one was composed exclusively of Germans, the other of non-Germans. The Germans, among whom were kind scholarly people such as Loder, Fischer, Hildebrand, and even Heym, were generally remarkable for their ignorance of the Russian language and their unwillingness to learn it, their indifference to the students, their spirit of western European servility and routine, their immoderate smoking of cigars, and the immense array of medals without which they were never seen. The non-Germans, on the other hand, knew no single living language except Russian, were patriotically obsequious, ecclesiastically clumsy, were looked upon with the greatest scorn, Merzlyakov[11] excepted, and instead of cigars they indulged in an immoderate quantity of liquor. The Germans mostly came from Göttingen, the non-Germans from priests' families.

—*Sochineniya* (Moscow, 1956), Vol. IV

NOTES: [1]Tsarskoe Selo Lyceum was opened in 1811 to give secondary education to children of the nobility and prepare them for careers as civil servants. The latter purpose, however, was not adhered to. Pushkin was a student there.

[2]The government police, or gendarmes, had light blue uniforms. Benkendorf was then police chief.

[3]Polezhaev, after graduating from Moscow University, was sent off to the army as a private for the anti-autocratic and atheistic sentiments in his poem "Sashka."

[4]General Pisarev became curator of Moscow University in 1825. He ordered the teaching of philosophy to be discontinued.

[5]Kostenetsky and the Kritsky brothers were members of secret societies founded after the December rebellion. A portrait (not a bust) of the Emperor Nicholas I had been defaced, with the exclamation: "Thus shall we hack down the tyrants of our country, all the Russian tsars!"

[6]Moscow University, in the eighteen-twenties and thirties, was a center of liberal and even radical thinking. The forbidden verse of Dekabrists circulated freely among the students.

[7]Nicholas Ogarev, Herzen's friend from childhood.

[8]In the open, free (in French in the text).

[9]See "A Provincial Town in the Early Nineteenth Century," pp. 21–23. A decree of 1809 had made the rank obtainable by university examination.

[10]In the guise of (in French in the text).

[11]Professor at Moscow University; also poet, critic, and translator.

■ ■ ■

THE ASSUMPTION CATHEDRAL AND THE TOWER OF IVAN THE GREAT IN THE KREML'

Early nineteenth-century painting

From *Tri veka*, ed. V. V. Kallash (Moscow, 1912), Vol. V

6

ART
AND
ESTHETICS

Until the first decade of the twentieth century, the term "Russian art" probably meant little, even to an enlightened public. Few nineteenth-century travelers in Russia had been interested in art; those who were did not see much beyond Petersburg and Moscow, and their eyes, which remembered Europe, caught chiefly the elements of "barbaric" splendor or imitation of Western models. Moreover, though many scholarly or enthusiastic studies of the artistic past were undertaken in Russia during the latter part of the nineteenth century, no systematic history of its development was written until the *Art Russe* of Viollet-le-Duc in 1877, a work which suffers from the fact that its author never set foot in Russia and which is concerned chiefly with architecture and decorative art.

Western Europe and America first became aware of Russian art in the beginning of the twentieth century through music and ballet, which brought in their wake the works of modern painters and the more picturesque aspects of folklore and costume. Here again the impression received was of wild exoticism, behind which the many-sided historical development of Russian art remained unperceived.

The diversity of development in Russian art is in fact considerable. This is especially true of architecture. A journey across space and time would reveal nearly as much variety and originality of achievement— if not such a height—in Russia as in Germany or England. The cupola-topped basilicas of Byzantine inspiration, the Armenian or Romanesque looking churches of the twelfth century, the elegant carved sandstone edifices of the Vladimir-Suzdal region, the late fifteenth-century "Italian" Kreml', the baroque buildings of seventeenth-century Moscow, the great rococo or classical palaces of Petersburg: all these may show adaptations of foreign techniques and styles—but no more so than Romanesque churches or Renaissance castles in western Europe. Less familiar to the tourist is "native" Russian architecture which proposes the wooden izba-like chapels of northern Russia, the brick sixteenth-century Moscow churches, the seventeenth-century Northern churches with their izba-inspired galleries and decoration; it offers the endless combinations in those two centuries of bulbs and pyramid-shaped roofs and the groupings of porches, spires, towers in a complex mass—the best example of which is visible in the nine chapels assembled under the name of Vasily the Blessed in the Red Square.

The Eastern tradition forbade sculpture, for which, moreover, stone or marble materials were rare; and before the end of the seventeenth century only a few churches were decorated with an embroidery-like pattern of carving in low relief. Glass was too precious for stained-glass art to develop, nor did the climate allow the large windows of the West. The painted image—icon or fresco—alone illustrated religious teaching. Like the

129

Byzantine models which inspired them, the icons stressed not the human emotions stirred by episodes from the sacred story, but the contemplation of the Divinity made visible. They speak of the mysteries by allusion, by the graphic and pictorial code that the West very early abandoned or subordinated to purely picturesque values. In the West, the religious vision was very soon impregnated with the personal, the individual, the realistic. Purely human emotions were expressed through the representation of the human body and by scenes from the Holy Books translated into the homely local idiom of costume and background, bringing the concept of the soul's struggle toward God down to earth. The western European felt amazement, fear, anger, amusement, and indignation as he gazed on the decoration of his church. And so, when art abandoned the symbolic expression of psychomachy to become a means of sensuous gratification or intellectual delight, the transition was easy: though the subjects might apparently change, the moral attitudes and the techniques were adaptable.

In Russia, however, the individual artist had been permitted no more scope than the celebrant of a sacred rite in his recitation of the holy text. Thus, when in the seventeenth century "modernist" icon painters began to introduce realistic traits into their works, the conflict with the old school was more than the standard quarrel between conservatives and adventurers in art: it represented an essential difference of vision.

What might have developed within the frame of religious art, how the old concepts and techniques might have evolved, is a matter for speculation only. The opposition between men such as Avvakum and the master Joseph sank into oblivion as the new century relegated all the cultural life of the past to the uneducated masses. The painters of the eighteenth and the early nineteenth century could find nothing significant in the former tradition. No transition was possible from the concept of a liturgic language to the ideal of enjoyment, and Russian painting went to school in Europe.

Icon painting, left to stagnate or borrow mechanically from an alien vision, degenerated into a mere craft, sterile and unimportant. Many of the finest examples of pre-seventeenth century icons and frescoes disappeared. The Old Believers, for whom religious and artistic conservatism coincided, preserved many icons by hiding them in their private chapels or semiclandestine meetinghouses. The richest Old Believers collected them, with a special fondness for the icons of the sixteenth- and seventeenth-century so-called "Stroganov school." At last, with the 1905 Tolerance Law, the old icons came out. Since this was a time of renewed interest in form, they were restored and admired, and played their part in the evolution of twentieth-century painting.

Nothing, at first glance, can seem further from the art of the icon than the realist school of painting in the latter part of the nineteenth century, the period when Russian art emancipated itself from the European-inspired classicism and academic romanticism. Yet the genre painters, the "Wanderers" and their sympathizers who dominated the Russian scene from the sixties to the nineties, share with the masters of the past a high conception of art. Like their forgotten predecessors, they wish to serve the good. With most of the young intellectuals of their time, with the musicians who are their contemporaries, they belong to that great movement of fusion with the people that gives the Russian culture of those decades its nobility. The language of their pictures is that of moral purpose, of social and political protest. By depicting everyday episodes, the heroic or pathetic past, the sorrowing people, the victims of government oppression, they seek to evoke pity, indignation, admiration, and sacrifice.

"What is art?" asked Tolstoy in 1897, at the end of a fifteen-year period of reflection on the subject. He answered that the essence of true art consists in the expression of feelings accessible to all, feelings which have the power to unite all people in religious, or brotherly, consciousness, and which are rendered in brief, clear, simple form, like the parables. The great icons, in their economy of means, carry that universal appeal. It is unfortunate that Tolstoy also offered as models the mawkish pictures of Jules Breton and Bastien-Lepage, which remind us forcibly of Gide's dictum that good feelings do not make good art. It is unfortunate, likewise, that for many nineteenth-century Russian painters, impatience with the problems of form and concentration on immediate meaning or usefulness proved fatal to their productions. Except in music, Russian art in the nineteenth century had not regained the harmony between spiritual purpose and achievement of its earlier ages.

KAZAN CATHEDRAL IN ST. PETERSBURG   Drawing by V. Patersen
From *Nevsky prospekt* (St. Petersburg, 1903)

WELCOMING THE ICON   Painting by K. A. Savitsky, 1878
From an album of reproductions of paintings in the Tretyakov gallery, Moscow

THE BUILDING OF THE CHURCH OF THE ASSUMPTION
Chronicle

> In 1472, Ivan III married Zoe Paleologue, niece of the last
> Byzantine emperor. She had taken refuge in Italy and was
> living in Rome. During the next fifty years or so, a succession
> of Italian architects came to Moscow, where they built or re-
> built the churches and walls of the Kreml' and of Kitay-Gorod.

■ ■ ■ In the year 6983,[1] the Grand Prince dispatched his envoy Semen
Tolbuzin to the city of Venice, to inform the prince of that city that he had
sent off his envoy Trevizan with many goods and silver to the value of
seven hundred rubles; he also requested Tolbuzin to seek out a master
church builder. Tolbuzin was received in Venice with great honors; he
took the money and chose a master builder by the name of Aristotle.[2]
"They have many builders," he said, "but not one wants to go to Russia;
this one has consented and I have agreed to pay him ten rubles a month.[3]
He is called Aristotle because of his skill. It is even reported that the
Turkish tsar in Tsargrad[4] wanted to employ him. Also, there is a church
in Venice, most wonderful and fair, St. Mark's, with Venetian gates of
skilled workmanship: these Aristotle made." Aristotle showed Tolbuzin
the following invention: he bade him to his house—a fine one with beautiful large rooms—and told him to take a bronze dish resting on four apple-
shaped supports, with a tin container inside the dish, like a washbowl; and
then Aristotle poured water, wine, or mead from the container: whichever
he wanted he could get.

Aristotle took along his son, Andrew, and a helper by the name
of Petrusha, and he came to Russia with Semen Tolbuzin.

He praised the smoothness of the walls of the Assumption
church,[5] but he thought the mortar was not strong enough and the stone
insufficiently hard. For this reason he built all the vaults of brick for, he
said, brick is harder than stone. He would not finish the north wall and
the choir, but started the work all over again.

He wrecked the church in the following manner:[6] he put up
three timbers and tied together their upper ends, then, crosswise, he sus-
pended from a rope an oak log with an ironclad end, and, by swinging
this, broke the walls. He removed some stones from the lower parts of
other walls, propped them up with timber, then burnt the timber, and the
walls collapsed. It was amazing to see that what had taken three years to
build he wrecked in a week and even less: the workers who carried away
the stones could not keep pace with him; otherwise, they say, he could
have finished in three days. The bookmen call such an oak log a ram: thus,
they say, did Titus destroy the walls of Jerusalem.

133

Aristotle gave the order to excavate over again and had oak piles driven in. He went to the city of Vladimir, praised the construction of the church,[7] and said: "This must be the work of our builders." He built a furnace back of the Andronicus Monastery in Kalitnikov, to fire bricks. He had them made narrower, longer, and harder than our Russian bricks; they have to be soaked in water before you can break them. He ordered the mortar to be mixed thick, with trowels; when dried overnight, it could not be broken off with a knife. He laid out the church oblong-shaped like a palace.[8]

The first year Aristotle raised the church from the ground. The mortar was mixed like heavy dough and applied with iron trowels; he ordered smooth stone to be laid inside. He built four round columns: these, he said, stand firmly; in the altar section he put two square brick pillars. He did everything with compass and ruler. . . .

In the year 6984, Aristotle raised the Church of the Assumption to the level of the niches which run round the walls. Inside the walls he put iron rods, and between the pillars, where in our churches there are oak logs, he put iron.

In that year Aristotle made a wheel; stones no longer had to be carried up, but were tied with ropes and raised up; and on top the workers fastened little wheels, such as carpenters call "squirrels" and use to lift earth to the top of the izba[9]—it was an amazing sight. He put four big stones on each pillar and connected them with arches, cutting the stones on each side to fit in the line of the arches, so that the whole looks like stone trees carved out of one block.

In the year 6986, the stone church of the Holy Virgin was completed. Aristotle built four cupolas, with the treasure room by the main drum; he made the choir gallery beside the altar as you come from the side doors, and he made stairs to the top of the church. But the top of the vaults is only one brick thick, and they leak when it rains. He made the pavement of small stones. In the sanctuary, above the Metropolitan's seat behind the altar, he carved in stone a Polish cross;[10] later the Metropolitan had it erased.

—*Khrestomatiya po istorii* SSSR (Moscow, 1951), Vol. I

NOTES: [1]1475.

[2]Rodolfo Fioravanti Aristotle, of Bologna, was a famous architect, engineer, and expert in hydraulics and fortifications. He had built the Palazzo Communale in Bologna, a fortress for Francesco Sforza in Milan, a bridge over the Danube in Hungary, and other buildings. He was about 61 in 1475. In 1479 he returned to Bologna, where he built the facade of the Podesta Palace.

[3]This was a considerable sum at the time. In Pskov, about the middle of the fifteenth century, one ruble would buy 35 sheep.

[4]Mahomet II.

[5]The three golden-domed churches in the center of the Kreml' are the Assumption, or coronation church; the Annunciation, or parish church of the tsars; and the Archangel Michael Church, or burial church.

[6]The reconstruction of the old Assumption church, built in 1326 (the first stone church in Moscow), had been started in 1472 by Russian craftsmen, but the edifice had collapsed in 1474.

[7]The twelfth century Assumption church in Vladimir.

[8]The term "palata," here translated as "palace," first used to designate a stone mansion or palace, later came to mean a reception chamber, a large official building, hall, or institution.

[9]Earth was used under the roof of an izba for insulation.

[10]A Roman Catholic cross.

■ ▩ ■

THE TROITSA MONASTERY IN 1858

T. Gautier

> The Emperor Alexander II invited the French writer Théophile Gautier to Russia to study and describe Russian works of art. Gautier, a man keenly interested in painting and an art critic after a fashion, made three trips to Russia and published his two-volume *Travels in Russia* in 1866.

■ ■ ■ On the other slope of the gully, on a wide plateau, the fortress-like convent of St. Sergius[1] rises picturesquely.

It forms an immense square surrounded by massive ramparts on which runs a roofed gallery pierced by barbicans, which shelters the defenders of the fort. The convent deserves this name, having sustained more than one attack.[2] Great towers, square or hexagonal, rise at the corners or flank the walls at intervals. . . .

Above the ramparts, in graceful and picturesque irregularity, rise the roofs and cupolas of the monastery buildings. The huge mass of the refectory catches the eye with its chequered and faceted walls and the bell turret of its elegant chapel. Near by, topped by the Greek cross, swell the five bulbous domes of the Church of the Assumption. A short way off, the tall many-colored steeple of the Trinity dominates the skyline with its tiers of turrets and lofty cross adorned with chains. Other towers, other belfries, other roofs emerge dimly over the walls. . . . Nothing is more delightful than those gilt spires and cupolas, touched with silver snow, as they spring from a mass of brilliantly colored buildings. They give the illusion of an Oriental city.

135

. . . Near the convent gates were set up stalls with petty wares and curios such as tourists like to buy as souvenirs. There were toys of primitive simplicity painted in amusingly barbaric colors, tiny white felt shoes trimmed with pink and blue, fur-lined mittens, Circassian belts, Tula forks and spoons[3] inlaid with platinum, models of the cracked Bell of Moscow,[4] rosaries, enameled medallions of St. Sergius, metal and wooden crosses on which a multitude of microscopic Byzantine figures mingled with inscriptions in Slavic characters, loaves of bread from the convent bakery with scenes from the Old and New Testament stamped on the crust—and heaps of green apples for which the Russians seem to have a particular fondness. . . .

The walls of Troitsa, which is almost a city, enclose nine churches, the tsar's palace, the archimandrite's residence, a chapter house, refectory, library, treasure room, monks' cells, sepulchral chapels, offices of all kinds. No symmetry has been sought for; each arose when and where needed, like plants growing where the soil is good. The look of the place is strange, novel, foreign. Nothing could be more unlike the picturesqueness of Catholic monasteries. . . . The Greek religion, which is less picturesque artistically, preserves the ancient Byzantine formulas and is not afraid of repetition, being more mindful of orthodoxy than of taste. Yet it achieves powerful effects of splendor and wealth, and its hieratic barbarity strongly impresses the untutored imagination. Even the most blasé tourist cannot help being struck with wonder when, at the end of an avenue of trees bright with frost, he sees those churches, painted blue, vivid red, apple green, outlined in white by the snow, rising quaintly with their golden and silver cupolas from among the many-colored buildings all around.

—*Voyage en Russie* (Paris, 1895)

NOTES: [1]Sergius of Radonezh founded the Monastery of the Trinity in the fourteenth century. The monastery rapidly gained power and wealth. It was a cultural center in the sixteenth and seventeenth centuries and later. In 1814, the Moscow Slavonic-Greek-Latin Academy was transferred to the monastery. The Soviet regime, after closing the Academy in 1918, restored it in 1944. The monastery is now a museum in the town of Zagorsk (formerly Sergiev Posad). The churches, towers, and walls of the monastery were built from the fifteenth to the eighteenth centuries.

[2]The monastery sustained a long siege by Polish troops during the Time of Troubles.

[3]Tula, south of Moscow, has long been famous for its metal works and arms factories. Tula samovars were also renowned.

[4]Cast in the eighteenth century, the "Tsar-Bell" fell during a fire, and a piece cracked. It now stands on a pedestal in the Kreml'.

MOSCOW AND PETERSBURG ARCHITECTURE
I. Grabar

■ ■ ■ One of Peter's undertakings played a decisive role in the history of Russian architecture and determined all its future development: the foundation of Petersburg and the transfer of the capital to the new city. From then on all our architecture was fatally destined to follow two parallel courses—the Moscow road and the Petersburg road.

. . . By itself the difference in topographical conditions sufficed to make Moscow architecture absolutely unlike that of Petersburg. On one hand, we have an old city, picturesquely spread on "seven hills," with patriarchal manners, a stubborn attachment to the past, a population that had elaborated its architectural tastes and practice in the course of several centuries and had expressed them in a complex and complete system; on the other, a giant city newly raised on a flat place, "on the marsh," with straight streets regularly planned; a city which at first was built anyhow, in haste, and later perseveringly renovated through the century—with elaborate palaces that have few equals in Europe rising as if by magic formula in place of variegated earthen houses. All this was to lead inevitably to dissociation in the development of our architecture.

We already know what excellent constructors, what experienced Russian craftsmen could be found in Moscow at the end of the seventeenth century. However, Peter did not call any of them to build the new capital, for he did not wish it to recall Moscow in any way. Instead he invited more and more builders from other countries. Meanwhile, the Moscow craftsmen went on building in the same baroque style that the foreigners were following in Petersburg, but with a noticeable deviation toward provincialism, which gave their work a kinship with the native Moscow architecture. Compared to the buildings of the same period in Petersburg, their Muscovite air is as typical as a Dutch, German, or Italian air is typical of Petersburg.

—*Istoriya russkogo iskusstva* (Moscow, 1909), Vol. III

■ ■ ■

PETERSBURG MONUMENTS
F. F. Vigel

■ ■ ■ Autumn was just as clear, still, and warm as summer had been; many thought this was due to the comet, which still shone ominously over us. This autumn was marked by two events in the capital: the completion and consecration of the Kazan Cathedral and the foundation of the Tsarskoe Selo Lyceum.

. . . When the Emperor Paul had completed his wonder-palace, now known under the name of Mikhailovsky or Engineer Castle,[1] and settled for a brief period in the temple he had thus erected to himself, he turned to the idea of building another temple to the Divinity, and shortly before his death he laid the foundations of the Kazan Cathedral. Even under Elizabeth, the previous structure stood nearly at the edge of the still-growing city, by a muddy stream called the Black Creek, which now, dredged but still dirty, is the Catherine canal. Like a few other churches of the kind still existing in Petersburg, it was merely a spacious, oblong, shed-like stone edifice, topped by a rather high wooden cupola; behind it spread a wide empty space destined to be the site of its splendid successor.

Count Alexander Sergeevich Stroganov was put in charge of the project. He was a constant patron of artists and an amateur of art, though I do not know the extent of his competence on the subject; combining a foreign education and tastes with Russian habits and hospitality, he lived in a lordly manner, and on Sundays entertained in his mansion not only the wellborn but the talented also. He was an enlightened, intelligent, and distinguished old gentleman; however, he was also a sufficiently adroit courtier to keep on good terms with all the favorites of the tsars and enjoy the good graces of four crowned heads. He succeeded in eliminating from the project a protégé of Paul's, the architect Brenna, who could hardly have been even an average house painter in Italy, and replacing him by his own house-trained Voronikhin.[2]

Paul had no taste at all, and Alexander I had a great deal; but in the first years of his reign he had a passion for columns and had to have them everywhere, and for this reason he kept the plan his father had approved, since columns were there in great abundance.[3]

All the enclosed space around the building—and likewise, when the work approached its completion, access to its interior—remained open to curious spectators; not as in some building yards into which only a few elect persons are allowed to peek at work that has been going on for decades, as if it was feared that well-dressed people would carry off the bricks and lime that lie around, or because quack builders wished to veil the wonders they perform under a screen of mystery. I sometimes penetrated into the unfinished edifice, and could not help marveling at the wealth lavished on its interior decoration. The figured marble pavement, the polished monoliths of immense size that made up the long colonnade, the silver latticework, doors, and chandeliers, the icons covered with gold and strewn with diamonds, all combined to amaze the entering visitor. However, certain persons ventured to compare the architect to an inexperienced cook who, by filling all his preparations with pepper, ginger, cinnamon, and all sorts of spices, hopes to impart a wonderfully pleasant taste to his dishes.

138

Ten years exactly after the coronation of the emperor Alexander,[4] on the fifteenth of September, the new temple was consecrated. Anybody in uniform, with no exception, was permitted to enter the church. I had no uniform, and I stood modestly outside in the crowd of civilian frockcoats and peasant caftans.

The opening of the Tsarskoe Selo Lyceum in October was not such a brilliant affair. I do not know who had first thought of founding the establishment or had suggested the idea—apparently it was the Emperor himself. In the first happy years of his reign, he was delighted with his popularity. . . . Wearied of the pomp and magnificence in which he had grown up, he had always loved simplicity, both in his dress and in his way of life. Among all his palaces, he had chosen for his summer residence the most private one, the quite forgotten Kamennoostrovsky palace.[5] This lasted until the Tilsit treaty, after which his preference went to Tsarskoe Selo.

A strange fate was that of that imperial town and its palace. Never attractive to the tsars at the beginning of their reign, it always became their favorite refuge in their last years. Its site, near the Moscow high road, had been a gift of Peter the Great to Catherine I: she secretly had lime trees planted and a tall, though not spacious, house erected on the grounds. In August 1724, she entertained her benefactor there for the first time; Peter was extraordinarily pleased with everything and announced his intention of becoming not only a visitor, but a frequent resident. In January he died. For a few years Catherine II preferred the Peterhof[6] view on the seashore to the other places of entertainment in her capital, until she formed an attachment to Tsarskoe Selo; then she put her powerful hand to it and performed miracles there, as in all that she undertook. Consquently, her son, who was but a child when she ascended the throne, imagined that all of Tsarskoe Selo was her creation. Of course, it was not filial tenderness that made him give up Tsarskoe Selo completely and refuse to assign any sum for its upkeep. It fell into a decay; nettles overgrew it, slime covered it, rot and ruin overcame it, and this threatening destruction was sadly depicted by the singer of Catherine, Derzhavin,[7] in his poem "The Ruins." Paul's entourage began to be sorry for the Russian Versailles; they persuaded him that his grandmother and great-grandmother had done as much for it as his mother had, and in July 1800 he yielded to their arguments and took up his residence there. He stayed until September and, passing with his usual rapidity from one feeling to another, found the place delightful, far better than his Pavlovsk, and declared his intention to live there two months every summer. He could not carry it out: in March he departed this life.

139

—*Zapiski* (Moscow, 1928)

NOTES: [1]Built by the architect Brenna on plans by Bazhenov.

[2]Andrey Voronikhin (1760–1814): a house serf, possibly an illegitimate son of Count A. S. Stroganov and a companion to his son. He was freed in 1786. He had traveled and studied both in Russia and Europe.

[3]Paul I wished Kazan Cathedral to resemble St. Peter's in Rome.

[4]1801: Coronation of Alexander I; 1811: Consecration of Kazan Cathedral.

[5]Built by Bazhenov.

[6]Now Petrodvorets.

[7]See "The Hermitage Under Catherine II," note 5, p. 59.

■ ■ ■

ON ICON PAINTING
Council of the Hundred Chapters

The Council's answer on icon painting and holy icons

■ ■ ■ According to the tsar's orders, the Metropolitan, the archbishops, and bishops in the sovereign city of Moscow and in all cities will see to it that the various church rites, and especially all that concerns the holy icons and the icon painters, follow the holy rules: that the painters behave as they should and represent fittingly the bodily image of our Lord God and Savior Jesus Christ and the Most Pure Mother of God and the Heavenly Hosts and all saints who have pleased God from all time.

It behooves the painter to be meek, humble, pious; he must not be a chatterer or a jester; he must not grumble or envy, not drink, rob, or murder; especially must he take every precaution to keep body and soul clean. If he is not able to remain pure to the end, let him take a wife in wedlock, and consult his spiritual fathers frequently, confiding in them and living in accordance to their instructions and advice, in fast and prayer, in temperance and lowly wisdom, without shamefulness or scandal.[1] Let him paint with the greatest care the image of our Lord Jesus Christ and His Most Pure Mother, and the holy prophets, and apostles, and sacred martyrs, men and women, and prelates and blessed Fathers, conforming to their accepted image, likeness, and model, following the works of old painters and drawing from good models.[2] If our present-day master painters live faithful to the promises they made and observe the precepts and are zealous in the service of God, the tsar will favor them and the prelates care for them and esteem them above ordinary people.

140 Also these painters must take pupils, examine them in every way, instruct them in piety and purity, and bring them to their spiritual fathers. These will instruct them, according to the statutes they hold from the prelates, in the manner of life of a Christian, without shamefulness or

scandal. Let the apprentices learn attentively from their masters. If God reveals the secret of such work to an apprentice, the master will take him to the prelate; the prelate will examine whether the work done by the apprentice follows tradition and pattern, will inquire whether he lives in purity and piety, according to the precepts and without scandal; then, blessing him, he will instruct him to continue in piety and persevere in his holy work with all diligence. And the prelate will honor the apprentice just as he honors the master, above ordinary people.

After this, the prelate will instruct the master not to give preference to a brother or son or kinsman. For if God does not open the secret of such work to a man, and he paints badly or lives in disregard of the precepts, but his master declares him to be talented and worthy, and substitutes for his work the work of another, then the prelate, after investigation, will place this master under due interdict, so that others may take fear and refrain from following his example. The apprentice will then be forbidden to continue painting icons. But if God reveals the art of icon painting to an apprentice, and he lives rightly, but his master, out of envy, maligns him to deprive him of the honor he, the master, receives, then the prelate, after investigation, will place the master under due interdict, and the apprentice will receive all the more honor. If one of these painters conceals the talent God has given him and does not let his apprentice benefit from it, God will condemn such a man, with him who hid his talent, to eternal torment. If a painter or one of his apprentices does not live according to the precepts, is addicted to drink, to impurity, to scandal, the prelate will put him under interdict, bar him from icon painting, and forbid him to continue his work, mindful of what has been said: "Cursed is he who does God's work with negligence!"

Concerning those who until this day have painted icons without studying, according to their own fancy and art, not conforming to pattern, and who have bartered[3] them cheaply to simple people, ignorant peasants: they will be placed under interdict and made to study under good masters. If God grants the gift to one and he paints according to pattern and likeness, let him paint; the one to whom God will not grant the gift will be forbidden all such work, in order not to offend God's name by his painting. If any do not give up, let them be submitted to the tsar's wrath and be judged. If they say: "This is our livelihood," pay no attention to this argument, for they speak without knowledge and do not see their sin. Not all men can be icon painters; God has granted men various handicrafts, and men can turn to those for their nourishment and subsistence, without painting icons and putting God's likeness to shame and discredit.

Also the archbishops and bishops in all cities, villages, and monasteries of their jurisdiction are to examine the icon painters, inspect their work themselves, choose, each in his see, the most renowned, and order them to supervise all others so that none mediocre or unsuitable should be among them. The archbishops and bishops will themselves

141

supervise the painters they have made responsible and take strict care about this matter, giving the supervisors more consideration and honor than to ordinary people. Both lords and people of low condition are to hold those painters in great respect and esteem for the holy work they do.

Also the prelate will see to it with great care that talented painters and their apprentices paint from the old models and refrain from all invention and fancy in representing the Divinity; for Christ our God is pictured in the flesh, but not in his Godhood, as St. John Damascenes said: "Do not picture the Divinity, do not lie, blind ones; verily God is invisible and hidden, but when I represent his bodily image in the flesh, I worship, and believe, and glorify the Virgin who bore the Lord."

If a man who has learned from skilled and capable masters conceals the talent God gave him and does not instruct and guide others, may he who hid his talent, be condemned by God, to eternal torment; for this reason then, painters, teach your apprentices without malice so that you may not be doomed to eternal torment.[4]

—*Russkaya khrestomatiya*, ed. F. Buslaev (Moscow, 1912)

NOTES: [1]Icon painting was a liturgic art, a divine service like the priest's.

[2]Andrey Rublev's work was the model proposed by the Church to Russian icon painters.

[3]It was not considered fitting to use the word "sell" for icons, which were consecrated objects—hence "bartered."

[4]The recommendations given here (chap. xliii of the Stoglav) were implemented by the composition of manuals or guides for the painting of icons in the Church tradition. This chapter was often used as a preface to such books.

■ ■ ■

AGAINST THE NEW SCHOOL OF ICON PAINTERS
Avvakum[1]

■ ■ ■ Through God's permission, in our Russian land, there has been an increase of icon painters who work in unseemly fashion. The painters are of inferior rank, but the high Church authorities favor them, and all together they progress toward the abyss of perdition, holding on to one another, as it is written: "If the blind lead the blind, both shall fall into the ditch, for they stagger in the night of ignorance;[2] but he who walks by day will not stumble, for he sees the light of this world"; and this means that he who is enlightened by reason has his eyes open to the tricks and spells of the heretics; he has an exact understanding of all newfangled things, nor does he flounder in the councils that sinners devise. But this is what is done in our time: the image of our Savior Emmanuel is painted with a puffy face, red lips, curly hair, thick hands and arms, swollen fingers, fat thighs, and the whole of him paunchy and fat like a German; nothing lacking but a sword at his hip! All this is painted from carnal notions, for the grossness of the flesh is dear to heretics and they have repudiated higher things. But our Lord Christ had all the finer qualities and thus do the theologians teach us. Read in *Margaritae*[3] what John Chrysostomes says on the Nativity of the Virgin; there he depicts the likeness of Christ and our Lady: it's a far cry from what the heretics have imagined nowadays. And all this has been invented by that fierce dog Nikon, the fiend:[4] he wants lifelike painting, he wants everything done in the Frankish or German manner.[5] For when the Franks paint the image of the Annunciation of our Blessed Lady, they show her pregnant, with her belly hanging over her knees—in the wink of an eye Christ is to be found all grown in the womb! Among us too, in Moscow, in the book *The Sceptre*[6] you will find the same, word for word: Christ, from his conception, was a grown being, as if ready to be born. Or, in another place, it says "like a man of thirty." Now look, good people: as if a man was born with teeth and beard! I ask you all, great and small: has this ever been since the beginning of time? Those enemies of God, they have even printed worse things than the Franks. But we, Orthodox believers, confess our faith as the saints have taught us, John Damascenes and others: Christ our Lord was perfect in his limbs and joints from the moment of his conception, but his blessed flesh grew for nine months as customary, and he was born an infant, not a man of thirty. Now the icon painters, referring to that book [*The Sceptre*], will start to paint Christ at birth with a beard, and all will be well! And Our Lady at the Annunciation will be pregnant, as with the pagan Franks. And Christ on the cross will be all bloated; the dear one, they paint him plump and fat, with legs like logs. Alack, alack, poor Russia, whatever did you want with German manners and uses!

> —"The Epistles of Avvakum," *Khrestomatiya po drevney russkoy literature*, ed. N. K. Gudzy (Moscow, 1955)

NOTES: 1See "The Life of Archpriest Avvakum," pp. 90–96.

2Matthew 15:14.

3A compilation of thirty sermons of St. John Chrysostomes. The Moscow edition (1641) added some other sermons and also a life of the saint.

4In reality, Nikon was against the new style, in which he saw "Latin" influences. He had ordered "new" icons to be burnt, over the tsar's protests.

5"Fryaz" and "Nemets": the two terms refer to foreigners, Fryaz being applied more to Latins and Europeans who came to Muscovy through the south, while the term Nemets describes northern Europeans, such as the majority of the foreigners

143

living in the "Nemetskaya Sloboda" in the second part of the seventeenth century. At the time Avvakum was writing, the term Fryaz was giving way to Nemets, following the shift in the composition of the foreign colony in Moscow.

6*The Sceptre of Government,* by Simeon Polotsky, directed against the Old Believers; published in 1667.

■ ■ ■

A DEFENSE OF THE NEW STYLE IN ICON PAINTING

I. Vladimirov

In spite of both Nikon's and Avvakum's denunciations, new influences were making themselves felt in art in the seventeenth century. Moscow called on icon painters from the flourishing cities of northern Russia to restore the frescoes in the Kreml' churches, thus enlisting the services of artists from the so-called Stroganov school and also of men who had been exposed to foreign influences along the trade route from the White Sea to Moscow. At the same time, foreign painters were working in Tsar Alexey's palaces. The best-known of the Russian icon painters of that time was Simon Ushakov (1626–86). A friend of his, Iosif Vladimirov, here defends the new style in an "Epistle to Ushakov," addressing an enemy of "worldly painting."

■ ■ ■ Do you really mean to say that only Russians have the gift of painting icons and that we should admire only Russian icon painting without respecting or adopting anything from other lands? . . . Ask your father and the elders; they will tell you that in all our Christian Russian churches all the sacred vessels, the chasubles and omophorions,[1] the embroidered clothes for icons and altar, all the cunningly wrought materials and gold lacework and precious stones and pearls, all this you receive from foreigners and bring into the church to adorn altar and icons, without calling any of it improper or evil. . . .

You demand of the painter in our times that he paint gloomy and unlovely figures? . . . Where can be found any precept to say that the saints' faces should be depicted swarthy and dark? Is the whole of humankind created on the same pattern? Were all the saints swarthy and gaunt? If here on earth their flesh was indeed mortified, up in Heaven they have been reborn and they shine in soul and body. What demon is it that bears a grudge against truth and casts spells on the luminous persons of the saints? Who among right-thinking beings will not laugh at such foolish-

144

ness, as if it were more fitting to prefer darkness and gloom to light? . . .
No, such is not the custom of a wise artist. What he sees or hears, he
traces in his images and faces, making them resemble the objects of sight
and hearing. He shows that many saints, men and women, were fair to
look at, both in the Old Testament and in our new times of Grace. . . .

How can you not fear, unworthy one, to gaze on the blessed
faces and to harbor evil thoughts in your heart? It is not fitting that a true
and pious Christian be tempted even when he gazes on wantons. That
temptation may arise from holy icons is a most brazen and vile thought.
The body, not the spirit, has inspired those men, in their foolishness, to
such thoughts: malice has blinded them.

—P. Milyukov, *Ocherki po istorii russkoy kultury* (Paris, 1931), II, 2

NOTES: [1]A vestment of the Greek and Russian Church, like the pallium in the
Latin Church.

■ ■ ■

ICON PAINTING IN THE TROITSA MONASTERY IN 1858
T. Gautier

■ ■ ■ Five or six monks of various ages were painting in a large, well-
lit room with bare walls. One of them, a handsome fellow with a black
beard and a swarthy complexion, who was putting the finishing touches to
a "Mother of God," impressed me by his solemn consecrated expression and
the pious care he gave to his work. . . . He was obviously more concerned
with religious feeling than with art: he painted as a priest celebrates mass.
. . . His Mother of God resembled a Byzantine empress as she stared at us
with the serious majesty of her great black eyes. The portions to be covered by the silver or gilt metal plate[1]—cut for the face and hands to show—
were as carefully executed as if they were destined to be seen.

Other pictures in a more or less advanced state, representing
Greek saints[2] and in particular St. Sergius, founder of the convent, were
being completed by the laborious hands of the monastic artists. These
paintings, intended for chapels or private houses, were on panels covered
with gypsum. They were rather smoky-colored, in no way different from

145

fifteenth- or twelfth-century paintings. The poses were just as stiff and constrained, the gestures as hieratic, the folds of clothing as regular, the flesh tints as tawny-brown; the doctrine of Athos was faithfully followed. The medium employed was egg-water[3] or tempera, which was later varnished. The halos and ornaments intended to be gilded were raised slightly in order to catch the light better. The old masters of Salonica, if they had come back to life, would have been satisfied with their Troitsa pupils.

But no tradition can now be faithfully adhered to. Less scrupulously strict adepts will sometimes slip in among the stubborn followers of the old formula. The new spirit forces its way through some chink into the old mold. Even those who wish to follow in the footsteps of the Athos painters and preserve the immutable Byzantine style in our own days cannot help having seen modern pictures which combine freedom of invention with the study of nature. It is difficult to keep one's eyes perpetually closed; even at Troitsa the new spirit had penetrated. Some monks complied with the rule; a few younger ones had abandoned egg-water for oil, and even though they kept their figures in the prescribed attitudes and in accordance with the ancient model, they relaxed so far as to give head and hands truer tints and less conventional coloring; they modeled the planes and attempted relief. Their female saints were more humanly pretty, the male less theocratically grim. . . .

This new manner, with its greater suavity and cheerfulness, has no lack of supporters, and examples of it can be seen in several modern Russian churches. But for myself, I prefer the old way by far. It is idealistic, religious, and decorative, with the prestige of form and color removed from vulgar reality. This symbolical way of presenting an idea by means of set figures, like a sacred writing whose characters may not be changed, strikes me as wonderfully suited to the decoration of a sanctuary. In spite of its rigidity, it allows a great artist to reveal himself through firmness of drawing, grandeur of style, and nobility of contours.

—*Voyage en Russie* (Paris, 1895)

NOTES: [1]The custom of covering the icon (leaving faces and hands visible) with precious silver or gilt plate began in the seventeenth century.

[2]Gautier means saints of the Orthodox faith; St. Sergius was Russian.

[3]The binding used to dissolve the pigment powder was composed of egg-yolk to which water and vinegar or kvas was added.

THE PAINTER FEDOTOV

V. V. Stasov

> V. V. Stasov (1824–1906) was an art historian, a critic, and an archaeologist. He was the self-appointed propagandist of the Peredvizhiniki (Wanderers) painters in the eighteen-seventies and eighties, and an ardent supporter of the musicians of the "Mighty Five" group. His fiery but humorless articles were widely read.

■ ■ ■ The first gleam of our new orientation in art came with Fedotov.[1] But this was a man who had nothing in common with the Europe of his time, knew nothing about it, and had not the slightest suspicion of what was being done, thought, or accomplished there. He had no knowledge of its books or pictures. What he knew in art was limited to what he could see at the Hermitage, the Academy, or in the studio of the "great" Brullov.[2] And in all these places, there was not a single trait of the new Europe; it was all old and arch-old: either the long-past classicism of the great and little masters of former centuries or the swollen and awkward romanticism of recent times. Moreover, the new departures in the West were little known in Europe itself; how then could anything about them have reached the ears of a poor retired officer of the Guards who, until the age of thirty, had spent his life between the Cadet School and the barracks, who had been nowhere and heard nothing? I knew Fedotov myself in the forties; I remember him distinctly. I was acquainted with him during his best and most vigorous years, when he was working on "The Major's Proposal." This picture was practically painted under my eyes. More than once, from Fedotov's own lips, I heard the doggerel rhymes he loved to recite, explaining the subject of his picture. I was present while he looked for types and details.[3] I recall his stories, his humor, his cheerfulness, his wit, and keenness of observation, all that made him so attractive to those who knew him then. He had graduated first of his class from the Cadet School; both there and later, he was fond of reading; however, he had received no real education and he grasped everything by sheer native talent and quickness. . . .

Another curious fact is that Fedotov did not understand Gogol[4] and had very little sympathy for him. What, it seems, would be more natural than for Fedotov, with his talented nature, to love Gogol passionately, to feel his genius instinctively, even more than did the Russia of his time, crazy as it was then about Gogol? Besides, apparently they had much in common in their temperaments and tendencies. Ignorance of the facts would easily lead one to imagine that Fedotov was directly inspired by Gogol and, gripped by his powerful spirit, strove to represent in colors what Gogol depicted in words of fire. And yet Fedotov neither liked nor understood Gogol: his friend and biographer Druzhinin tells us so. Why

147

was this? Because he found an excess of caricature everywhere in Gogol. What a strange trait of Fedotov's nature, what evidence of its insufficiency and poverty, that he found "caricature" in Gogol, and turned from the works of this genius on that account, while at the same time filling a good half of his own works with that same caricature! But at least this fact shows us that Fedotov was as little influenced by Gogol as he was by the new French realists. As an artist, he stood by himself.

What did he like in art, what did he strive for, what did he wish? His favorites were the old Dutch painters, whose numberless little pictures at the Hermitage he studied for days at a time. He also had a passion for Hogarth, whom he knew from prints endlessly studied. . . . Born with a strong gift of observation, Fedotov first applied this talent to painting caricatural portraits of the individuals he saw at school and in the regiment, that is, in army life; later he started to paint pictures of regiment scenes in which the characters were still exclusively soldiers, officers and generals in barracks, at camp, or in the palace; but all this was mostly depicted in an indiscriminating and flattering spirit. Finally, dissatisfied with the narrowness of such limits, he resigned from military service and became a painter of the "little" scenes that occur among the people and the class of society with whom he was in constant contact. The mood of Hogarth and the old Dutch painters expressed itself strongly here; and soon to this was added the unpretentious magazine-like illustration of everyday life that he found and liked in Gavarni,[5] the fashionable favorite of the Russian as well as of the Parisian public in the forties. Skill and brilliance, wit, a certain adroit grasp of the typical, lightness and gaiety, a superficiality that skimmed the surface without plumbing the depths, all this charmed Fedotov and corresponded to certain aspects of his nature, while other aspects remained deeply bound with the Dutch and Hogarth. And, as it happened, all those various elements fused into a most original whole. But Fedotov would have remained a minor, lightweight artist, a rather pleasant illustrator and a fair painter-moralist if he had not painted two pictures: "The Decoration" and "The Major's Proposal."

With these two works everything changes. The former light sketches, the careful but uninspired copies from nature—all that glittered and fluttered, butterfly-like—withdrew into the background, and a talented, significant art came to the fore. Fedotov suddenly touched deep notes, unsounded before him in Russian art. In one canvas, "The Decoration, or The Morning of a Newly-Rewarded Chinovnik," shown at the 1848 exhibition, he presents our terrifying official of the thirties; in the other, "The Major's Proposal," our terrifyingly brutal officer of the thirties and forties: the two huge sores of our old Russia, expressed in deep, stupendous, infinitely truthful traits. Look this chinovnik in the face: here we have a crafty, hardened nature, a corrupt bribe-taker, the soulless slave of his superior, one who can no longer think of anything except what can give him money and a medal for his buttonhole. He is ferocious and merciless, he will drown anyone and anything—and not one fold of the rhinoceros hide on his face will quiver. Malice, arrogance, soullessness, the worship of his decoration as the highest and unanswerable argument, a totally degraded life—all this is present on the face, in the pose, and in the figure of this hardened chinovnik, as he stands in his dressing gown, barefooted, curlers in his hair and his decoration on his chest. It was deeply appreciated by the Russian public, who crowded to the exhibition where the picture was first shown; but the censorship of the time also recognized its significance, and when a print was made from the picture the decoration was absent— the new "knight" simply indicated his chest. The painting was mutilated— but who cared about that? True, even earlier, in the catalogue of the Academy exhibition, the title of the picture had been sensibly given as "Result of a Celebration and a Scene." So everyone was led to understand that there was no more to it than a man in his cups having a tiff with his cook. There was apparently nothing else worth reflecting on. And thank Heaven that it was so: without this protective blind, Fedotov's picture would have been forbidden and might have disappeared entirely.

Fedotov's other painting, "The Major's Proposal, or Mending One's Fortunes," shown at the 1849 exhibition, is in the same serious mood. Here again we glimpse a grim tragedy behind the entertaining screen of appearances. At a first glance, we might be only amused by the Major twirling his moustache in front of the mirror in the hall, before entering the room where the merchant's family and the fiancée are awaiting him; we might be only amused by each member of the family—the practical-minded mother, and the over ripe, affected fiancée; we might find amusement, nothing more, in the storekeeper father, wearing the coat he has put on for the first time in his life, at his wife's orders; we might find the whole house, with its half-village, half-inn atmosphere, amusing and nothing more. But amusement disappears and laughter is forgotten when you think of what this scene signifies: here are two hostile camps at war with each other; here are enemies, seeking how best to cheat each other, soulless, coarsened, vile, and furiously selfish, ready to use any means, fair or foul. This is no laughing matter. Here for the first time Fedotov's gifted brush has shown with depth and power that "dark realm"[6] which, a few years later, was to be presented on the stage by Ostrovsky's mighty talent.

—*Twenty-five Years of Russian Art* (1882–83),
Izbrannoe (Moscow, 1950)

NOTES: [1]Pavel Andreevich Fedotov (1815–52), the "founder of critical realism in Russian painting," according to Soviet criticism, was the son of a poor *chinovnik*, or government employee. He served in the Guards in Petersburg, attended classes at the Academy of Arts, and was encouraged to paint by Brullov (see note 2). In 1844 he resigned, with the rank of captain. His exhibition of 1848 won him public favor.

149

[2]Brullov (1799–1852) artist, painter of the then widely admired "Last Days of Pompeii" (1833).

[3]Fedotov himself, in his autobiography, writes: "The studio sees only a tenth part of my labors; my chief work takes place in the streets and in other people's houses. I learn from life; incessant observation is my task."

[4]Nikolay Vasilevich Gogol (1809–52), author of the satirical play *The Inspector General* (1836) and the picaresque epic novel *Dead Souls* (1842). It was at a reading of a fragment of *Dead Souls,* some years before its publication, that Pushkin exclaimed: "God! how sad is our Russia!"

[5]Gavarni (1804–66) was a French illustrator, whose series on students, "grisettes," street women, carnival revellers, and so forth, were extremely popular.

[6]An expression of the critic Dobrolyubov on the world depicted in the plays of Ostrovsky, a world of savage family tyranny and sordid greed.

■ ■ ■

THE ESTHETIC RELATIONS OF ART TO REALITY
N. G. Chernyshevsky

As were many of the intelligentsia of his time, Chernyshevsky (1828–89) was the son of a priest. The public discussion of his doctoral dissertation, *The Esthetic Relations of Art to Reality*, at the University of St. Petersburg in 1855 was a significant event for progressives. From 1853 to 1862 Chernyshevsky was one of the directors of the journal *The Contemporary*. He was arrested in 1862, and while in prison he wrote and published the novel *What's To Be Done?* This was passed by the censor as being so dull that it would disgust everybody, but it rapidly became the gospel of radical youth. Both Marx and Lenin greatly admired Chernyshevsky. The following passage is the conclusion of his dissertation.

■ ■ ■ Here are the main conclusions to which this investigation has brought us:

(1) The definition of beauty, "Beauty is the full manifestation of a general idea in an individual aspect," does not stand up to criticism; it is too broad, being the definition of the formal striving of all human activity.

(2) The real definition of beauty is such: "Beauty is life"; a beautiful being for a man is that being in whom he sees life as he understands it, just as a beautiful object is that object which reminds him of life.

(3) This objective beauty, or beauty in its nature, must be distinguished from perfection of form, which consists in unity of idea and form or in the fact that an object completely fulfills its destination.

150

(4) The sublime does not affect man by awaking the idea of the absolute; it very rarely awakes such an idea.

(5) Man sees the sublime in what is far greater than the objects or far stronger than the facts with which man compares it.

(6) The tragic has no essential link with the concept of fate or necessity. In real life the tragic is for the most part accidental; it does not originate from the nature of preceding moments. The form of necessity in which art clothes it is the result of the traditional principle of art: "the denouement must proceed from the plot," or of the misplaced subservience of the poet to certain conceptions of fate.

(7) The tragic, according to the conceptions of the new European culture, is "the terrible in the life of man."

(8) The sublime (and its moment, the tragic) is not a variation of beauty; the ideas of the sublime and of the beautiful are totally separate; there is neither inner link nor inner opposition between them.

(9) Reality is not only more vivid, it is more perfect than fancy. The images of fancy are only a pale and nearly always unsuccessful transformation of reality.[1]

(10) Beauty in objective reality is completely beautiful.

(11) Beauty in objective reality satisfies man completely.

(12) Art is certainly not born of man's need to compensate for the insufficiencies of beauty in reality.

(13) The creations of art are inferior to beauty in reality, not only because the impression produced by reality is more vivid than the impressions produced by creations of art but also because the creations of art are inferior to beauty in reality (just as they are inferior to the sublime, the tragic, the comic) from the esthetic point of view.

(14) The field of art is not limited to the field of the beautiful in the esthetic sense of the word, of the beautiful by its living essence and not only by the perfection of its form: art reproduces all that is interesting for man in life.

(15) The perfection of form (unity of form and idea) does not constitute the characteristic trait of art in the esthetic sense of the word (fine arts); beauty as unity of idea and image, or as the full realization of an idea, is the purpose toward which art, or "ability" in the broadest sense of the word, strives—the purpose of all the practical activity of man.

(16) The need that gives birth to art in the esthetic sense of the word (fine arts) is the very same that often expresses itself in portrait painting. A portrait is painted not because the features of the living person do not satisfy us, but in order to assist our memory of the living person when he is not before our eyes, and to give some idea of him to those who have had no occasion to see him. By its reproductions art only reminds us of what interests us in life, and strives to acquaint us to a certain degree with those interesting aspects of life which we would have no occasion to experience or observe in reality.

151

(17) The reproduction of life is the general characteristic sign of art that constitutes its essence; often works of art have another significance—the explanation of life; frequently they also have the significance of a judgment on the manifestations of life.[2]

—*Izbrannye sochineniya* (Moscow, 1934)

NOTES: [1]In the body of his thesis Chernyshevsky amplifies this by saying that "as regards beauty of contours there is not a single statue in Petersburg that is not far inferior to an innumerable quantity of living people," and that "in comparison with the living lines of body and face, the colors of painting are a coarse and pitiful imitation."
   [2]Though Chernyshevsky rightly points out against the tenets of "art for art's sake" that "man's works must have their goal in men's needs and not in themselves," his concept of art as primarily utilitarian and secondarily ethical and educative indicates that his views of man's needs were limited.

■ ■ ■

THE VALUE OF ART

D. I. Pisarev

The name of Pisarev (1840–68) is linked with the theory of the common good and with antiesthetic intolerance. His adoption of the word "nihilism" in his famous article on Turgenev's *Fathers and Sons* made him the model of the "intellectual terrorists" of the eighteen-sixties. Pisarev himself called his attitude toward life "thinking realism." A great admirer of Darwin, Pisarev preached self-development and a pitiless struggle with all the accepted values of society: "What can be broken must be broken . . . just strike left and right; no harm will or can come of it." Esthetic values were among those he attacked most furiously.

■ ■ ■ From the very beginning of this article,[1] I have discussed poetry only. Concerning all other arts—plastic, tonic, mimic—I will express myself briefly and clearly. I feel the deepest indifference toward them. I definitely do not believe that these arts contribute in any way whatsoever to the intellectual or moral advancement of humanity. Human tastes vary infinitely: one likes to drink a glass of vodka before dinner; another to smoke a pipe after dinner; a third to amuse himself in the evening with a fiddle or a flute; a fourth to be enraptured or awed by the screeching of Aldridge[2] in the role of Othello. All right, this is all very well. Let them have a good time. I can understand all that. I also understand that two amateurs of vodka or of the 'cello enjoy talking about the perfections of their cherished object and of the means to be used in order to make the cherished object still more perfect. Such specialized conversations may give birth to specialized associations. For instance, "The Association of Vodka Amateurs," "The Association of Theatergoers," "The Association of Flaky-

152

Dough Pirozhki Fanciers," "The Association of Music-Lovers," and so on, ad infinitum. Such associations may have their regulations, their elections, their debates, convictions, reviews. Such associations may deliver patents for genius. As a consequence, there may appear among us great men of the most varying kinds: the great Beethoven, the great Raphael, the great Canova, the great chess-player Murphy, the great chef Dussot, the great billiard-player Turia. We can only rejoice at this abundance of human genius and prudently pass by all these "associations of amateurs," carefully hiding the smile that appears on our lips in spite of ourselves and that might vex many simpletons. Besides, we will not go so far as to deny completely the practical utility of painting. The drawing of plans is essential to architecture. Sketches are necessary in nearly all works on natural history. At the present minute, I have before me the wonderful, illustrated *Lives of Animals* by Brehm,[3] and this book shows me graphically to what degree a talented and educated artist's pencil can help the naturalist in the spreading of useful knowledge. But then neither Rembrandt nor Titian would have drawn pictures for a popular work on zoology or botany. As for Mozart and Fanny Elssler, Talma, or Rubini, how they could have contrived to apply their great gifts to any sensible job, I cannot in the least imagine. I wish the estheticians of *The Epoch*[4] and of *The Readers' Library*[5] would help me in this difficult circumstance.

The frivolous tone of this chapter should not anger the lovers of all sorts of art. Liberty and tolerance first! They find pleasure in blowing in a flute or in strutting about the stage as Hamlet, or in flecking a canvas with oils; well, I find mine in demonstrating in a sarcastic tone that they are no earthly use to anybody and that there is no reason to set them up on a pedestal. But nobody intends to disturb them in their pastimes. Nobody is dragging them by the scruff of their necks to do some useful job. You are enjoying yourselves—all right, have a good time, dear children!

—*Sochineniya* (St. Petersburg, 1900–1901)

NOTES: [1]"The Realists," published in 1864 in *The Russian Word* (1859–66), a radical journal to which Pisarev contributed his chief articles.

[2]Ira Aldridge: a Negro actor, born in Baltimore in 1807. After acting in the United States and Europe, he went to Russia in 1858. He died in Lodz in 1867. His greatest success was in the role of Othello.

[3]A German naturalist, whose *Lives of Animals* was very popular.

[4]A journal founded by Dostoevsky in 1863.

[5]*The Readers' Library* (1834–65) was a conservative publication, especially popular among provincial readers. In the eighteen-sixties, it held "art for art's sake" views.

THE LADY MOROZOVA, NOVEMBER 18, 1671   Painting by V. I. Surikov, 1887
From an album of reproductions of paintings in the Tretyakov gallery, Moscow

THE MAJOR'S PROPOSAL   Painting by P. A. Fedotov, 1848
From an album of reproductions of paintings in the Tretyakov gallery, Moscow

THE DESTRUCTION OF ESTHETICS

D. I. Pisarev

Critical opinion was generally hostile to Chernyshevsky's *Esthetic Relations of Art to Reality* on its first publication. However, when a second edition appeared in 1865, the intellectual climate had changed, and the interest it excited was for the most part favorable. In his article "The Destruction of Esthetics," written on this occasion, Pisarev takes the opportunity, while commenting on Chernyshevsky's thesis, to express his own, more radical, views on art. This article was published in the *Russian Word* in 1865.

■ ■ ■ The author [Chernyshevsky] finds in poetry the inevitable short-coming: that its images always appear pale and indefinite when we start comparing them with life. "The image in a work of poetry," he says, "bears the same relation to the real, living image as the word to the real object that it designates—it is no more than a pale, general, indefinite intimation of reality."

If any one should doubt that this idea is correct, let me propose the following proof. We know that the highest form of poetry is the drama; we know that the best dramas in the world were written by Shakespeare; there is nothing higher in poetry than Shakespeare's dramas; consequently, if the images in Shakespeare's dramas turn out to be pale and indefinite intimations of reality, it will not be worthwhile to discuss any other poetical works. But everybody knows that all dramas, and Shakespeare's among them, attain a certain definiteness, bringing them closer to reality, only when they are acted on the stage; everybody knows too that only remarkable actors can play Shakespearian roles in a satisfactory manner; that is to say, a whole new branch of art is essential in order to give the poetical images a certain definiteness; intelligence, talent, and education are essential in order to understand and interpret the "pale and indefinite intimations of reality." This understanding and interpretation is the problem before the talented actor; and he acquires a universal reputation by his solution of this problem. Consequently, it is indeed a very difficult problem, and the intimations are indeed "pale and indefinite." But this is not all. Everybody knows that the same role is played by various actors in quite various ways, and yet in an equally satisfactory manner. One understands a character thus, another differently, a third again in his own way; and if all are equally talented, the most attentive and exacting spectator is perfectly satisfied; that is to say, all the actors have a correct understanding of the role, and so the poetical image is comparable to the indeterminate

155

equation which, as we know, allows a number of solutions. After this, it seems to me, it is difficult to doubt that poetry, by its very essence, can give only pale and indefinite intimations of reality.

—*Sochineniya* (St. Petersburg, 1900–1901)

■ ■ ■

ON "THE LADY MOROZOVA"

V. V. Stasov

■ ■ ■ Surikov[1] has now created a picture which, in my opinion, is the best of all our paintings on subjects from Russian history. . . . From my first glance at this canvas I was impressed to my very soul. . . . Russian history, the seventeenth century in Russia, comes to life and breathes in this picture. As you gaze at it, you are carried back to the old Moscow, the Moscow that was still half a village and yet glittered with fair churches; you seem to be part of those people, to share the burning interests of their days. The crowd moving before our eyes is filled with the concerns and emotions of those times. The whole population of Moscow has poured out of their houses onto the snowdrifts heaped up high on the streets. Young and old, rich and poor, the glorious aristocrats and the ignorant populace, all have rushed out of their homes to throng the street, the church steps, the fences. An awesome, a stirring scene is being enacted in Moscow. A great lady, the famous boyarynya Morozova,[2] known to all the city, is being taken to the torture, to frightful torments, to an underground prison where she is fated to disappear and die. But first, all Moscow must see her, must sneer and scoff at her, make her feel the weight of popular hatred and retribution. She must be humiliated and spat upon by all the city. This is why she is being driven round on that sleigh. A squad of *streltsy*[3] marches ahead, others walk on the sides, in their red caftans, with axes on their shoulders. But the wishes and hopes of her all-powerful enemies are not fulfilled. Moscow and the people do not all consent to make a mock of Morozova. Only the most obtuse, brutish, coarse, and half-animal of the mob, incapable yet of any understanding, and also the aristocracy of the time—boyars in gold and braid—and ignorant priests laugh and rejoice as the unfortunate woman is driven by in the fateful sleigh. The mass of the people, all "the humiliated and insulted,"[4] all the "little ones," gaze on their lady with deeply shocked and sorrowful feelings. They know one thing only: how good and wonderful she was, how kind to everyone, how she felt for their needs, and how she stood up for the old

156

life, the old traditions that are so dear and precious to all. Here in the dense crowd meet and mingle Morozova's sister, Princess Ukhtomskaya, in the costly garments of the seventeenth century, all in velvet, precious furs, pearls, and silk, and rich burgher women in embroidered bonnets and kerchiefs, in brocade sarafans[5]—but the greater number are nuns, monks, novices, *yurodivy*,[6] beggars, peasants, and peasant women who secretly or openly cherish the old life and faith. Even the little boys watching the show from the fences they have clambered on are not all indifferent idlers, they are not all harsh mockers staring at the sleigh and shouting with stupid laughter. Among them are young lads whose hearts are wrung with pity, whose wide-open eyes gaze sorrowfully at the poor victim. What a rich variety of characters, feelings, moods—what a diversity of mental development! This is the real people, the real human multitude with its hundred spiritual distinctions and capacities. All the best and highest Russian artists—Repin,[7] Vereshchagin,[8] Perov,[9] Schwartz,[10] Vladimir Makovsky,[11] Pryanishnikov,[12] and others—have turned their gifts and hearts to this people, have striven to grasp and reveal its life, its scenes, its events. Surikov has proved their worthy companion. Moreover, among the general chorus, he can show up the soloists. . . .

The lady Morozova is the real center of the picture, she draws all eyes. Exhausted by suffering, the poor woman has lost all her former beauty, and the only thing that is left is her indestructible energy, the character and strength of soul that nothing can break. This is the woman whom Avvakum, the leader of the fanatics of the time, called " a lion among sheep." Her hands are chained, her whole body seems to be broken by tortures and torments, but her spirit is strong and victorious. Her eyes, like glowing coals, burn from under her nun-like coif and black veil, her whole body seems to rise from the straw of the sleigh, her hand is raised high in the two-finger sign of the cross (symbol of all her beliefs and hopes), she is wrapped in an ecstasy, she is preaching, she is striving to kindle all hearts.

We can no longer be moved by the interests that thrilled this poor fanatic two hundred years ago; other problems, broader and deeper, confront us. But still we cannot help respecting the fortitude of this woman, her indestructible mind and heart. We shrug our shoulders at her strange delusions, the vain purposeless martyrdom. But we cannot join the jeering boyars and priests, we cannot share their fierce brutish joy. We gaze with pity on those boys, on the peasant who, sitting in the front of the sleigh, drives the horse and shakes the reins with his thick-mittened hands to hurry it, while he shows all his teeth in a gaping grin and laughs with the crowd. These are the people who "know not what they do." We can only feel pity, sorrow, and pain as we think of them. But our eyes seek out something else: the drooping heads, the lowered eyes with their quiet suffering gleam, all the meek souls who were then the best and most lovable,

157

but subjugated and downtrodden, and so prevented from saying their own word—how faithfully this depicts poor Russia, the old grieving oppressed Russia!

I have tried to outline the chief points of Surikov's picture and to give the reader at least a faint notion of its possible significance and merits. But I am far from judging it perfect. It seems to me to have some shortcomings, too. Thus, I think its chief defect lies in the absence of virile, strong characters in all that crowd. True, Avvakum said that there were only "sheep" around Morozova. We cannot believe this now. . . .

Beside this chief defect, I might point to a few others: an excessive sharpness and some lack of harmony in the colors, a motley effect, a rather careless drawing, an absence of air in some parts of the picture. But I do not wish to dwell on such details, for I am too deeply impressed with the great, the extraordinary qualities of this painting, which thrill our imagination and grip our feelings.

—"The Wanderers' Exhibition, 1887",[13] *Izbrannoe* (Moscow, 1950)

NOTES: [1] V. I. Surikov (1848–1916) was born in Siberia of an old Cossack family. He painted chiefly historical pictures. The most famous are: "The Morning of the Streltsy's Execution" (1881), "The Lady Morozova" (1884), "The Conquest of Siberia by Ermak" (1895), "Stepan Razin" (1899).

[2]Morozova (1631?–75) was one of the richest noblewomen of the time. A zealous Christian, she became Avvakum's penitent and ardent supporter. She was arrested in 1671 and died, after many hardships and tortures, in 1675.

[3]The streltsy were a military body founded about 1550 by Ivan IV.

[4]Allusion to the title of Dostoevsky's novel, published in 1861.

[5]A long, belted, sleeveless gown, traditional in old Russia.

[6]See the "Life of Archpriest Avvakum," p. 96.

[7]I. Repin (1844–1930). His famous pictures are: "The Volga Boatmen" (1873), "The Zaporozhe Cossacks" (1878–91), "Ivan the Terrible and His Son" (1885), "Mussorgsky" (1881).

[8]Vereshchagin (1842–1904) painted chiefly pictures on war themes, with a strong emphasis on the horrors of war.

[9]Perov (1833–82), a realistic and satirical painter.

[10]Schwartz (1838–69), an historical painter.

[11]Makovsky (1846–1920), a painter of genre and social protest pictures.

[12]Pryanishnikov (1840–94), genre painter. All the painters named here were members of the Wanderers' group (see note 13) or sympathized with the Wanderers' aspirations.

[13]In 1863, thirteen students of the Academy of Fine Arts in Petersburg left the Academy as a protest against the subject imposed for the final prize competition, "The Gods Feasting in Valhalla." They organized a community out of which, in 1870, grew the Society of Wandering Artists, which dominated Russian painting for the next twenty years. The art of the Wanderers, like that of many writers and musicians of the time, aimed at recovering lost unity with the people. It did so by its wandering exhibitions, the choice of its subjects (modern life, genre, history, social and political protest), and its resolutely realistic technique. Socialist realism finds its precursor in the Wanderers.

158

MUSSORGSKY ON MUSIC

M. P. Mussorgsky

> Like the writers and painters of his time, Mussorgsky, (1839–81), one of the most talented representatives of the national tradition in Russian music, was deeply concerned with realism, with the "living thoughts" of people, with the most intimate "traits of human nature and human masses."

■ ■ ■ At present I am resting, and so I have been raking hay, making preserves, and putting up pickles—comment cela vous plaît?[1] The haying was quite successful, the preserves and pickles are very good. I am now thinking over the second act of *Marriage*.[2] I probably won't write any little pieces, I'm not in the mood, and yet, who knows, perhaps I shall! I am observing colorful peasant women and typical peasants—both may come in handy. What a wealth of fresh aspects, untouched by art, in the Russian nature, what a wealth of them, so vivid, so wonderful! I have pictured a fragment of what life has given me in musical images for the people I cherish; I have spoken to them of my impressions. If God grants me strength and life, I shall speak more grandly; after *Marriage*, the Rubicon will be crossed, but *Marriage* is a cage in which I am imprisoned until I am tamed, and then—to freedom! All this is what I desire, but it does not yet exist, though it must. It's frightening! because something that may come to life may also not be, since it's not achieved yet. Here is what I wish: my characters must speak on the stage as living people speak, but besides, the character and vigor of their living intonations, supported by the orchestra which makes up the musical canvas of their words, should attain their purpose directly; that is, my music must be the artistic reproduction of human speech in all its finest inflections: *the sounds of human speech*, as external manifestations of thought and feeling, should become, without exaggeration or violence, genuine, accurate music, that is, artistic, highly artistic. This is the ideal I strive for ("Savishna," "The Orphan," "Ieremushka," "The Child").[3]

Well then, I am now working on Gogol's *Marriage*. As you know, the effect of Gogol's words depends on the actor, on his true intonation. Well, I want to fix Gogol into place, and to fix the actor into place; that is, to say in music what cannot be said in any other way, and to say it as Gogol's characters wish to speak. This is why I am crossing the Rubicon with *Marriage*. This is living prose in music, not the scorn of poet-composers for common human words when they are not dressed up in heroic robes—this is respect for the human language, the reproduction of simple human speech.

159

—"Letter to L. I. Shestakova,[4] July 30, 1868,"
Pisma i dokumenty (Moscow, 1932)

NOTES: [1]In French in the text.
[2]Mussorgsky's recitative opera based on Gogol's work was never finished. The Soviet composer Ippolitov-Ivanov completed it, and it was performed in 1931.
[3]From Mussorgsky's cycle of songs on peasant life, composed in the sixties.
[4]Lydia Shestakova was the sister of Glinka and a friend and protector of the young composers of the time.

■ ■ ■

THE NEW RUSSIAN MUSICAL SCHOOL

V. V. Stasov

■ ■ ■ Glinka[1] thought he was creating nothing more than the Russian opera, but he was mistaken. He was creating the whole of Russian music, the whole Russian musical school, a whole new system. In the fifty years that have elapsed, our music and our school have grown and developed in their wonderful, original beauty, talent, and strength.

For a long time they were not recognized; they were looked down upon and scorned. As late as 1860, Dargomyzhsky[2] wrote: "How many registered experts we have who question the possibility of the existence of a Russian school, not only in singing, but even in composition! However, the school has emerged. It is too late to suppress it. Its existence is already inscribed on the 'Tables of Art.'" Yes, the Russian school has existed ever since Glinka, with specific features that distinguish it from other schools.

What forces have engendered the particularity of our school; what elements have given it its exceptional orientation and its original traits?

The first is lack of prejudice and of blind faith. Beginning with Glinka, the Russian musical school is characterized by its complete independence of thought and opinion regarding any earlier music. It bows to no universally recognized authorities. It insists on seeing for itself, on making sure by itself, and then only does it consent to accept the greatness of a composer or the significance of a work. Such independence of thought is rare even among contemporary European musicians; fifty years ago it was still more unusual. Only a few, such as Schumann, ventured to express a personal criticism of universally accepted and worshipped celebrities, while the majority of Western musicians believed blindly in all authorities and shared all the tastes and prejudices of the crowd. On the contrary, the new Russian musicians are terribly "irreverent." They refuse to believe in any tradition until they themselves decide what to hold high in their esteem. . . .

Then, beginning with Glinka, all the best Russian musicians have had very little faith in school learning and have failed to consider it

160

with the servility and superstitious respect which are still accorded to it in many parts of Europe. It would be ridiculous to discount science or learning in any field, whether music or other; but the new Russian musicians, not having in their background, under the guise of a historical foundation inherited from former centuries, the long chain of scholastic training of Europeans, look science in the eye fearlessly. . . . They respect it, use its advantages, but without exaggeration or worship. They deny the necessity of its dryness or pedantic excesses, deny its acrobatics, which are so highly prized by thousands of Europeans, and do not believe that one should drag out long docile years in the study of its sacred mysteries. . . .

Neither did Dargomyzhsky's successors and comrades in later times waste long years in vain, as the Germans do. They learnt the grammar of music simply and quickly, as any other grammar; but that did not prevent them from learning it thoroughly. This attitude toward the false "wisdom" so honored by the music schools saved the Russians from pedantic and routine compositions—we have none of that kind in our modern school. This is one of the traits that distinguish it from European schools.

Another trait characterizes our new school: the urge to be national. This began as early as Glinka and has continued ever since. Such an urge exists in no other European school. Historical and cultural conditions among other peoples were such that the folk song—expression of the spontaneous artless musicality of the people—has practically disappeared long since in most civilized nations. Who in the nineteenth century knows or hears French, German, Italian, or English folk songs? Of course they have existed and at some period they were in common use, but they have been leveled by the scythe of European culture, so hostile to the fundamental original modes of life; and now it takes the efforts of musical archaeologists and curious travelers to discover fragments of old folk songs in remote provinces. Our case is entirely different. The folk song still sounds everywhere. Every peasant, carpenter, stonecutter, doorman, cabman, country woman, laundress, cook, nurse, and nursemaid brings it from his home to Petersburg, to Moscow, to any city, and you can hear it there the year around. Just as a thousand years ago, each worker, man or woman, in Russia, sings numberless songs as he works. The Russian soldier goes to battle with a folk song on his lips. The songs are familiar to us all and no archaeological research is needed to know and love them. This is why every Russian born with a creative musical soul grows up from the first days of his life in a deeply national musical environment. Moreover, nearly all the most important Russian musicians were born not in the capitals, but inside Russia, in provincial cities or on their fathers' estates; and they spent their childhood there (Glinka, Dargomyzhsky, Mussorgsky, Balakirev, Rimsky-Korsakov). Others spent several years of their youth in the provinces or outside the cities, in frequent and intimate contact with folk songs and folk singing. Their basic musical impressions were national. If there has been no artistic development of folk music with us be-

161

fore, the fault must be sought in the unfavorable conditions of Russian life in the eighteenth and nineteenth centuries, when all that was of the people was trampled underfoot. Yet the national element in music was so close to all, it was such a general basic need, that even under Catherine, in the age of court perukes and powder, now one, now the other of our composers attempted to introduce national melodies into his mediocre operas, copies of the mediocre operas of the West. Such was later the case with Verstovsky.[3] National elements appeared there in the most unfortunate aspect, still there they were, showing a desire that existed in no other nation. But as soon as there was the very slightest change, as soon as there began to be talk of the national in life and literature, as soon as it began to arouse sympathy again, there immediately appeared gifted people with the wish to create music in those national Russian forms that were nearest and dearest to them. No doubt European composers (at least the best of them) would have followed the same road as ours did, beginning with Glinka; but such a road was no longer open to them. This is proved very obviously by the avidity with which they have always grasped at anything national in music, even if it was foreign, even if it was trifling. Remember how Beethoven used Russian folk songs for his themes, Schubert Slovakian ones, Liszt Hungarian? And yet they could create neither Russian nor Slovakian nor Hungarian music. Music is not a matter of themes only. To be national, to express the national spirit and soul, music must address itself to the very root of the life of the people. . . .

It was different for the Russian composers. They are not outsiders, they are at home in the world that brought to light our Russian and Slavic melodies; thus they can use them freely, they can let them come forth in all the truth and strength of their coloring, temper, and character. What Glinka did is now universally known and recognized. He opened a new road, created a national opera in forms to be found nowhere else in Europe. Glinka's successors followed in his steps, supported by the example and initiative of his genius.

Connected to the national Russian element is another, the Eastern element, which gives the new Russian school a distinctive character. Nowhere in Europe does it play such an outstanding role. Some of our musicians have seen the East themselves (Glinka and Balakirev have been in the Caucasus); others, though they have not traveled there, were surrounded all their lives by impressions of the East and could express them vividly. This is nothing strange, since the East has always been part of all forms of Russian life and has given them a distinctive coloring. Glinka felt this when he said in his *Notes:* "Undoubtedly our Russian song is a child of the North, but it has been through the hands of the natives of the East." Just as the Eastern element imbues many of Glinka's best works, so it can be found in those of his followers. It is ridiculous and shortsighted to see in this (as our musical critics often have) only a strange whim of Russian composers.

162

Lastly, one strong, typical characteristic of the Russian musical school is its extreme tendency toward "program music."

After living in Paris several months, Glinka suddenly wrote his friend Kukolnik in April 1845: "Studying Berlioz' music and observing local audiences has brought me to important conclusions. I have decided to enrich my repertoire with a few concert pieces for orchestra under the title *Fantaisies Pittoresques*. It seems to me that one can unite the demands of art and those of the times, and with the help of improved instruments and performances write pieces equally significant to connoisseurs and to the ordinary public. I shall start on the *Fantaisies* in Spain; the originality of the local melodies will be a great help." This was the origin of *Jota* and *Night in Madrid*—later of *Kamarinskaya*.

These were not only talented works; they had another significance: they were the prototypes of program music in Russia. In this Glinka followed the trend of the century, which found expression first in Beethoven, then in Weber, Berlioz, Mendelssohn, and later still in all the important new composers—Liszt, Wagner, and others.

What Glinka had begun, his heirs and successors continued. With very few exceptions, Russian symphonic music is program music.

Such are the chief distinguishing characteristics of the Russian musical school. In noting them, I have no thought of setting it up over other European schools—this would be a ridiculous and absurd task. Each nation has its great people and its great achievements. But I deemed it indispensable to outline the particular traits and tendencies of our school, which are naturally most interesting and important.

—*The Messenger of Europe* (1882–83), *Izbrannoe* (Moscow, 1950)

NOTES: [1]M. I. Glinka (1804–57). His most famous work is the opera *Ivan Susanin* (1836). Another opera is *Ruslan and Ludmila*, based on a poem by Pushkin.

[2]A. S. Dargomyzhsky (1813–69) was a composer of operas, the most famous being *Rusalka*, on a poem by Pushkin, and *The Stone Guest*.

[3]Verstovsky (1779–1862) composed songs, vaudevilles, and operas. The best known of the latter is *Askold's Tomb* (1835).

■ ■ ■

7

NATIONAL
CONSCIOUSNESS
AND
IDEOLOGIES

The first part of the nineteenth century in Russia is full of passionate efforts to define the national essence. Separated for centuries from the development of European life, the Russians had, as early as the Muscovite period, striven to establish consciousness of their own historical destiny. Fifteenth-century works such as the *Tale of the White Mitre*, in which the Constantinople Patriarch, foreseeing the fall of his city, sends his mitre to Novgorod; or the *Relation of the Vladimir Princes*, which traces the origins of the Russians from Prus, brother of Caesar Augustus; or the legend that the apostle Andrew, "the first called," had Christianized the Russians—all tended to establish a claim to a privileged position in the European Christian family. These tales culminated in the famous Church-inspired theory of the Third Rome—Moscow—after which no fourth would come. However, such figments, even though some gained a certain popularity in the sixteenth century when Moscow tsars established themselves as autocratic sovereigns of a centralized land, remained instruments of political thought and did not spread far beyond the ecclesiastical circles which had brought them forth.

Moreover, no real effort at self-understanding is perceivable in these theories. They were prompted by self-assertion rather than self-knowledge and were founded largely on fear, scorn, and ignorance of the other European states. No real confrontation of ideological principles took place, and no definition emerged.

After Peter had sent a Russian elite to the school of European society and learning, there came a time when his efforts fructified—a small minority felt it had achieved Europeanism. The Russian European no longer felt the need to identify or assert himself, since the body of European culture was behind him to give him ready-made definitions. Apart from a condescending interest in the native pastoral entertainments of dancing and singing that survived from the past, he would have agreed unhesitatingly with the entry found in some editions of Voltaire's *Philosophical Dictionary*: "RUSSIA: see Peter the Great."

This unquestioning acceptance of a changed identity could not last. With the Napoleonic wars, the December 1825 uprising, and the infatuation with German romantic philosophy, the younger generation of educated Russians had to recognize that Russia was indeed different from its now uncrowned teacher. At the same time they became aware of their dissociation from their own people, who with the 1812 campaigns had briefly moved into the foreground of the historical scene. Recognition of this double dissociation and the effort to reach unity focused Russian thought during the nineteenth century on moral as well as historical problems.

167

The study of the past, in the modern sense, began in the eighteenth century, when Tatishchev first used the chronicle sources with a measure of critical judgment. But the monumental *History of the Russian State* by Karamzin, the first eight volumes of which were published in 1816, was the work that really revealed old Russia to the nineteenth century, making its author, in the words of Pushkin, "the Columbus of the Russian past." Karamzin's *History* started a rash of historical novels, but its chief value lay in the fact that it provided early discussions on the nature of the Russian "principle" with their fundamental elements.

Though a passionate interest in history existed in most European countries during the nineteenth century, in Russia it was marked by a special existential urgency: in the minds of Russian thinkers, Russia was literally deciding its future destiny by rediscovering and mapping the road it had already traveled. As the century progressed, the chief landmark on that road, the reign of Peter the Great, took on a symbolical significance: attitudes toward Peter exemplified the various positions in the philosophy of Russian history. As he was seen as the creator or violator of Russia, so was the Church viewed as the villain or hero of Russian life; the situation of the peasant, as the mortal sin or the special blessing of the Russian state; the ways of Europe, as the roads to life or to death.

In the middle of the century and later, the argument assumed greater complexity. Though the echoes of the old quarrels lingered, new generations were more directly concerned with the present and future. New labels were popular: the superfluous man, the repentant nobleman, the nihilist or thinking realist, the populist. The emerging intelligentsia, a term which then combined the notion of culture (or semiculture) with that of progressive thinking and plebeian origin, defiantly called themselves nihilists and, in the name of life and Darwin, threw overboard all accepted values, recognizing only the data of experience and the purpose of common usefulness. The guilt-ridden privileged classes, superfluous in a state that had distrusted them since 1825, felt personally responsible for the unhappiness of the people, whom liberation from serfdom in 1861 did not free from misery and oppression. The impulses of nihilism and repentance joined in the populist movement, in which the early nineteenth-century yearning for lost unity takes the form of a passionate attempt at fusion with the masses.

"Go to the people! There is your place," said Herzen in 1861 to students expelled from the University. Sharing with the intellectuals of western Europe a humanitarian idealization of the people, Russians, before the eighties, could understand by "people," nothing other than "peasants." The city proletariat, then beginning to develop, was still organically linked to its village origins—unless the village commune released a worker from his tax obligations, he was still listed "peasant" in his papers. On the other

168

hand, the study of folklore was a recognized university subject—the peasant culture, in all its wealth, unfolded before large groups of city students. The contrast of past strength and beauty with present degradation could but breed, together with pity, indignation and a tender admiration. By sharing the peasants' sufferings, learning from their virtues, helping them to emerge from their night, Russians hoped to regain the lost unity of soul and advance on the road toward the Russian ideal. Thus would be solved the moral as well as the historical problems of the native land—a hope not destined to fulfillment.

THE EMPEROR PETER THE FIRST   Portrait by **Kupetsky**
From *Nevsky prospekt* (St. Petersburg, 1903)

EPISTLE TO THE GRAND-PRINCE VASILY IVANOVICH
The Elder Philotheus

> The name of Philotheus (Filofey), Elder of a Pskov monastery, is generally linked to the theory of "Moscow, the Third Rome," in which Moscow is held to be the heir to the Roman Empires of the West and East. Philotheus expressed this idea with great force in epistles addressed to the grand-princes Vasily Ivanovich and Ivan Vasilevich (Ivan IV) in the first part of the sixteenth century. The theory had been formulated in 1492 by the Metropolitan Zosima, who had celebrated Ivan III as the new "Tsar Constantine of the new city of Constantine—Moscow." In making such claims, the Russian Church took its inspiration from the writings of the southern Slavs who, in the fourteenth and early fifteenth centuries, before the Turkish conquest, had already aspired to the Byzantine succession.

■ ■ ■ My greetings to you, who have been set up by the Most High, Almighty, All-sustaining hand of God, by Whom princes reign, by Whom the great grow powerful and the strong write down the law; to you, most illustrious Lord Grand-Prince, who sit on the high throne, Orthodox Christian Prince and Sovereign of all, Ruler of the sacred thrones of God's holy universal and apostolic Church, the Church of the Most Holy Mother of God, of Her glorious and venerable Assumption,[1] the Church which has shone forth instead of those in Rome and Constantinople. For the churches of old Rome fell through the impiety of the Apollinarian heresy;[2] the portals of the churches of the second Rome, the city of Constantine, have been hacked through by the hatchets of the sons of Hagar.[3] But now shines the holy oecumenic apostolic Church of the third new Rome of your sovereign realm; it shines brighter than the sun, over the whole earth, unto the limits of the universe through the Orthodox Christian faith. . . .

As I wrote to you earlier, thus I say now: remember and hearken, pious Tsar—all Christian realms have gathered in your one realm; two Romes have fallen, but the third stands and there will be no fourth; your Christian realm will be replaced by no other.

—Khrestomatiya po istorii SSSR (Moscow, 1951), Vol. I

NOTES: [1]The Mother of God was considered to be the protector of Muscovy. **171**
[2]The followers of Apollinarius (fourth century) believed that the Incarnation did not imply the real humanity of Jesus, since in him the divine Word took the place of human reason. They held that his sufferings had thus been apparent only.
[3]The Turks.

RUSSIA AND EUROPE

P. Ya. Chaadaev

Petr Yakovlevich Chaadaev (1794–1856), a brilliant officer in the Guards, resigned in 1820 and spent six years in western Europe, where, before returning to Russia, he met such famous thinkers as Lamennais and Schelling. In 1836, the journal the *Telescope* published the Russian text of Chaadaev's "Philosophical Letter to a Lady," which Chaadaev had written in French in 1829. The letter was a bitter and eloquent denunciation of Russian moral and social inferiority, which Chaadaev attributed mainly to refusal of the European historical tradition represented by Catholicism.

The reaction to the "Letter" was overwhelmingly hostile. Most readers were indignant. The *Telescope* was stopped by the authorities, its editor banished, and Chaadaev himself was declared "unbalanced" and placed under house arrest and medical supervision.

No other letters by Chaadaev were published in Russia during his lifetime. The French texts or Russian translations of his works (*Letters* and *Essays*) have since appeared in Paris and Russia.

Chaadaev's views on Russian history and destiny, which made him unpopular at the time, found sympathy with Westernizers of the eighteen-forties, such as Herzen. The questions he asked: "Has Russia shared in European history?" and "Should Russia share in the life of Europe?" concerned all Russian thought in the nineteenth century.

■ ■ ■ It is one of the most deplorable aspects of our singular civilization that we still have to discover truths elsewhere accounted most trivial, even among nations far less advanced in certain regards than we are. The reason is that we have never moved with other nations; we belong to none of the great families of mankind; we are neither of the West nor of the East, and we have the traditions of neither. Situated as if outside the times, we have never been reached by the universal education of mankind.

The admirable sequence of human ideas through the centuries, which has developed the human mind to the condition it has now reached in the rest of the world, has had no effect upon us. What elsewhere has long constituted the very essence of society and life is only theory and speculation among us. For example, you, Madam, are happily in a position to gather all the good and true in life, to be aware of all that provides the sweetest and purest advantages of the soul, yet, one must ask you, what have all those advantages given you? You still seek what should fill not only your life, but your day. The very things that elsewhere make

172

up the necessary frame of life, in which all the day's events find their place so naturally, a condition as indispensable to a sane moral existence as wholesome air is to a sane physical existence, are totally lacking in our midst. You understand, I am not speaking of moral principles or philosophical maxims, but merely of a well-regulated life, of those habits, those routines of the mind which give it its freedom and imprint a regular movement to the soul.

Look around you. Does not everyone have a foot in the air? It is as if we were all on a journey. No sphere of determined existence for anyone, no good habits for anything, no rule in anything; not even a domestic hearth; nothing to inspire attachment or to arouse sympathy, no continuity, no permanence; all goes by, all flows along without leaving a trace either outside or within yourself. In our houses, we seem to camp; in our families, we seem to be outsiders; in our cities, we are nomads, more so than those who graze their horses in our steppes, for they feel closer to their deserts than we do to our cities. Do not imagine this to be a trifling point. Poor souls that we are, let us not add to our other miseries that of misjudging ourselves; let us not aspire to the life of pure spirits; let us learn to live sensibly, in our given reality. But first, let us speak of our country: this will not be a digression. Without this preamble, you could not understand what I have to tell you. . . .

Nations live only through the strong impressions that past ages leave in their minds and through contact with other people. In this same manner each individual experiences his relationship with all mankind.

What is the life of man, asks Cicero, if the memory of earlier events does not link present to past? But we, born like illegitimate children with no heritage, no link with the men that came before us on this earth, we have nothing in our hearts of the teachings that preceded us. Each of us must strive by himself to restore the broken family thread. What among other nations is habit, instinct, we must hammer into our heads. Our memories do not go beyond yesterday; we seem to be alien to ourselves. We move so strangely in time that, as we progress, our yesterdays escape us forever. This is the natural consequence of a culture that is all importation and imitation. There is no inner development, no natural progress among us; new ideas sweep away the old, because they do not derive from them, but are dropped on us from outside. Since we adopt only ready-made ideas, that ineradicable impress created by their natural development which gives them their force does not touch our intelligence. We grow, but do not mature; we move, but sideways—we draw no nearer to our goal. We are like children who have not been taught to think for themselves; grown to be men, they have nothing of their own; all their science is on the surface of things; their whole soul is outside them. Such exactly is our case.

173

Peoples are moral beings, just as individuals are. Centuries educate them, as years do persons. It can be said, in a way, that we are an exceptional people. We belong to those nations that do not seem to be an integral part of humanity but exist only to teach some great lesson to the world. The teaching we are destined to give will assuredly not be lost; but who knows on what day we shall find ourselves back in the bosom of humanity, or what miseries will be our lot before our destinies are fulfilled? . . .

I ask you, where are our sages, where are our thinkers? Who has ever thought for us, who thinks for us nowadays? And yet, situated between the great divisions of the world, between Orient and Occident, one elbow leaning on China and the other on Germany, we should combine in our nature the two great principles of intelligent creation—imagination and reason—and unite in our civilization the histories of the entire globe. Such is not the role allotted to us by Providence. Far from it, Providence seems to have had no concern at all for our destiny. Suspending, in regard to us, its benevolent action on men's minds, it has abandoned us wholly to ourselves; it has refused to have anything to do with us, to teach us anything. The experience of centuries means nothing to us; ages and generations have gone without fruit for us. It would seem, to look at us, that the universal law of humanity has been revoked in our case. Solitary in the world, we have not contributed a single idea to the mass of human ideas; we have in no wise assisted the human mind's progress, and whatever part of it has come to our share we have distorted. Nothing, since the first moment of our social existence, has ever emanated from us for the common good of men; not one useful thought has germinated on the barren soil of our country; not one great truth has sprung from our midst; we have not taken the trouble to imagine anything ourselves; and, from all that others have imagined, we have only borrowed deceptive appearances and superfluous luxury.

A strange thing! Even in the all-embracing world of science, our history is linked to nothing, explains nothing, proves nothing. If the hordes of barbarians that convulsed the world had not run over our land before swooping on the Occident, we should barely have provided a chapter to universal history. In order to attract attention, we have had to stretch from the Bering Straits to the Oder. One day, a great man wished to civilize us, and to give us a foretaste of enlightenment he threw the cloak of civilization to us; we picked up the cloak, but left civilization alone.[1] Another time, another great prince, associating us with his glorious mission, led us victoriously from one end of Europe to the other; returning home after this triumphal march through the most civilized countries in the world, the only things we brought back were ideas and aspirations which resulted in a calamity that set us back half a century.[2] There is something in our blood that repels real progress. In a word, we have lived and live only to present some great lesson to the remote posterity that will be able to discern it; today, in spite of all fine words, we are a blank spot in the realm of intellect. I cannot weary of admiring the vacancy and amazing solitude of our social existence. Doubtless an unfathomable destiny has its share in this, but, as in all that concerns the moral order, man also is responsible. Let us question history again: she it is who explains peoples.

While the structure of modern civilization was arising from the struggle between the energetic barbarity of Northern peoples and the lofty idea of religion, what were we doing? Driven by a fatal destiny, we turned to wretched Byzantium, object of those peoples' profound scorn, for the moral code that was to educate us. A moment before, an ambitious spirit had severed this family from universal brotherhood:[3] the idea thus distorted by human passion was the one we adopted. The life-giving principle of unity was then the inspiration for everything in Europe. Everything derived from it, everything focused upon it. The whole intellectual movement of those times had as its only aim the unity of human thought, and all activity originated in the powerful need to arrive at a universal idea, which is the genius of modern times. Alien to this admirable principle, we became the prey of conquerors. And when we were freed from the foreign yoke, and, had we not been separated from the common family, could have profited by the ideas that had meanwhile appeared among our Western brothers, we fell into a still harsher servitude, sanctified as it was by the fact of our deliverance.

What bright lights had then already emerged in Europe from the seeming darkness that had covered it! Most of the knowledge that the human mind boasts nowadays had already been conjectured; the character of society had already been fixed; and, by turning back to pagan antiquity, the Christian world had rediscovered the form of beauty that it still lacked. Estranged by our schism, nothing reached us of what happened in Europe. We took no part in the great deeds of the world. The eminent qualities with which religion had endowed modern nations and which, in the eyes of sane reason, raised them as high above the ancients as these rise above the Hottentots and Lapps, the new forces with which it had enriched human intelligence, the manners which, through submission to a disarmed authority, had become as mild as earlier they had been harsh: none of this had emerged among us. Though we bore the name of Christians, while Christianity was majestically progressing along the path traced by its divine founder, while it drew generations in its wake, we remained inert. While the whole world was building itself anew, nothing was being erected in our midst; we huddled as before in our thatch and log hovels. Christians though we were, the fruit of Christianity did not ripen for us.

I ask you, is it not absurd to suppose, as is generally done in our country, that this progress of European nations, so slowly achieved through the direct and obvious action of one single moral force, can be appropriated by us at one stroke, without even taking the trouble to find out what is its nature?

175

Christianity cannot be understood if one does not realize that it has a purely historical aspect which is such an essential part of the dogma that it contains, so to speak, the whole philosophy of Christianity, since it reveals what Christianity did for men and what it is to do for them in the future. Thus the Christian religion appears not only as a moral system conceived in the perishable forms of the human mind, but as a divine, eternal power, acting universally in the world of intelligence, and whose visible action must be a perpetual teaching for us. . . .

But after all, you will say, are we not then Christians? And can one be civilized only in the European fashion? Certainly we are Christians; but then, so are the Abyssinians. Certainly one can be civilized in a manner different from that of Europe: are not the Japanese civilized? . . . Do you believe that it will be the Japanese and the Abyssinian civilization that will bring about the order of things which I discussed just now and which is the ultimate destiny of humankind?

—*Sochineniya i pisma P. Ya. Chaadaeva,* ed. Gershenzon (Moscow, 1913)

NOTES: [1]Cf. Kireevsky's phrase in *The Nineteenth Century* (1832): "Having shaved our beard, we have not yet washed our face."
[2]The December uprising in 1825.
[3]Allusion to the Eastern schism.

■ ■ ■

RUSSIAN LIFE AND THE RUSSIAN CHURCH
P. Ya. Chaadaev

Chaadaev's second "Philosophical Letter" was published for the first time in a Russian translation from the original French in volumes twenty-two to twenty-four of *Literaturnoe nasledstvo* (Moscow, 1936), with notes by M. D. Shakhovskoy. The date of composition cannot be determined with any certainty, but according to Shakhovskoy, it was probably written very soon after the first Letter, in 1829 or 1830.

■ ■ ■ If I expressed my thought successfully the other day, you must have realized that I am far from reducing our deficiencies to a mere lack of knowledge. True, even in this we are not too rich, but for the moment we must be satisfied to do without the vast spiritual wealth that has accumulated over the centuries in other countries where it is available to humanity: another task awaits us. Besides, even if we admit that study and meditation might gain us the knowledge we lack, where could we find the living traditions, the vast experience, the deep understanding of the

176

past, the solid intellectual habits—all results of a tremendous concentration of human capacities—that is, everything that makes up the moral nature of the peoples of Europe and gives them their real superiority? So, then, we are not faced with the task of broadening the scope of our ideas, but with that of correcting them and giving them a new direction. As for you, Madam, what you need first is a new sphere of existence, in which the new thoughts sown by chance in your mind and the new demands those thoughts have bred in your soul can find their effective application. You must create a new world for yourself, since the world in which you live has become alien to you.

Let us begin with the fact that the state of our soul, however lofty its temper, necessarily depends on its environment. For this reason, you should determine clearly what can be done, considering your position in society and in your own family, to harmonize your feelings with your mode of life, your ideas with your family relations, your beliefs with the beliefs of those that surround you.

Indeed, many evils arise from the very fact that what takes place in the depths of our mind is in sharp opposition to the necessity of submitting to social conventions. You say that your financial means do not allow you to live comfortably in the capital. Well, you have a charming country estate: why should you not settle there till the end of your days? This is a fortunate necessity, and it is in your power to extract from it all the profit that you could obtain from the most edifying precepts of philosophy. Make your retreat as attractive as possible, decorate it handsomely, even give it—why not?—a certain refinement and elegance. Do not consider this a form of sensuality; you will not be concerned with vulgar pleasures, but with the possibility of concentrating entirely on your inner life. I beg of you, do not despise these outer details. We live in a country that is so poor in manifestations of the ideal that if we do not surround ourselves in our home life with some measure of poetry and good taste we may easily lose all refinement of feeling, all notion of elegance. One of the most striking traits of our peculiar civilization is our neglect of the conveniences and pleasures of life. We are satisfied with struggling more or less successfully against the excesses of the seasons, and this in a country about which one may wonder in all seriousness whether it was intended for the habitation of reasonable beings. Since we have in the past been imprudent enough to settle in this cruel climate, let us at least try now to organize our existence so as to forget some of its harshness. . . . There is a real cynicism in that indifference toward the pleasures of life that certain of us consider meritorious. One of the chief reasons that hinder progress among us consists in the absence of any influence of art on our domestic life. . . .

Naturally, any one who would follow his beliefs with enthusiasm will encounter obstacles and resistance among that mass whose inertia nothing has ever shaken. You will have to create everything, Madam, even the air you breathe, even the soil you must tread. This is literally so. Those slaves who serve you, are they not the air around you? Those furrows that other slaves have dug in the sweat of their brows, are they not the earth that bears you? How many things, how many miseries are contained in the mere word "slave"! This is the magic circle in which we struggle without the power to escape; this is the odious reality which breaks us all. This is what reduces to naught our noblest efforts, our most generous impulses; this is what paralyzes our will and soils all our virtues. Weighed down by a fatal guilt, what soul, fine though it may be, will not wither under such an unbearable burden? What man, be he ever so strong, living in eternal contradiction with himself, thinking in one way and acting in another, will not finally be abhorrent to himself? I have returned, as you see, without noticing it, to my first point: allow me to dwell on it a little longer, and I shall come back to you later.

Where lies the cause of this terrible ulcer that debilitates us? How could it happen that the most striking trait of a Christian society is just the one that the Russian people have renounced in the very bosom of Christianity? How is it that religion has had this reverse effect upon us? I do not know, but it seems to me that this alone might cause us to question the Orthodox faith of which we boast. You know that not one philosopher of antiquity attempted to imagine a slaveless society or found any arguments against slavery. Aristotle,[1] the recognized representative of all the wisdom that existed in the world before the coming of Christ, stated that some people are born to be free, others to bear fetters. As you also know, even the most stubborn sceptics admit that we owe the abolition of serfdom in Europe to Christianity. More, we know that the first instances of serfs' emancipations were religious acts, performed in front of the altar, and that in the majority of emancipation deeds we meet the formula: *pro redemptione animae*—for the redeeming of our soul. Finally, we know that the clergy led the way everywhere by freeing their own serfs and that the Roman pontiffs were first to bring about the abolition of serfdom in the territory submitted to their spiritual rule. Why, then, did not Christianity have the same consequences among us? Why, on the contrary, was the Russian people subjected to slavery only after it had become Christian— to be precise, in the reigns of Godunov and Shuïsky? Let the Orthodox Church explain this.

Let it say why it did not raise its maternal voice against this hateful abuse of one part of the nation by the other.[2]

—*Literaturnoe nasledstvo* (Moscow, 1936)

178

[1] *Politics*, i. 2.
[2] Since the French text of this letter was not available, except for fragments, this text has been translated from the Russian.

■ ■ ■

RUSSIA'S HISTORICAL DESTINY

P. Ya. Chaadaev

> In *Apologia for a Madman* (1837) Chaadaev for the first time
> speaks of Russia with some hope for its future and even some
> respect for its Church. At the same time, he expresses strong
> misgivings and scorn for the ideologies of the Slavophils.

■ ■ ■ Do you believe that if he [Peter the Great] had found in his
nation a rich and fertile history, living traditions, deep-rooted institutions,
he would not have hesitated to cast it into a new mold? Do you believe
that, confronted by a strongly outlined, strongly marked nationality, his
founder's instinct would not, on the contrary, have led him to ask this very
nationality for the instruments of his country's regeneration? Would this
country, on the other hand, have allowed itself to be dispossessed of its
past and to have an European past imposed, so to speak, upon it? But
this was not the case. Peter the Great found his country a blank sheet of
paper; with his strong hand he wrote on it the words: "Europe and the
West," and ever since we have belonged to Europe and the West. Do not
doubt it: however great this man's genius and the tremendous energy of
his will, his work was possible only in a nation whose past did not im-
periously determine its further progress, whose traditions had no power
to shape its future, whose memories could be erased with impunity by a
bold legislator. If we were so docile when the voice of the prince called
us to a new life, it is apparently because nothing in our earlier existence
justified resistance. The deepest trait of our historical nature is the lack of
spontaneity in our social development. Look carefully, and you will see
that each important fact of our history has been imposed upon us, that
almost every new idea is an imported idea. But there is nothing to offend
national feeling in such a point of view; if it is correct, we must accept it,
that's all. There are great nations, just as there are great historical characters, who cannot be explained by the normal laws of reason, but who are
decreed by the supreme logic of a mysterious Providence: so it is with us;
once again, national pride has nothing to say in this. The history of a
people is not merely a succession of facts, it is also a sequence of ideas. A
fact must be expressed by an idea; a thought, a principle, must inform
events and strive to emerge from them. Then the fact is not wasted, it
has made its mark on intelligences, it has remained engraved in hearts,
and no force on earth can tear it out. Such history is not made by his-
torians, it lies in the force of circumstances. The historian finds it ready-
made and records it; but whether he comes or not, it exists by itself; and
each member of the historical family, however obscure, however insignificant, bears it in the depths of his being. This history we do not possess.

179

We should learn to reconcile ourselves to its absence and not stone those who were first to discover our lack.

Our fanatic Slavs[1] may well, now and then, in their various excavations, dig up curious objects of interest for our museums and libraries; but one may doubt, I believe, that they will ever succeed in extracting from our historic soil anything to fill the emptiness of our souls, to condense the vagueness of our minds. . . .

The life of nations has something in common with that of individuals. All men have lived, but only the man of genius or the man who is placed in certain particular conditions has a real history. If, for instance, a people, through a combination of circumstances not of its own creating, through a geographical position not of its own choosing, spreads over an immense stretch of land without being conscious of what it is doing, and if one fine day it turns out to be a powerful nation, this will certainly be a surprising fact, and one may admire it to one's heart's content: but what is history to say about it? Actually this is a purely material fact, a geographical fact of tremendous proportions, no doubt, but nothing more. History will take note of it, will record it in its annals, then will close the book on it, and that will be all. The real history of this people will begin only from the day when it has grasped the idea entrusted to it, which it is called upon to bring about, and when it starts to pursue this idea with the persevering though hidden instinct that leads nations to their destiny. That is the moment to which I aspire, with all the powers of my heart, for my country. . . .

More than any of you, believe me, I cherish my country; I have its glory at heart; I can appreciate the eminent qualities of my nation. But it is true also that the patriotic feeling which inspires me is not exactly the same as the one whose shouts have disturbed my peaceful existence and cast anew on the ocean of human miseries the skiff I had run aground at the foot of the Cross. I have not learned to love my country with closed eyes, a bowed head, a shut mouth. I believe one can serve one's country only by seeing it clearly; I think the time of blind infatuation is over, and nowadays truth is what one owes first to one's country. I love my country as Peter the Great taught me to love it. I do not, I confess, have that smug, lazy patriotism which manages to see everything through rosy spectacles, which falls asleep on its illusions and which, unfortunately, afflicts too many of our fine brains today. I think that if we have come later than others, it is in order to do better than others, to escape falling into their faults, their mistakes, their superstitions. In my opinion, it would be a strange misjudging of the role that is assigned to us to reduce us to a clumsy repetition of the long series of follies committed by nations less favored than we are, to a fresh beginning of all the calamities that have befallen them. I think we are in a fortunate situation, provided we know how to appreciate it.

—*Sochineniya i pisma P. Ya. Chaadaeva*, ed. Gershenzon (Moscow, 1913)

180

NOTES: [1]The term in French is *Slavons*, Slavonians, which was then frequently used to designate the group later called Slavophils.

■ ■ ■

RUSSIAN MESSIANISM
V. F. Odoevsky

> Prince V. F. Odoevsky (1803–69) was in his youth a member of the philosophical society "Liubomudrie," which studied and discussed the German philosophers Kant and, especially, Schelling. Odoevsky blends the ideologies that Slavophils and Westernizers were later to develop separately. He believed that the future belonged to Russia, by virtue of her all-embracing strength and love; but he also admired Peter as the organizer of that strength. The book *Russian Nights*, from which the following extracts are taken, was written in the eighteen-thirties, though it was not published until 1844.

■ ■ ■ Let us then dare to utter a word which now may seem strange to many, while it will sound almost too obvious at some future time: "The West is perishing!"

Yes, it is perishing! While it assembles its petty treasures, while it gives itself up to its despair, time moves on. Time, which has its own life distinct from that of nations, moves on; it will soon overtake decrepit Europe and will perhaps bury it under the same layer of inert ashes that covers the huge edifices of ancient America's nations—nations without a name. . . .

It seems sometimes, in happy moments, that Providence itself arouses in man the dormant feeling of faith and love for science and art; sometimes, remote from the storms of the world, it preserves a people whose destiny is to point once more toward the direction humanity has lost and to take the first place among nations. But only a new, an innocent nation is worthy of this lofty deed; in it only, or through it, can be conceived a new world embracing all the spheres of the mind and of social life. . . . Where is now that part of the world which Providence has marked for such a lofty accomplishment? Where is now the people that preserves the secret of the world's salvation? . . .

In the time of fear and death, the Russian sword alone cut the knot that bound trembling Europe, and even now the gleam of the Russian sword shines portentously[1] in the gloomy chaos of the old world. . . .

181

All manifestations of nature are symbolic of one another: Europe called the Russian its *savior*; the name conceals an even higher vocation, whose might is to extend to all the spheres of social life: it is not only the *body* of Europe that we must save, but its soul too!

We have been set on the border of two worlds—the past and the future; we are new and fresh; we have taken no part in the crimes of old Europe; before us is being enacted its strange, mysterious drama, the solution of which lies hidden, perhaps, in the depths of the Russian spirit. We are merely witnesses; we are impassive, for we are already accustomed to this strange sight; we are impartial because we can often foresee the denouement, for we often recognize the parody mingled with the tragedy. . . . Yes, it is not in vain that Providence brings us to these Saturnalia, as the Spartans of old led their youths to gaze upon drunken barbarians!

We are called to a lofty deed, a difficult achievement! We must bring everything to life! Our spirit must be engraved in the history of the human mind as our name is written on the tablets of victory. Another higher victory—the victory of science, art, and faith—awaits us on the ruins of decrepit Europe. Alas! it may be that our generation is not fated to accomplish this high deed! We are still too close to the scenes that our eyes looked on, we have still hoped, we have still expected something fine from Europe! Our clothing still wears traces of the ashes it has stirred up. We still share in her sufferings! We have not yet isolated ourselves in our nativeness. We are an untuned string—we have not yet understood the sound that we are to bring forth in the universal harmony. . . .

You of the new generation, you will see a new sun—but you will not understand our sufferings, you will not understand our age of contradictions! . . . Combine, then, in yourselves the experience of age and the strength of youth; do not spare your efforts. Rescue the treasures of science from under the tottering ruins of Europe and, fixing your eyes on the last convulsive movements of her expiring life, seek inspiration in your own feelings; cast forth upon the world your very own native achievements; and, in the sacred threefold unity of faith, science, and art, you will find the tranquillity that your fathers prayed for. The nineteenth century belongs to Russia! . . .

Our earth has seen a great naturalist, Peter the Great was his name; the subject of his experiments was a wonderful organism, worthy of his spirit. Peter the Great fathomed the structure of that wonderful world; he saw its huge dimensions, its giant strength; he discovered in it sturdy, well-tempered cogwheels, robust points of support, fast-working gears—but this huge system lacked a pendulum, and therefore its powerful components achieved results contrary to their nature. The feeling of strength developed into that total insouciance which has devoured the Asiatic tribes; the many-sidedness of the spirit, manifested in an admirable receptivity akin to the feeling of truth, could find no food for itself and withered in inactivity; a few more centuries—instants in the life of a people—and this powerful world would have worn itself out with its own might. But Peter the Great knew nature and man, and he did not despair; he saw at work in his people elements which had nearly disappeared among other nations; he saw the feelings of love and unity, strengthened by agelong struggles against hostile forces; he saw the feelings of piety and faith that sanctified agelong sufferings; all that was needed was to curb the excessive, to arouse the dormant. And the great man in his wisdom inoculated his people with the lesser Western elements which it lacked: he sobered the feeling of wild valor through organization; he broadened the national egotism, confined in the sphere of its beliefs, by the sight of Western life; he gave receptivity the nourishment of knowledge. It was a powerful inoculation: as time went by, the alien elements were assimilated and subdued the native—and new, fiery blood flowed in the great veins of the giant. All his feelings found release in action; his soft muscles tautened; he remembered the obscure dreams of his infancy, the promptings of a superior force; he rejected some, gave substance to others—breathed freely with the breath of life, raised his mighty head over the West, bent upon it the gaze of his clear guiltless eyes, and fell into deep meditation.

The West, absorbed in the world of its own elements, elaborated it carefully, forgetting the existence of others. Wonderful indeed was its work, which brought forth splendid deeds; the West has produced all that its elements could yield—but no more. In its uneasy and hurried activity, it has developed certain things and stifled others. Balance has been lost, and the inner sickness of the West is reflected in the disturbances of the populace and in the dark, purposeless discontent of its elite. The feeling of self-preservation has become touchy selfishness and hostile mistrust of one's neighbor; the need for truth has been distorted into coarse demands for tangibility and petty minuteness. Busy with the material conditions of material life, the West invents laws for itself without seeking their roots in itself; not the elements of the spirit, but those of the body imbue the world of science and art. Lost is the feeling of love, of unity, of strength even, for hope in the future has disappeared; in its materialistic intoxication, the West dances in the graveyard of its great thinkers' thoughts and tramples into the earth those that would exorcise its madness with a powerful and holy word.

The West, in spite of all its greatness, has lacked another Peter to inoculate it with the fresh and powerful lifeblood of the Slav East in order to achieve the full harmonious development of the fundamental elements common to humanity.

Meanwhile, what the hand of man has not accomplished is brought about by the passing of time. . . . The West feels the coming of the Slav spirit; it fears it, as our ancestors feared the West. A confined organism does not willingly accept elements alien to it, even though they might help to maintain its existence—but at the same time it turns unwillingly and unconsciously toward them, as a plant to the sun.

Do not fear, brothers in mankind! There are no destructive elements in the Slav East—learn to know it and you will be convinced of this. You will find in us partly your own strength, preserved and multiplied; you will find also our strength, which you do not know, and which will not decrease from being shared with you. . . . You will become convinced that there exists a people whose natural impulse is that all-embracing many-sidedness of the spirit[2] which you vainly attempt to arouse by artificial means.

—*Russkie nochi* (Moscow, 1913)

NOTES: [1]Allusions to Napoleon's defeat in Russia in 1812 and the role played by Alexander I in 1815.

[2]In *The Brothers Karamazov* and the "Pushkin Speech" (1880), Dostoevsky expresses similar ideas about the "all-embracing and loving Slav spirit."

■ ▨ ■

MOSCOW AND PETERSBURG

A. I. Herzen

A contrasting of Moscow with Petersburg was a frequent theme in Russian literature during the first half of the nineteenth century. The theme is indicated in Pushkin's *The Bronze Horseman* (1836). Later, the comparison between the old and the new capital served as a way of posing the problem of Russia's historical destiny.

Herzen's article was written in 1842, but because of censorship circulated only in manuscript form. Three years later, the critic Belinsky, in his turn, wrote an essay on "Petersburg and Moscow," which stressed more strongly the "new hope, the fair future" represented by Petersburg.

■ ■ ■ You too, my dear friends, you are angry because, from the bank of the Volkhov[1] where I have settled, I speak of nothing but the past, as if we had no present, as if a secret limit had been set for us in history—to confine us in our research to the origin of Russia—as if the most important fact and event in our history was a birth certificate, after which we lived so humbly that there's nothing more to tell. . . . Here I'll stop you. If I have started talking about the past, it's for this very reason that, it seems to me, we did not live in it, but merely somehow existed. Still, if you wish, let's forget about the past!

184

To talk about the present of Russia is to talk about Petersburg, about this city with no history in either direction, the city of the present, the city which alone, on this huge section of the planet that is called Russia, lives and acts on the level of contemporary and national needs. Moscow, on the contrary, claims old ways of life, a supposed link with the past; it preserves memories of some bygone glory; it always looks back; though caught in the movement of Petersburg, it follows reluctantly, with its back turned to the goal and to any European initiative. Petersburg lives only in the present; it has nothing to remember except Peter; its past is all lumped in one century; it has no history and no future either—every autumn may bring the storm that will submerge it.[2] Petersburg is the everyday currency that cannot be dispensed with; Moscow is a rare coin, but though it may be precious to the collector, it is out of circulation. So, let's talk of the city of the present, of Petersburg.

Petersburg is an extraordinary thing. I have studied it, investigated it in its academies, its offices, its barracks, and its hotels, but to little result. A man of no occupations, not caught in the whirl of civilian affairs or in the parades and maneuvers of *peaceful military activities*,[3] I had leisure—by retreating, so to speak, to one side—to examine Petersburg; I saw various classes of people—people who can with an Olympian movement of the pen award a Stanislas medal[4] or dismiss from office; people who write endlessly—civil servants; people who hardly ever write—Russian literary men; people who not only never write, but never read either—high-ranking officers of the Guards; I saw lions and lionesses, tigers and tigresses; I saw people who were unlike any beast or man, but were at home in Petersburg like fish in water; lastly, I saw poets in the Third Section[5] of the Special Office and the Third Section of the Special Office in charge of poets; but Petersburg remained a mystery as before. Even now, when it has begun to disappear from my eyes in the fog in which God wraps it the year around in order to conceal what's happening there from distant observers, I can find no means of solving the riddles of the existence of a city founded on all sorts of contradictions and extremes, both physical and moral. . . . This, by the way, is one more proof of its contemporaneousness: all our history since Peter I is a riddle; our present way of life is a riddle—this ill-assorted patchwork of mutually-destructive forces, of opposite trends, from which at times something European emerges, something broad and human breaks forth, to drown again, whether in the swamp of the Slavic character's inert passiveness (which accepts everything apathetically—knout and book, rights and deprivation of rights, Tatars and Peter—and so, in fact, accepts nothing at all), or in the waves of barbarous fancies about an exceptional national essence[6]—fancies which have recently crawled out of the grave without being any the wiser for their stay under the damp earth.

The day when Peter saw that the only salvation for Russia was to cease being Russian, the day when he decided that we should enter

185

universal history, determined the necessity of Petersburg and the super-fluity of Moscow. The first inevitable step for Peter was to move the capital away from Moscow. With the foundation of Petersburg, Moscow became secondary; it lost its former meaning for Russia and vegetated in insignificance and emptiness until the year 1812. Perhaps, in some future time . . . who knows what may happen? There will certainly be many good things in the future. But we are speaking of the past and the present. Moscow meant nothing to humanity, and for Russia it was like a whirlpool that sucked in the best forces of the country and could do nothing with them. After Peter, Moscow was forgotten and accorded only the respect and attentions that we grant an old grandmother who is no longer allowed any share in managing the estate. Moscow served as a relay between Petersburg and the next world for our retired gentry, as a foretaste of the peace of the grave. It felt no indignation against Petersburg; on the contrary, it followed in Petersburg's footsteps, aping and distorting its fashions and manners. All the younger generation at that time served in the Guards; whatever talent came to light in Moscow went to Petersburg to write, serve the government, be active. All of a sudden, this Moscow with its Kreml', whose very existence had been forgotten, became involved in the history of Europe. Burnt at the right moment, it was rebuilt at the right moment. Its name was mentioned in the bulletins of the Great Army. Napoleon rode along its streets. Europe remembered it. Fantastic stories about its reconstruction circulated all over the world. Every ear rang with stories of the beauty of this phoenix rising from its ashes. Yet, we must confess, that reconstruction was a bad job; the architecture of the houses is ugly and frightfully pretentious; the houses, or rather manors, are small, stuck with columns, weighed down with pediments, hemmed in with fences. What must Moscow have looked like before if this was an improvement? There were some good people who thought that such a violent jolt would shake Moscow out of its sleep; it was believed that a native and cultured originality would develop there, but the old dear merely stretched forty versts from Troitsa in Golenishchev to Butyrki[7] and now slumbers once more. And today there's no Napoleon on the horizon!

In Petersburg, the people, taken together or separately, are most unpleasant. It is impossible to love Petersburg, but I feel that I could live in no other city of Russia. In Moscow, on the contrary, everybody is most kind, only they bore you to death: in Moscow there is a sort of half savage, half civilized "gentry" mode of life that is obliterated in the contiguity of the Petersburg crowds; it is pleasant to observe, just as any other idiosyncrasy, but you get sick of it at once. The Russian gentry do not know comfort; they are rich but dirty; in Moscow they are provincial and puffed up, and for this reason they are perpetually on thorns, eager to catch up with Petersburg usages—but Petersburg has no usages of its own. Petersburg has no originality, no idiosyncrasy, while in Moscow everything is original, from the bizarre architecture of Vasily the

Blessed to the taste of *kolachi*.[8] Petersburg is the embodiment of the general abstract notion of a capital city; it differs from all European cities because it resembles all of them collectively; while Moscow is different in that it resembles none, but is the giant development of a rich Russian village. Petersburg is an upstart; it has no memories sanctified by centuries, no heart-ties with the country it was raised from the marshes to represent; it has a police, government offices, a merchant class, a river, a Court, seven-story houses, the Guards, sidewalks on which you can walk, gas-lamps which really light the streets, and it is satisfied with its comfort, which has no roots and stands, like itself, on piles that hundreds of thousands of workers drove in at the price of their lives.

A dead calm prevails in Moscow; people there are idle systematically; they merely live and relax before work. After ten you won't find a cab in Moscow; in some streets you won't meet a soul; at each step you are reminded of the isolated Slavonic-Oriental way of life. In Petersburg there's the eternal clatter of "vanity of vanities," and everybody is so busy that they don't even live. Petersburg's activity is senseless, but the habit of activity is a great thing. The lethargic sleep of Moscow gives Muscovites their Pekin-Kukunor character of stagnation. The Petersburg citizen's aims are limited or vulgar, but he strives for them successfully; he is dissatisfied with the present; he works. The Moscow citizen, in the extreme nobility of his soul, has no aim at all; he is generally satisfied with himself, or, if not, he is incapable of extricating himself from general, indeterminate, and indistinct thoughts to find out what's wrong. In Petersburg all literary men are hucksters; not one literary circle there is held together by some idea: they all center round some individual or profit. The Petersburg literary men are less cultured by half than the Moscow writers; when they come to Moscow they are astonished at its intelligent gatherings and conversations. But there is no literary activity except in Petersburg. There journals are published; there the censorship is more intelligent; there Pushkin, Karamzin wrote and lived; even Gogol belonged to Petersburg more than to Moscow. In Moscow you can find people with deep convictions, but they sit inactive; in Moscow there are literary circles that spend their time in disinterestedly proving to each other some useful thought, such as that the West is rotting while Russia flourishes. In Moscow one single journal is published, and even that is called the *Muscovite*.[9]

The Moscow citizen likes medals and ceremonies, the Petersburg man, positions and money; Moscow cherishes aristocratic connections, Petersburg cultivates people in office. If a Moscow man receives the medal of "Stanislas on the neck,"[10] he wears it on his paunch; the Petersburg man wears his "Vladimir"[11] medal like a dog's collar with a lock, or like a broken rope on a man just dropped from the gallows. You can live two years in Petersburg without finding out its religion; even the Russian churches there have put on a Catholic air.[12] The day after your arrival in Moscow the bronze voice of Orthodoxy will strike your ear. In Moscow

187

a great number of people go to church every Sunday and holiday; some even go to matins. In Petersburg no member of the male sex goes to matins, and mass is attended only by Germans in their kirche and by peasants from out of town. In Petersburg there is only one relic—Peter's cottage; in Moscow repose the relics of all the Russian saints who couldn't find a place in Kiev, even those whose death is still a matter of discussion, such as the tsarevich Dimitry. All this holiness is guarded by the Kreml' walls; the walls of the Peter and Paul fortress guard prison cells and the Mint.

Remote from political animation, living on stale news, having no key to the government's actions and no instinct to decipher them, Moscow argues, grumbles, criticizes freely. Suddenly some Ivan Alexandrovich[13] on a grand scale appears—Moscow bows to the ground, welcomes the visitor, gives him balls and dinners, and repeats his witticisms. Petersburg, the center of all events, has no welcome for anything or anybody, no surprise at anything: if the whole Vasilevsky island was blown up, this would cause less excitement than the arrival of Khozrev-Mirza[14] to Moscow. Ivan Alexandrovich has no importance in Petersburg: you can't bluff anyone there by force or authority; they know where force is and who has it. In Moscow, even today, every foreigner is taken for a great man; in Petersburg every great man is taken for a foreigner. In all its life Petersburg has rejoiced but once: it was very much scared of the French, and when Wittgenstein[15] saved it, it ran out to welcome him. You can tell good old Moscow through the papers to weep on such a day and to rejoice on another: all the governor general has to do is give orders for the regimental band to come out or a church procession to take place. But Moscow weeps when there is a famine in Ryazan; Petersburg doesn't, because it is totally unaware of the existence of Ryazan—or if it does have some dim notions about the central provinces, it certainly doesn't know that people there eat bread.

The young man in Moscow disregards conventions, he plays the liberal, and it's just in those liberal sallies that you see the perennial Scyth. This liberalism passes as soon as the Moscow people get a taste of the secret police. The young Petersburg man is conventional as an official paper; at sixteen he acts the diplomat and even something of the spy, and he remains firm in his role all his life. In Petersburg everything happens at a wonderful speed. Polevoy[16] became a faithful subject of the Emperor five days after he arrived in Petersburg; in Moscow he would have felt some shame and would have played the freethinker for five years or so. As a general rule, our flimsy Moscow liberals, once they are in Petersburg, begin to look for a position, to curse education, and to bless military parades. Petersburg hastens the breaking of the shell, but the kind of chicken that is hatched is not its concern. Belinsky, who in Moscow had preached nationality and autocracy, was not a month in Petersburg before he outdid Anacharsis Cloots himself.[17] Petersburg, like all positive people, will not listen to chatter, but demands action, which is why noble Moscow talkers often turn into the vilest doers. In Petersburg you can say that there are no liberals, but if any do crop up, they don't get to Moscow, they are sent straight from here to hard labor or the Caucasus.

The destiny of Petersburg has something tragic, gloomy, and majestic. It is the cherished child of a northern giant, in whom were concentrated the energy and cruelty of the French Convention of 1793 and its revolutionary strength—the cherished child of a tsar who renounced his country for its own good and oppressed it in the name of Europeanism and civilization. The sky of Petersburg is eternally grey; the sun that shines on wicked and good alike does not shine on Petersburg; its marshy soil gives forth vapors; a damp sea wind whistles in its streets. I repeat, each autumn it may expect the gale that will submerge it. Moscow's destiny has something mediocre, petty; its climate is not bad, but neither is it good; its houses are not high, nor are they low. Look at the Moscow citizens in Novinskoe or in Sokolniki[18] on the first of May: they are neither hot nor cold; they're just comfortable, and satisfied with the fair booths, the carriages, and themselves. And now look at Petersburg on a pleasant day. The wretched inhabitants rush out of their lairs, hurry into their carriages, and gallop off to their country cottages or to the islands; they drink in the green and the sun, like the prisoners in *Fidelio,* but the habit of worrying does not leave them; they know that it will rain in an hour, that the next day, convicts of government offices, hired servants of bureaucracy, they will be back at their desks. A man who shivers in the frost and damp, who lives in perpetual fog and hoarfrost, looks differently on the world; this is evidenced in the government, which has taken its hostile and gloomy temper from the hoarfrost around it. An artist who grew up in Petersburg has chosen for his brush the fearful image of a savage, senseless force destroying people in Pompeii—such is the inspiration of Petersburg![19] In Moscow there is a fine view every mile, while you can walk from one end to the other of Petersburg without finding a single view that would even be passable; but, your walk over, you must return to the Neva bank and say that all the prospects in Moscow are nothing in comparison. In Petersburg people like luxury, but do not care for the superfluous; in Moscow it's that very "superfluous" that is reckoned as luxury. This is why every Moscow house has columns, which you don't find in Petersburg; each Moscow citizen has several lackeys, ill-dressed and idle, but the Petersburg man has one, clean and skillful.

We must admit that it's impossible to have received a more contrasting education than Petersburg and Moscow. All its life Petersburg has seen nothing but palace upheavals, overthrows, and celebrations, and it has no knowledge of our traditional life. Moscow, which grew under the Tatar yoke and took possession of Russia, not by virtue of its own merit but through the insufficiency of the other provinces, has stopped at the last page of the Kotoshikhin times and has only hearsay knowledge of

189

later upheavals. A courier comes in his own time, bringing a document, and Moscow believes what the printed word says: who is tsar and who is not; that Biron[20] is a good man, and later that he's a bad man; it believes that God has come down on earth to install on the throne Anna Ioannovna, then Anna Leopoldovna, and then Ioann Antonovich, and then Elizaveta Petrovna, and then Ekaterina Alexeevna in Petr Fedorovich's place.[21] Petersburg knows perfectly well that God won't mix in that murky business: it has seen the orgies of the Summer Garden, the Countess Biron sprawling in the snow, and Anna Leopoldovna asleep with her lover on the balcony of the Winter Palace and later exiled; it has seen the funerals of Peter III and Paul I. It has seen much and knows much.

I have nowhere fallen into such frequent and numerous sad thoughts as in Petersburg. Oppressed with painful doubts, I have wandered on its granite embankments and been near to despair. I owe such minutes to Petersburg and they have made me love it, just as I have become indifferent to Moscow because it cannot even torture and torment. Petersburg will make any honest man curse this Babylon a thousand times; in Moscow you may live for years and never hear a curse except in the Assumption Cathedral.[22] That's what makes it worse than Petersburg. Petersburg keeps you in a state of physical and moral fever. In Moscow your health improves to such a degree that the movements of your organism take the place of all life activities. In Petersburg . . . you cannot find a single fat man. All this makes it clear that if a man wishes to live both in body and spirit, he will choose neither Moscow nor Petersburg. In Petersburg he will die before his life is half over, in Moscow he will become an imbecile.

"What the devil," you will say, "you've talked and talked, and I can't even tell which you prefer." Be sure that I can't tell either. First, it's impossible now to choose either Petersburg or Moscow for a residence; but since there is a fate that chooses our place of residence for us, that's a settled affair; secondly, all that lives has such a multitude of aspects so amazingly welded in one whole that any sharp-edged judgment is a one-sided absurdity. There are some aspects of Moscow life that one can like, just as there are some in Petersburg; but there are far more of the kind that make you dislike Moscow and detest Petersburg. To be sure, you can find good things everywhere, even in Pekin and Vienna, just as there were three good men for whose sake God forgave several times the sins of Sodom and Gomorrah—but he did no more than forgive. We shouldn't get excited over this: wherever many people live, wherever people have lived long, you will find something human, something solemn and poetic. Solemn are the peal of Moscow bells and processions in the Kreml'; solemn are the great parades in Petersburg; solemn are the gatherings of Buddhists in the East as they read their holy books by the light of a hundred and twelve torches. We're not satisfied with this poetical aspect, we would like . . . there are so many things we would like.

They are now prophesying a railway between Moscow and Petersburg.[23]   God speed!   Thanks to this, Petersburg and Moscow will find themselves on the same level, and no doubt caviar will be cheaper in Petersburg, while in Moscow they'll know two days earlier what numbers of the foreign journals are forbidden.   Well, that won't be so bad!

—*Sochineniya* (Moscow, 1955)

NOTES: [1]Herzen was then in forced residence in Novgorod, on the river Volkhov.

[2]Petersburg had known several disastrous floods.   One of the most famous, in 1824, was described by Pushkin in *The Bronze Horseman*.

[3]Herzen's italics.

[4]The order of Stanislas, originally a Polish order founded in the eighteenth century, had been assimilated into Russian orders by Nicholas I.

[5]The Third Section: the government office in charge of the "gendarmes," or political police.

[6]Allusion to Slavophil theories.

[7]Troitsa ... Butyrki: respectively southwest and north of Moscow in the nineteenth century—now part of the city.

[8]White bread, in the shape of a pretzel.

[9]Or rather the *Moscow Citizen*: a journal (1841–56), founded by Pogodin, of official, conservative tendencies.

[10]The second class of the Stanislas order was worn round the neck.

[11]The Vladimir order had been founded by Catherine II and rewarded soldiers, artists, commoners, and civil servants.   The second class insignia was worn round the neck.

[12]Allusion to the Kazan Cathedral, inspired by St. Peter's in Rome.

[13]Ivan Alexandrovich Khlestakov, the "Inspector General" in Gogol's comedy.

[14]Head of the Persian Embassy to Russia in 1829, after the death in Persia of the Russian ambassador, the writer Griboedov.

[15]In 1812 General Wittgenstein was in command of the army corps that protected Petersburg.

[16]N. A. Polevoy published the *Moscow Telegraph*, which was closed by the government in 1834.   Polevoy later supported government policy.

[17]A Prussian baron, active in the French Revolution, and one of the founders of the cult of the goddess Reason.   Guillotined in 1794.

[18]Moscow suburbs in the nineteenth century, the scene of traditional merrymaking in the spring.

[19]Allusion to Brullov's picture "The Last Days of Pompeii."

[20]Biron (1690–1772): the favorite of Anna Ioannovna; he gave the Russian language the word "Bironovshchina," perpetuating his reputation for cruelty and oppression.

[21]Anna Ioannovna: Anna I, empress of Russia from 1730 to 1740; Anna Leopoldovna: regent from 1740 to 1741; Ioann Antonovich: an infant of one year, nominal emperor during his mother's regency in 1740–41, imprisoned and later killed by his guards; Elizaveta Petrovna: empress from 1741 to 1761; Ekaterina Alexeevna: Catherine II; Petr Fedorovich: Peter III, killed in 1762.

[22]The anathema on various enemies of Russia and the Russian faith, for example on the false Dimitry.

[23]The railway line between Petersburg and Moscow was opened in 1851.

191

ORTHODOXY, AUTOCRACY, NATIONALITY

S. S. Uvarov

> S. S. Uvarov was Minister of Public Education from 1833 to 1849, during the reign of Nicholas I. Although official opinion was mistrustful of the Slavophil ideology, the government thought it could find uses for some of its elements. Hence Uvarov's formula, "Orthodoxy, Autocracy, Nationality," the emphasis being, of course, on the central member of the "Trinity."

■ ■ ■ Amid the rapid decay of religious and civilian institutions in Europe and the universal spread of destructive notions, in view of the sad occurrences that surround us on all sides, it was necessary to fortify our Fatherland on the firm foundations which are the basis for the prosperity, the strength, and the life of the people; to find the principles that constitute the distinguishing character of Russia and belong to her exclusively; to gather into one whole the sacred remains of her native essence and cast on these the anchor of our salvation. Fortunately, Russia has kept a warm faith in the saving principles without which she cannot prosper, gain strength, or live.

Sincerely and deeply attached to the Church of his fathers, the Russian has, from the earliest times, looked upon it as the pledge of social and family happiness.

Without love for the faith of its ancestors, a people, just as an individual, is bound to perish. A Russian devoted to his country will no more consent to the loss of one of the tenets of our *Orthodoxy* than to the theft of one pearl from the crown of Monomakh.[1]

Autocracy constitutes the chief condition of the political existence of Russia. The Russian colossus stands on it as on the cornerstone of its greatness. This truth is felt by an overwhelming majority of Your Majesty's subjects: they feel it fully, though they are placed in various walks of life and differ in their education and in their relations to the government. The saving conviction that Russia lives and is preserved by the spirit of a strong, humane, enlightened autocracy must permeate public education and develop with it.

Besides these two national principles, there is a third, no less important, no less powerful: *nationality*. The question of nationality does not have the unity of the preceding one; but both take their origin from the same source and are linked on every page of the history of the Russian Empire. All the difficulty concerning nationality consists in harmonizing old and new conceptions; but nationality does not compel us to go back or

192

to stand still; it does not require immobility in ideas. The government system, as the human body, changes its aspect with time; features alter with years, but their character must not alter.

—"Report to the Emperor, 1843," *Khrestomatiya po istorii SSSR* (Moscow, 1953), Vol. II

NOTES: [1]The crown of Monomakh, supposedly a gift of Emperor Constantine to Vladimir Monomakh, is a crown, or rather headdress, of Oriental craftsmanship of the fourteenth century, which served as coronation crown until 1724. It is of gold filigree work, topped with a cross and edged with sable.

■ ■ ■

MOSCOW IN THE FORTIES

A. I. Herzen

■ ■ ■ On my return from Novgorod to Moscow, I found both camps ready for battle. The Slavs were in full fighting array, with their light cavalry under the command of Khomyakov,[1] with the extraordinarily heavy infantry of Shevyrev and Pogodin,[2] with their skirmishers, their auxiliaries, their ultra-Jacobines who rejected everything later than the Kiev period and their moderate Girondines who rejected only the Petersburg period. They had their chairs at the University, their monthly review which appeared regularly with two months' delay but never failed to appear finally. With the main corps were to be found the orthodox Hegelians,[3] the Byzantine theologians, the mystical poets, a great number of women, and so on, and so on.

Our war kept the literary salons of Moscow extremely busy. Indeed, Moscow was then entering that era of intense intellectual interests when, politics being banned, literary questions become vital. The publication of a remarkable book was an event; criticisms and anticriticisms were read and commented upon with the same attention that, once upon a time, was accorded in France and England to parliamentary debates. The oppressed state of all other spheres of human activities threw the educated elements of society into the world of books and, indeed, there only, muffled and half-expressed, sounded a protest against the tyranny of Nicholas, the protest that was heard louder and more openly on the day after his death.

In Granovsky,[4] Moscow society hailed Western thought for its eagerness for liberty, for its struggle to gain intellectual independence.

193

With the Slavophils, it protested against that arrogance of the Petersburg government that insulted national feeling.

At this point I should make a reservation: in Moscow I knew two groups, two poles of its social life, and it is only of those that I can speak. At first I was immersed in the society of old men: officers of the Guards in Catherine's times, friends of my father, and other old men, his brother's friends, who had found a peaceful refuge in the shelter of the Senate. Later I knew only young Moscow: its literary and worldly circles—and it is of the latter I am writing. What vegetated or lived between the elders of pen and sword, who were awaiting a funeral fitting to their rank, and their sons and grandsons, who sought no rank and were busy with books and ideas, I neither knew nor cared. This intermediate sphere, the real "Nicholas" Russia, was colorless and vulgar—it lacked the Catherinian originality, the bravery and dash of the 1812 men, as well as our aspirations and interests. It was a pitiful, depressed generation, among whom struggled, stifled, and perished a few martyrs. When I speak of the Moscow parties and dinners, I speak of those in which Pushkin used to reign; where before our time the Dekabrists set the tone; where Griboedov laughed; where M. F. Orlov and A. P. Ermolov[5] found a friendly welcome because they were out of official favor; where, finally, Khomyakov would argue until four in the morning, having started talking at nine; where K. Aksakov,[6] wearing a murmolka,[7] raged in the defense of Moscow, although nobody attacked it; where Redkin logically demonstrated the existence of a personal God, ad majorem gloriam Hegelii; where Granovsky appeared with his quiet but firm speech; where everyone remembered Bakunin and Stankevich;[8] where Chaadaev, dressed with scrupulous care, with his delicate waxen face, angered the dazed aristocrats and the orthodox Slavophils by sharp remarks, set in an original mold and purposely iced; where the young-old man Turgenev[9] gossiped pleasantly about all the celebrities of Europe; where Botkin[10] and Kryukov pantheistically savored the stories of M. S. Shchepkin;[11] and on which, finally, sometimes fell Belinsky, like a Congreve rocket, burning all that happened to be in the vicinity. . . .

Nicholas died; a new life brought the Slavophils and ourselves beyond the limits of our disputes; we held out our hands to them, but where are they now?—Gone! . . .

The Kireevsky brothers, [12] Khomyakov, Aksakov have done their work; whether their lives were long or short, they could tell themselves in full consciousness as they closed their eyes that they had accomplished what they wanted to do; and though they had been unable to halt the "feldjäger" troika started by Peter, in which Biron sat beating the coachman to make him gallop across the fields and crush the people, at least they had halted runaway public opinion and caused every serious-minded person to stop and think.

With them begins the break in Russian thought. And when *we* say this, we can hardly be suspected of partiality.

194

Yes, we were enemies, but most strange ones: we loved the same thing, but not in the same way.

Both they and we had received into our hearts, from our early years, a strong, instinctive, physiological, passionate feeling, which for them was a memory, for us a prophecy: the feeling of boundless, all-absorbing love for the Russian people. And, like Janus or the two-headed eagle, we looked in opposite directions while our heart was one.

They transferred all their love, all their tenderness to their oppressed mother. For us, educated outside our home, this link had weakened. We were in the hands of a French governess. We only learnt later that our mother was not this French person, but a downtrodden peasant woman; and this we guessed by ourselves because of the resemblance in our features and also because her songs were dearer to us than vaudeville. We then felt a strong love for her, but her life was too restricted for us. We stifled in her little room: nothing but darkened faces gazing from silver frames, priests and parish clerics who frightened the unhappy woman already oppressed by soldiers and scribes. Her eternal lament for lost happiness tore at our heart; we knew that she had no bright memories, but we also knew that her happiness lay in the future, that in her bosom pulsed the germ of a new life, the life of our younger brother, to whom we would yield our birthright without asking for a mess of pottage in return. But for the time being:

> Mutter, Mutter, lass mich gehen,
> Schweifen auf den wilden Höhen![13]

Such was our family quarrel about fifteen years ago. Much water has since flowed under the bridge. Time, history, experience have brought us closer, not because we have joined them or they us, but because both they and we are now nearer genuine understanding than when we were pitilessly tormenting one another in journal articles, though I do not recall that even then we doubted their ardent love for Russia, or they ours.

Because of this mutual faith, of this common love, we too have a right to salute their graves and throw our handful of earth on their dead, with the sacred wish that on their tombs, on our tombs, may, strong and unconfined, flourish young Russia.

—*Sochineniya* (Moscow, 1956), Vol. V

NOTES: [1]A. Khomyakov (1804–60) is often called the father of Russian lay theology.
[2]Shevyrev was a professor at Moscow University; Pogodin, the editor of the *Moscow Citizen* (the *Muscovite*).
[3]Hegel's philosophy of history and his *Logic* were made popular by Redkin, professor of law at Moscow University, who published a summary of Hegel's *Logic* in the *Muscovite*, and also by the brilliant history professor Kryukov.

[4]Granovsky was professor of history at Moscow University from 1839 to 1855. A Westernizer, he attacked Pogodin and even the government. Dostoevsky has unkindly and unfairly caricatured him in *The Demons* as Stepan Verkhovensky.

[5]Orlov, a Dekabrist sympathizer; General Ermolov, famous for his campaigns in the Caucasus.

[6]Konstantin Aksakov, son of the writer S. T. Aksakov, himself a writer and active Slavophil.

[7]The murmolka was the traditional Russian headdress for men that went out of fashion in the early eighteenth century; some Slavophils attempted to revive the style.

[8]Stankevich, who died at the age of 27, was the heart and mind of a group which counted Bakunin and Belinsky among its members.

[9]This is *not* the novelist, but a historian and archaeologist.

[10]A member of the group around Belinsky and Bakunin.

[11]M. S. Shchepkin (1788–1863), a famous actor, born a serf.

[12]The Kireevsky brothers, Peter (1808–56) and Ivan (1806–56). The first was a distinguished collector and student of folklore; the second, a philosopher, friend of Odoevsky whose article in the *European* (1832) is one of the first expressions of Slavophilism.

[13]Schiller, "The Alpine Hunter" (1804).

■ ■ ■

A REBUKE TO SLAVOPHILS

P. Ya. Chaadaev

Once again, two years before his death, Chaadaev expressed his philosophy of Russian history. This time, he used the Crimean War as the occasion to attack the national arrogance and Messianism of the Slavophils.

■ ■ ■ No, a thousand times no, it was not thus that we loved our country in our youth. We desired its well-being, we wanted it to acquire good institutions, sometimes we even went so far as to wish that it might have, if at all possible, a little more liberty. We knew it was great, mighty, full of promise; but we did not believe it to be the most powerful and fortunate country in the world. We were far from imagining that Russia represented some mysterious abstract principle containing the final solution to the social problem; that it formed a separate world by itself, the direct and legitimate heir to the glorious Eastern Empire and to all its claims and virtues; that its special mission was to absorb all the Slav peoples into its bosom in order thus to accomplish the regeneration of mankind. Above all, we did not think that Europe was ready to collapse into

196

barbarity and that our task was to save civilization with the remnants of the very civilization that once had served to rouse us from our ancient torpor. We treated Europe politely, even respectfully, for we knew that it had taught us many things, among others our own history. When by chance we defeated it, as did Peter the Great,[1] we said: "This, gentlemen, we owe to you." And thus, one fine day, we reached Paris, which made us welcome, as you know, forgetting for a time that at bottom we were young upstarts and that we had contributed nothing yet to the common fund of nations, not even a poor little solar system like the Poles, our subjects; not even a wretched algebra like the Arabs, those infidels whose absurd and barbarous religion we are now fighting. We were made welcome because we were found to have good manners, because we were polite and unassuming, as befits a newcomer whose only claim upon public regard is a well-set-up figure. You have changed all that; very well; but, I beg of you, let me love my country as did Peter the Great, Catherine, and Alexander. The time is not far, I hope, when such patriotism may be found to be as deserving as another.

Observe that any government, apart from its own particular orientation, possesses the instincts proper to its nature as an animate and intelligent force created to live and act. For instance, it feels, or does not feel, supported by its subjects. Now, the Russian government in this case knew itself to be in perfect agreement with the general wishes of the country; hence, to a great extent, the fatal thoughtlessness of its politics in the present crisis. Who is unaware that the so-called national reaction has reached a point of actual monomania among our new doctors? There was no question, as earlier, of the prosperity of the country, or of civilization, or of any progress whatever; it was enough to be Russian: this name alone contained all imaginable blessings, salvation included. All sorts of wonderful elements unknown to the rest of the universe were allegedly to be discovered in the depths of our rich nature; all the serious and fruitful ideas that Europe had taught us were repudiated; an attempt was made to institute on the soil of Russia a whole new moral order that relegated us to some strange Christian Orient, invented for our particular use, without our suspecting in the least that by isolating ourselves morally from the peoples of Europe we were also isolating ourselves politically, that once our fraternity with the great European family was broken, none of those peoples would hold out their hand in the hour of danger. Finally, the most valiant among the partisans of the new national school did not hesitate to welcome the conflict in which we found ourselves engaged as the fulfillment of their backward-looking utopias, the dawn of our return to the tutelar regime renounced by our fathers in the person of Peter the Great. Too ignorant, too frivolous to appreciate or even to decipher these learned hallucinations, the government, I know, did not approve them; sometimes it even delivered at random a brutal kick to the most forward or the least careful of the blessed cohort; but nevertheless it was convinced

197

that, on the day when it would fling its glove at the impious and decadent West, the sympathies of all the new patriots who take their incompleted studies, their inarticulate wishes, for the real national policy, would not fail them any more than would the docile support of the populace, the latter being the constant accomplice of all patriotic dreams expressed in the banal idiom used in such circumstances. And this is how, one fine day, the vanguard of Europe found itself in the Crimea.

—"Letter to an Unknown Correspondent, 1854," *Sochineniya i pisma P. Ya. Chaadaeva*, ed. Gershenzon (Moscow, 1913)

NOTES: [1]Allusion to the victory of Poltava over Charles XII's Swedes in 1709.

■ ■ ■

THE YOUNGER GENERATION IN THE SIXTIES
S. V. Kovalevskaya

Sophia Vasilevna Kovalevskaya (1850–91) was the daughter of General Korvin-Krukovsky. Among the friends of the family were some of the most cultured and interesting personalities of the time: the surgeon and educator N. I. Pirogov, the editor of the *Readers' Library* and Professor of Arabic Literature O. I. Senkovsky, and others. In 1868, Sophia Korvin-Krukovskaya married the paleontologist V. O. Kovalevsky. This was a fictive marriage, such as many girls entered into in order to be free of parental authority. S. Kovalevskaya left Russia in 1869 to study in European universities. She became a well-known mathematician and taught at the University of Stockholm. Her sister Anna (the Anyuta of this text) wrote for Dostoevsky's journal the *Epoch*, was admired by Dostoevsky, and later married a French socialist. Sophia's "Reminiscences of Childhood," written in 1889, were first published in the *Messenger of Europe* in 1890.

198

■ ■ ■ We can say that during the period from the early eighteen-sixties to the early seventies all the educated circles of Russian society were concerned with one question only: the rift between old and young. An inquiry about any family of the nobility at that time would always receive the same answer: the parents had quarreled with their children. And these quarrels did not arise from any concrete, material reasons; the causes were purely theoretical and abstract. "They disagreed in their views," that was all. But it was enough to make the children leave their parents and the parents renounce their children.

The children, especially the girls, were stricken then by a kind of epidemic: running away from home. Our immediate vicinity had as yet been spared, all was quiet; but rumors were already spreading from other localities: such or such a squire's daughter had run away—this one abroad, to study, another to Petersburg, to the "nihilists."

The chief scare of all the parents and tutors in our neighborhood was a certain mythical commune, which apparently had been set up in Petersburg.[1] All the young girls who wished to leave their homes were, so people asserted, being recruited into this commune, where young people of both sexes lived in complete communism. There were no servants; the young ladies of the nobility scrubbed floors and cleaned samovars with their own hands. Of course, none of those who spread the rumors had ever set foot in that commune. Where it was situated and how it managed to exist in Petersburg under the very nose of the police, nobody knew exactly, but nevertheless its existence was never doubted.

Soon symptoms of the times began to appear in the immediate vicinity of our home. The parish priest, Father Philip, had a son who until then had always gladdened his parents' hearts by his good behavior and obedience. All of a sudden, after graduating from the seminary with the highest honors, this exemplary youth inexplicably turned into a rebellious son and categorically refused to enter orders, though a lucrative parish was his for the asking. His Lordship the Bishop himself had summoned him and besought him not to leave the bosom of the Church, hinting clearly that he only needed to express a wish and he would be appointed parish priest in the village of Ivanovo (one of the richest in the province). Of course, in that case, he would be expected first to marry one of the former incumbent's daughters, since it is a long-established tradition that a parish serves as dowry for one of the late pastor's daughters. But even this attractive prospect failed to tempt our young *popovich*.[2] He preferred to go to Petersburg, enroll in the University on his own, and condemn himself to tea and dry bread for the four years of his studies.

Poor Father Philip grieved over his son's unreasonableness, but he might have taken comfort if the boy had enrolled in law school, this being, as everyone knows, the best "money-maker." Instead, his son enrolled in the natural sciences, and during the very first holidays he started to pour out such nonsense about men coming from monkeys and about Professor Sechenov[3] proving that there was no soul, but only reflexes, that the poor stunned batiushka grabbed a holy-water sprinkler and began to swing it at his son.

199

In former years, when the young popovich had returned home on vacation from the seminary, he had never failed to come and offer his congratulations on all our family celebrations. At our party dinners he sat at the lower end of the table, as befitted a young man of his condition, heartily tucking-in the name-day pie, but not mixing in the conversation.

This summer, at the first name day to be celebrated after his arrival, the popovich was conspicuous for his absence. However, one fine day he appeared unexpectedly at our house, and on being asked by the servant what his business was, replied that he had come to pay a visit to the general.

My father was already sick of hearing about the "nihilist" popovich; he had not failed to observe his absence on his name day, though of course he had in no way betrayed his awareness of such an insignificant circumstance. Now he was indignant at the young upstart's daring to come on a casual visit, as an equal, and he decided to teach him a lesson. So he ordered the servant to tell him that "the general received business callers and applicants for favors only in the morning, before one o'clock."

Faithful Ilya, who always caught his master's slightest hint, delivered his message in the exact spirit in which it had been given. But the popovich did not show the least confusion and took his leave, remarking in a nonchalant tone: "Tell your master that I'll never set foot in his house again." Ilya delivered this message also, and you can imagine the scandal that the young fellow's impertinence caused in our house and in the whole neighborhood.

But the most amazing was when Anyuta heard about the incident, she ran to Father's study and exclaimed, breathless and flushed with emotion: "Why, Papa, did you insult Alexey Philippovich? It's dreadful and despicable of you to insult an honorable man in this fashion."

Papa looked at her in stupefaction. His surprise was so great that at first he could find no words to answer the insolent girl. However, Anyuta's courage had already collapsed and she ran off to her room as fast as she could. . . .

Anyuta expressed her protest against the insult the young popovich had suffered by meeting him whenever she could, either at neighbors' houses or on her walks.

Our coachman Stepan told in the servants' hall how he had seen with his own eyes the young lady strolling in the woods with the popovich. "That was a real funny sight. Our baryshnya walking without a word, her eyes on the ground, playing with her sunshade. And he striding along beside her on his long shanks, for all the world like a spindly crane. There he was, spouting away, waving his hands; or else he'd grab a ragged book out of his pocket and start reading out loud like a teacher in school."

It must be admitted that the young popovich bore little likeness to the fairy-tale prince or medieval knight that Anyuta used to dream of.

His awkward lanky figure, long scrawny neck, and pale countenance framed by thin sandy hair, his big red hands with flat nails which were not always immaculately clean, but chiefly his unpleasant vulgar pronunciation which clearly revealed his clergy origin and his seminary education, all this could not make a very glamorous hero of him in the eyes of a girl with aristocratic habits and tastes. It was difficult to suspect any romantic grounds for Anyuta's interest. Obviously the reason lay elsewhere. . . .

Indeed, the young man's chief prestige in Anyuta's eyes was the fact that he had just arrived from Petersburg and brought back the very latest ideas. Moreover, he had even had the happiness to see with his own eyes—from a distance, it was true—many of those great men whom the younger generation then venerated. That was quite sufficient to make the young man himself interesting and attractive. But besides, Anyuta could, through him, obtain various books otherwise not available to her. At home we received only the most dignified and staid publications: the *Revue des Deux Mondes* and the *Athenaeum* among foreign journals, the *Russian Messenger*⁴ among Russian ones. As a great concession to the spirit of the times, my father had that year consented to subscribe to Dostoevsky's *Epoch*. But Anyuta now got journals of another calibre from the young popovich: the *Contemporary*,⁵ the *Russian Word*, each number of which was an event for the youth of that time. Once he even brought her a number of the illegal *Bell*.⁶

—*Vospominaniya i pisma* (Moscow, 1951)

NOTES: ¹This commune existed: it was the Znamenskaya Commune, founded by the writer Sleptsov.

²Priest's son.

³Sechenov (1829–1905), physiologist; author of several scientific works, among them *Reflexes of the Brain* (1863). His wife's first fictive marriage with a certain Bokov and the life of the trio Bokov-Bokova-Sechenov may have inspired Chernyshevsky's famous novel *What To Do?*, though it is more likely, according to recent Soviet research (*Oktyabr*, November 1959), that the members of another such trio (Mikhailov-Shelgunov-Shelgunova) were its prototypes.

⁴A conservative journal founded by Katkov in 1856. Turgenev's *Fathers and Sons*, Tolstoy's *War and Peace*, and other novels were published in it.

⁵Journal founded by Pushkin in 1836. In the fifties and sixties it became the organ of the young radical generation. Closed by government order in 1866.

⁶Herzen's journal, published in London and Geneva from 1857 to 1868. It was widely, though clandestinely, read in Russia.

201

ARREST OF A PROPAGANDIST Painting (1880–89) by I. E. Repin
From an album of reproductions of paintings in the Tretyakov gallery, Moscow

POPULISM IN THE SEVENTIES

V. G. Korolenko

During his studies, first at the Technological Institute in Petersburg, then at the Agricultural and Forestry School in Moscow, V. G. Korolenko (1853–1921) began to take an interest in populist ideologies and activities. As a result, he spent many years in forced residence in northeast Russia and Siberia. In addition to numerous essays and articles on conditions in the Russia of his time, Korolenko wrote many charming or moving stories and novels. From 1905 to 1919, he wrote *The History of My Contemporary*, which comes close to being an autobiography.

■ ■ ■ One day Grigorev[1] gave me a number of an illegal newspaper published abroad (the *Tocsin*,[2] I believe), with an article by Tkachev.[3] Tkachev was a rather well-known writer, who had contributed to the *Cause*[4] and had emigrated after the Nechaev trial, in which he had been implicated with his common-law wife, Dementeva. They had both occupied a particular position in the Nechaev[5] trial, and there were many discussions about them and also about common-law marriage. Tkachev's article, which Grigorev now gave me to read, was polemical, directed against Lavrov,[6] who, after escaping abroad from his place of banishment in the Vologda province, had founded the periodical *Forward*. I knew of Lavrov from his "Historical Letters," printed in the *Week*[7] and later published separately in a book which had been taken out of circulation because of censorship. (In our unofficial library, it had been sewn together from the *Week*.) Tkachev joined issues with Lavrov, whose program called on youth to "go to the people" for the propagation of Socialist ideas. Besides, he demanded that the propagandists should undergo a preliminary intellectual preparation which required considerable labor and time. Tkachev considered this superfluous. His point of view was different. Like Lavrov, he urged going to the people, but moved by a revolutionary impulse, he urged the preaching of immediate rebellion. In the center of his article, written with great beauty and passion, he placed the image of the suffering people martyred on the cross. And so, he wrote, it is suggested that we study chemistry in order to investigate the composition of the cross, botany in order to determine the nature of the wood, and anatomy to find out what tissues are damaged by the nails. No, we are in no condition to investigate. We are in the grips of one single passionate desire—to free the victim from the cross now, with no delay, with no preliminary useless research.

I quote from memory and cannot of course render Tkachev's passion. I remember that at first it was this very passion that impressed me. In such a tone, I felt, should a real revolutionary speak. Grigorev did not argue, but soon he gave me a copy of *Forward*, which carried Lavrov's program and one of his articles, "A Conversation of Logical People." I read the whole at one sitting and found myself completely conquered by the harmonious system of revolutionary populism. I had liked Tkachev's short article merely as a beautiful literary production. The program and articles in *Forward* immediately stirred thoughts and feelings then developing in the depths of my being as the result of all the spontaneous impressions received from life and literature.

I shall not expand on the subject of populism. It is easy now to sum up both the moral truth (though many nowadays incline to deny it) and the errors of that movement. Among its mistakes, the chief one was of course its naïve vision of the people (which then signified mainly the peasantry)—its vision of potential wisdom, which slumbered in the consciousness of the people and only awaited the definitive formula to manifest itself and crystallize all of life according to its pattern.

From the time of emancipation, the notion of the "people" had loomed extremely large in the thoughts of all Russian society. Like a cloud, it stretched on our horizon; we gazed at it, attempting to make out the shapes that swarmed in that dim mass, to distinguish or divine them. Various groups saw various things, but all gazed with interest and alarm, and all appealed to popular wisdom—not to speak of the Slavophils, in

203

whose philosophy the people occupied such an enormous place. Even Katkov[8] and the conservatives pointed to the "wisdom of the people" who, according to them, supported the foundations of the existing regime in full consciousness. For Dostoevsky, the people were "a God-bearer," while as late as the eighties Ivan Aksakov,[9] in his newspaper, liked to quote on various pretexts the aphorisms of the "dear little Russian muzhiks," even though those "dear little muzhiks" were in fact "fat purses," born in the peasant class but long since advanced to the condition of merchants. That did not matter. The mere fact of peasant origin gave a sort of patent for the possession of genuinely popular wisdom. In a story by Zlatovratsky[10] *(Hearts of Gold)*, we see an intellectual of peasant birth in the medical student Bashkirtsev. He is almost inarticulate, but everyone feels that he knows something that is outside the ken of the other seditious intellectuals and that, when the necessary moment comes for him to speak, he will utter some really new "word."

The comparison arises involuntarily between this hero of a rather feeble populist novel and Karataev in one of the greatest works of Russian literature, *War and Peace*. Karataev also is incapable of uttering a correct clause, but Pierre Bezukhov remembers his brief utterances all his life, striving to interpret them in some mysterious and almost mystical sense. This attitude toward the Karataev spirit was doubtless inherent to Tolstoy himself, and along with him to practically all the Russian critics who touched on *War and Peace*.

This is why the system of revolutionary populism so rapidly and completely conquered the minds of our generation. The life of a society has its forebodings. Indeed a cloud loomed on the horizon of our life after the emancipation. As yet, one could not see the lightning flashes or even hear remote thunderclaps, but its mysterious shadow already lay on all the objects of our still bright and sparkling life, and our eyes turned to it in spite of ourselves. Youth, the most impressionable and sensitive element of society, drew its conclusions.

Social injustice was a fact that stared you in the face. Those who suffered most from it were those whose labor was the hardest. And all, irrespective of tendencies, admitted that among those masses was maturing or had already matured a "word" that would solve all doubts.

This feeling was then widely diffused in the consciousness of Russian society, and from this our generation—which in the seventies was approaching the crossroads to careers—merely drew the most logical and honest conclusions. If the premises were correct, the conclusion was indeed clear: we should "renounce the old world,"[11] leave "the rejoicing, idly chattering, with hands stained in blood" to go where "rough hands toiled" and where, besides, was maturing some mysterious formula for a new life.

Was this naïve? Yes, but the naïvete was shared by the least romantic representatives of educated Russian society. Part of the legal literature, and all the illegal, drew from this the logical, most morally honest conclusions. And youth contributed its native enthusiasm. Revolutionary populism was ready. Old Lavrov and old Mikhailovsky[12] found clear formulas for the theory: "Oh, if I could sink," wrote Mikhailovsky in the seventies, "melt in this coarse grey mass of the people, sink without return, but keeping that torch of truth and ideal which I have managed to obtain at the expense of that very people! Oh, if all of you, my readers, made the same decision, especially those whose torch burns more brightly than mine. . . . What an illumination that would be, what a great historical celebration it would mark! None could be its equal in history."

This fiery tirade expresses the mood of all that generation and the whole theory of "going to the people" which the *Annals of the Fatherland*[13] developed in legal literature and *Forward* brought us illegally from abroad. Soon I was entirely in the grasp of the logic and harmony of this program, in which all the impressions life and literature had made upon me found their place. Populism gave our generation what the "thinking realists" of the preceding one had lacked: it gave faith in more than formulas, in more than abstractions. It gave our impulses a broad vital foundation.

Groups now met in Moscow and at the Academy and ardently discussed the Lavrov program. At that time, I enthusiastically discovered Mikhailovsky's articles and started to publicize them among my friends, showing them the direct link between his ideas and the subjects of our secret discussions. I had now found what I had vainly sought in Petersburg. How to live honorably and what to do were the themes of our simple and friendly talks during our secret gatherings. I no longer looked for the genuine "ideal" student. That elusive image had been replaced by the broader and more attractive image of the people, great and mysterious in its wisdom, the object of new aspirations and perhaps new illusions. At the same time, I had found much of what I had sought earlier in the student environment, but it had come to me more simply and in another guise.

—*Sobranie sochinenii* (Moscow, 1953), Vol. VII

NOTES: [1]A special friend of Korolenko's.

[2]A populist journal, founded by Tkachev and published in Geneva and London.

[3]P. N. Tkachev (1844–85) was arrested in 1869 for membership (with Nechaev) in a student revolutionary committee. He emigrated in 1873.

[4]A monthly published in Petersburg (1866–88).

[5]Nechaev became famous for his murder of the student Ivanov and his (or Bakunin's) *Catechism of a Revolutionary.*

[6]Lavrov (1823–1900) left Russia in 1869. His "Historical Letters" insist on the debt of the intelligentsia to the people.

[7]A liberal populist weekly.

[8]M. N. Katkov (1818–87) first contributed to the *Annals of the Fatherland*, later was the editor of the *Russian Messenger,* a liberal journal that became conservative in the early sixties.

[9]Ivan Aksakov, brother of Konstantin, wrote in several Slavophil papers, especially in *Moskva.*

[10]A minor Slavophil writer.

[11]A quotation from the "Workers' Marseillaise." The text was written by Lavrov and published in *Forward* in 1875. It was extremely popular in revolutionary circles in the eighties and nineties.

[12]N. K. Mikhailovsky (1842–1904), a liberal Populist, contributed to and later edited the *Annals of the Fatherland*; in 1892, he was editor of the *Russian Wealth,* which spoke against Marxist ideas.

[13]The *Annals of the Fatherland* was founded in 1818 and lasted until 1884. It had many ups and downs in the course of its long career. The writers Nekrasov and Saltykov became its co-editors in 1868.

■ ■ ■

A BRIEF HISTORY OF RUSSIA, 1147-1881

■ ■ ■ Moscow's official eight-hundredth anniversary was celebrated in 1947. The first known mention of a settlement of that name occurred in 1147, when, according to a chronicle, the Suzdal Prince, Yury Dolgoruky, sent his ally the Prince of Novgorod-Seversky the following message: "Come to me, brother, in Moscow." A few years later, about 1156, the same Yury founded the fortified enclosure that was to become the Moscow Kreml'. This was only one of the several strongholds that Yury built on the western borders of his lands. Its site was conveniently located at the crossing of the river and land roads to the more important cities of Vladimir in the east, Ryazan in the south, and Smolensk and Novgorod in the west and north. Moscow was also easy to defend; the Kreml' hillock stood in a natural circle of forests and swampy rivers that as late as the eighteenth century remained a conspicuous feature of the region's landscape.

The situation in the Russian territories in the twelfth century was one of dispersion and anarchy. Kiev on the Dniepr river, the former center of power and unity, had declined during the past century. Its lands had crumbled into an infinity of family estates endemically at war against one another, and it had suffered repeated raids by Asiatic nomad tribes on the lower Dniepr—the trading road to Byzantium. As Kiev declined, new principalities grew in Galich, Smolensk, Suzdal, and elsewhere. In 1169 Andrey Bogoliubsky of Suzdal sacked Kiev and, assuming the title of grand-prince, set up a new capital in Vladimir. Even so, Kiev might have retained its significance as the symbol of Russian unity had it not been destroyed by the Mongol (Tatar) Batyi in 1240. Nor did the northern principalities escape: Suzdal became a Tatar dependency, as did most of the Russian lands in the thirteenth century. Protected by its situation and insignificance, Moscow suffered less than most central Russian settlements. However, neither by itself nor as a part of the Suzdal-Vladimir realm could it establish any *modus vivendi* with the conquerors until Alexander Nevsky, the former prince of Novgorod, after defeating the Swedes and Teutonic Knights who had been threatening Russia from the west, became grand-prince in 1252. With Alexander ruling in Vladimir, negotiations with the Tatars resulted in the transfer of executive functions from the conquerors to the Suzdal princes. Eventually this gave them the controlling power over their rival princes.

For some hundred years after the Tatar invasions, however, Novgorod remained the most powerful center of political, economic, and cultural life in Russia. Its near-independence from the Tatars as well as its trading links with Byzantium and the West made it the source from which culture and wealth flowed into the Russian lands and justified its title of "Lord Great Novgorod." Meanwhile, the princes of Suzdal, serving as trustees for the Tatar Horde (then settled on the lower Volga) and enjoying the support of the only group to be exempted from tribute, the Russian Church, were busy enlarging their domains and wealth at the expense of their neighbors. In 1328, nearly two hundred years after the first mention of Moscow, Ivan Kalita (the Moneybag) moved his residence from Vladimir to Moscow; about the same time the seat of the Metropolitan was transferred; thus Moscow became a center of both material and spiritual power. The grand-princes of Moscow, as they now styled themselves, were soon strong enough to turn openly against the masters they had been "helping." The brilliant, if ephemeral, victory of Dimitry on the field of Kulikovo in 1380, after his enterprise had been blessed by the Church in the person of the respected hermit Sergy of Radonezh, gave Moscow a moral prestige equal to its increasing strength. From that time the "gatherers of the Russian lands" were on the way to becoming rulers of the Russian Orthodox realm. Their most serious rival, Novgorod, with its vast northern domain, was subjugated, ruined, and annexed in 1478, and its great bell, the symbol of its autonomy, was brought to Moscow to ring indistinguishably among Kreml' companions. In 1480, a century after the Kulikovo victory, the grand-prince Ivan III, not without hesitation, refused to pay homage to the Horde. Only the Crimean Tatars remained an annoyance during the next century, pushing as far as Moscow in their raids. The debris of the disintegrated Golden Horde, the Kazan and Astrakhan khanates, were respectively conquered and annexed in 1552 and 1556. The fall of Kazan is commemorated on Red Square by the Church of the Intercession (now known as Vasily the Blessed in memory of the "fool for Christ" who was buried there in the late sixteenth century).

After the middle of the sixteenth century, the Russians gradually moved into the "wild plain" of the south, pushing their military and agricultural advance on both sides of the Don, and preceded by independent adventurers or "Cossacks" as far as the North Caucasus and the river Ural. At the same time, other adventurers began the great march into Siberia.

In the west and north, however, other powers were threatening. At the end of the fifteenth century, the Lithuanian principality occupied extensive regions now making up most of the Ukraine, Belorussia, and part of western Russia. The southern part of this domain became Polish after the Polish-Lithuanian union of 1569. This union, though internally weakened by tensions between the Orthodox Lithuanians and the Catholic Poles, was engaged in nearly continuous hostilities with Russia from the sixteenth through the seventeenth centuries. The struggle over the Russian lands that formed a great part of Lithuania and the mutual fear and distrust between "Latin" and Orthodox powers were the main reasons for those wars. The dynastic crisis that resulted from the ending of the Rurik line in 1598 degenerated into civil war and was exploited by the Poles, who, supported by some of the Russian aristocracy, had hoped to turn Muscovy into a Polish-ruled kingdom. After the end of the Time of Troubles in 1613 and the ascension to the throne of the Romanovs, the Polish-Lithuanian threat gradually disappeared and Poland was forced onto the defensive in the Ukraine. In 1654, when the Cossacks of the Ukraine transferred their allegiance to Moscow, the balance of power shifted to the Russian side, and the old capital city of Kiev became part of the Russian realm.

With another enemy in the west, Sweden, the bone of contention was the possession of the Baltic regions which changed hands several times before finally becoming Russian under Peter the Great in the eighteenth century. This paved the way for the safe opening of relations with the West through the Baltic Sea.

In their wars against western neighbors for the possession of the border lands, the Moscow princes were strengthened by the feeling that they alone were the rightful heirs not only to all the country formerly governed by Kiev rulers, but also, through them, to Byzantium and Rome. The fall of Constantinople in 1453 had been seen by Russian Churchmen as the deserved retribution for the impiety of attempting union with the Papacy in 1439. In their view subjection to the Turks defiled the Greek Patriarchate. During the uncertain period that followed, the Moscow Metropolitans no longer were confirmed by Constantinople, and the Russian Church became, in fact, autocephalous. Its complete independence was consecrated in 1589, when the head of the Russian Church was raised to Patriarchal dignity. Forty-two years earlier, in 1547, Ivan IV had been crowned Tsar. His grandfather, Ivan III, after marrying the niece of the last Byzantine emperor in 1472, had adopted the two-headed Byzantine eagle as the arms of the Russian State. Muscovy, therefore, now had both a Caesar and a Patriarch: it was the true heir to the Eastern Roman Empire.

This final achievement was also a triumph for the Church-State alliance party within the Church itself over those members of the

209

clergy who, during the sixteenth century, supported the principle of the purity of the Church by renouncement of social and political power. However, the victory of the Church-State party was later to mean defeat for the Church as a whole: in the collaboration between Tsar and Patriarch, the former was to prove the stronger partner who would ultimately reduce the Church to the status of a Department of Civil Service. This, however, did not happen until a tsar came to power who no longer felt in his own person a deep communion with the Orthodox faith: Peter the Great.

As powerful landowners and councillors to the tsars, church dignitaries were part of the system that ruled Muscovy. The princes of Moscow, as we have seen, were only one branch of the Rurik family. In the fifteenth century many descendants of other ruling branches subjugated by Moscow were still alive. With cadets of the Moscow house, Lithuanian or Tatar princes who had accepted Moscow suzerainty, and boyars whose ancestors had fought in the Kiev princes' *druzhina* (band of warriors), they formed the aristocracy of the land. Their links to the Moscow princes were more personal than territorial and were not felt to be binding, but such relations could not long remain satisfactory. As in western Europe, the ruler needed the support of a class entirely dependent upon his favors. In the West, this class was the bourgeoisie. In Russia, it took the form of a service nobility created by the tsars through the distribution of lands and offices to military men. The lands were granted on tenure and at first were not hereditary. The new nobles were known as *dvoryane* from the word *dvor*, enclosure, manor, court, and—in their capacity as landowners— as *pomeshchiki*, from *pomeste*, landed estate, in opposition to the *votchina* or patrimonial domain of the old aristocracy. In a series of bloody purges during the reign of Ivan the Terrible, the old aristocracy lost most of its power, and though it tried to regain it during the Time of Troubles and later the attempts were finally defeated. The Boyar Council, the governing organ which traditionally deliberated with the tsar on his decisions, had to admit members of the new nobility into its ranks. By the end of the seventeenth century, it had become essentially passive, and the title of boyar could now be granted by the tsar, thus making boyars merely the highest-ranking members of a subordinate class.

The growing complexity of the Moscow administration necessitated the creation of government offices headed by boyars and secretaries and staffed by numerous scribes. This system, which reached its height in the second half of the seventeenth century, marked one more stage in the evolution of Muscovy to a bureaucratic absolute monarchy.

210

A Land Assembly, composed of delegates from various classes and regions, was first called by Ivan IV. For more than a century these assemblies, in which the new nobility formed a majority, served as instruments of the tsars' policy against the oligarchic claims of the boyars. They also helped to codify the condition of the mass of the working population, the peasantry. The first Land Assembly in 1550 modernized the 1497 Code of Ivan III; one of the last, in 1648–49, adopted a new Code. The 1497 Code had allowed a peasant two weeks a year in which, if he wished, he could change from one lord to another; that of 1649 forbade all such moves: thus, the process of emancipating the peasant which marked western European history was reversed in Russia.

Old Moscow, like Kiev, had a peasantry composed of slaves and free men, with an intermediate floating group of half slaves, free men who sold themselves into limited or life bondage for financial reasons or to evade military obligations. The free peasants, however, found it increasingly difficult to preserve their liberty. Moscow's continual territorial expansion, frequently into empty or sparsely settled areas, proceeded at a more rapid rate than the over-all population growth. This gave rise to a continuing flux and scarcity of agricultural laborers and resulted in the adoption of stabilizing measures by both landowners and government. When heavy taxes (often more than 50 per cent) did not prompt a farmer to flee his village into the "wild field," they plunged him into debt to his landlord. As the practice of granting lands to the new service nobility class did away with the old free lands, by the end of the sixteenth century most of the peasants were reduced to the condition of serfs, tied to their lord, if not to the land. Meanwhile, the service noble's tenure gradually became freehold hereditary possession. Time, then, intensified the peasant's dependence, and when slavery was finally abolished by Peter the Great, its disappearance meant little, for instead of a minority of slaves, nonproductive in regard to military service and taxes, the government and nobility acquired an immense force of taxable and draftable serfs. The eighteenth century only worsened the peasant's lot: by the end of it a peasant could be legally sold, with or without his family, sent off to other regions, beaten, tortured, or even killed by his owner. Although the crown peasants were slightly better off, they were perpetually in danger of being given away to the favorites of the moment. No wonder then that the seventeenth and eighteenth centuries were marked by repeated uprisings both in the cities, plagued by overtaxation and starvation, and in the villages. The two most famous, a hundred years apart, were headed by Stepan Razin and Pugachev.

By the end of the seventeenth century the idea of absolute monarchy had triumphed, but the tsar ruled over classes profoundly divided and hostile to each other. The unity of Muscovy was kept intact by the common faith that linked its people and by the desperate struggles for survival that had for previous years engrossed the nation.

Moscow succeeded Kiev; in turn, Moscow was replaced by St. Petersburg, founded in 1703 and proclaimed the capital in 1713. The reign of Peter I, known as the Great, seemed to open a road leading to unlimited progress. The title of tsar was officially changed to that of emperor in 1721, symbolizing the emergence of Russia as a modern European power. During this year the twenty-one-year-old war with Sweden was concluded and the eastern shores of the Baltic were annexed, opening an ice-free sea in the north to Russia.

The victories over powerful Sweden were won by a totally transformed army in which the old system of territorial militia under a complex seniority command had been replaced by compulsory service, modern equipment, and a policy of liberalized promotion. The Russian army of the eighteenth century conquered two-thirds of Poland for Russia, restoring to it Belorussia and adding Lithuania and Courland. It also dislodged the Turks from the northern shore of the Black Sea, where Odessa was founded in 1796. Access to the two seas was aided by the creation of a fleet, Peter's most cherished and perhaps most lasting achievement.

Peter's military and naval innovations and the wars he waged conditioned all his other activities. The nearly intolerable drain on the country's resources—almost two-thirds of the budget—demanded still heavier taxes, the burden of which fell chiefly on the peasants. The effort required to assimilate new knowledge and techniques in so short a time demanded the harnessing of all the forces of the country to the efficient service of the state. In Peter's mind, each class was to have its own compulsory task. The nobility served in the army and administration, which were strictly divided into parallel ranks by the "Table" of 1722. The peasants served the nobility. The merchants, also organized, served the material needs of the nation. Its spiritual needs were looked after by the clergy, which, however, Peter took care to place under state supervision by abolishing the Patriarchate in 1721 and instituting a Synod under a government officer. The total submission of the clergy to state control was to be achieved with the secularization of church lands in 1764. The administration of the country was put in the hands of collegial assemblies and boards functioning under a supreme Senate.

212

The structure was, in theory, complete and imposing. In fact, however, it was haphazardly constructed and expensive to maintain. At Peter's death the country was exhausted; its population had been reduced by nearly 20 per cent. To the existing hostility between privileged and nonprivileged groups were added the germs of mutual incomprehension and ignorance. Costume, language, beliefs, the whole concept of life now separated the Europeanized nobility from the rest of the country. Moreover, the sole justification for Peter's harshly regulated system—that of universal service to the state—was to disappear when on February 18, 1762, the nobility was freed from its obligations. A corresponding step in favor of the peasants would be taken on February 19, but ninety-nine years later.

In Russia as elsewhere, the eighteenth century was the epoch of women in power. A succession of palace conspiracies placed them on the imperial throne. The concept of legitimacy of rule, so important in an absolute, God-consecrated autocracy, was thus offended and confused, and impostors who had plagued Russia during the Time of Troubles reappeared and found a ready following among the oppressed peasantry.

One of the few sensible acts of Catherine II's son Paul was the institution of succession by direct descent from male to male. This tardy law, though it did not prevent the assassination of Paul himself, ensured an orderly succession of emperors during the nineteenth century. The descendants of Peter III and Catherine II, respectively three-quarters and one hundred per cent German, were called Romanovs only by convention. (Paul was presumably Peter's son, though the presumption is open to some doubt.) The reigns of Paul I, Alexander I, and Nicholas I, who followed each other from 1796 to 1855, can in fact be referred to as Prussian in more than just the physical sense. Military drill, omnipresent uniforms, the State's interference in all aspects of the subjects' lives (even to regulating the shape of their hats and the trimming of their whiskers), its claim to the directing of their very thoughts—such were the features of the times, as they had been under Peter. But the idea of all-embracing control, perhaps necessary at an earlier time, paralyzed the country. At first a facade of European prestige concealed the deadening process. Under Alexander I, Russia broke Napoleon's power and emerged as the liberator and arbiter of Europe—a role which, under Nicholas I, dwindled to that of gendarme. The crushing of the Polish rebellions did nothing to brighten the face Russia presented to the world. Under Nicholas' "knoutocratic" reign, a pall of oppressive boredom and fear lay over the nation. The

213

breadth and grandeur of Petersburg had for a time symbolized the expansion of Russian might, its break with the old closed-in Muscovy. Now the "Northern Palmyra" had become a huge barracks, and the Petersburg culture, which had shone for a century, sank into faceless and soulless officialdom.

Nicholas' reign closed with the disaster of the Crimean War. The social and political distress of the country could no longer be ignored. Since the beginning of the century, half-hearted measures had somewhat eased the serfs' condition. They could no longer be advertised for sale along with a parrot "able to speak Russian correctly" or a cow; the amount of work they were required to perform for a landlord was regulated; and they could be sold only with the land they tilled. Nevertheless they remained in bondage: forty-seven millions of them.

On February 19, 1861, after several years of preparatory work, the government of Alexander II emancipated the serfs. The reform was a compromise: personal liberty was granted, the peasants received free possession of their house and enclosure, but the land they had held under their landlords was transferred not to individual owners, but to the rural community, which remained collectively responsible for the instalments and the taxes due by its members. Nor were the peasants legally assimilated into the rest of the population. The emancipation satisfied no one: the landed nobility, on the whole, was impoverished; the peasants, frequently land-starved, remained on tenure, still underprivileged members of society.

Other social reforms were more successful, especially the judicial and administrative transformations, the latter instituting, under the name of *zemstvo*, the principle of self-government at the district and provincial levels. However, social reform alone was no longer sufficient. Even though autocratic rule might introduce long overdue changes, the principle of autocracy itself came under attack. In December 1825, for the first time, members of the class created by the Muscovite autocrats for their support rose to demand not new privileges, but a constitution. The rebellion was crushed, the Decembrists were hanged or sent to Siberia, and the mass of the population, which had not understood or had not sympathized, settled back into apathy. In the latter half of the century conditions were different; a revolutionary Russia made up of an intelligentsia of students and writers and of the first proletarians would no longer be satisfied with the gracious or grudging gifts of official liberalism. Terroristic acts multiplied, and on March 1, 1881, after several unsuccessful attempts, Alexander II was killed by a bomb. Before leaving his palace for the fatal drive, he had signed a rescript announcing the granting of a constitution.

Although the year 1881, four centuries after the refusal to pay homage to the Tatars that had established Russian independence, did not mark the final break between government and nation, Alexander II, the first emperor to grant a degree of liberty to the people of Russia, was also the first to fall victim to a plot, several of whose participants belonged to the people. His proposed constitution, timid as it was, was abandoned, and reactionary policies were adopted, policies that eventually helped to bring about the destruction of the regime.

CHRONOLOGICAL TABLES

■ ■ ■ FIFTEENTH CENTURY

1415–32		"The Mystical Lamb" (Van Eyck brothers)
1422–27	"The Trinity Icon," by Rublev, Russia's greatest icon painter	
1440	(*circa*)	First printing press in western Europe
1453		**Fall of Constantinople to the Turks**
1462–1515	**Reign of Ivan III**	
1472	Ivan III marries Zoe Paleologue, niece of the last Byzantine emperor	Height of Venice's power (second part of the fifteenth century)
1475–79	The Italian Fioravanti builds the new Church of the Assumption in the Kreml'	
1478	Novgorod falls to Moscow	"Spring" (Botticelli)
1482–1508	Italian and Russian architects build churches, palaces, and walls of the Kreml'	
1492–1504		Columbus' discoveries
1497	The Sudebnik (Code) of Ivan III	

■ ■ ■

■ ■ ■ SIXTEENTH CENTURY

1503	A Church council condemns the "Hermit" or non-worldly party	
1508–12		Frescoes of the Vatican (Raphael) and Sistine Chapel (Michelangelo)
1513		*The Prince* (Machiavelli)
1531		Henry VIII proclaims himself head of the Anglican Church
1532	Church of the Ascension in Kolomenskoe — first important brick and stone adaptation of wooden "pyramid" churches	
1533–84	**Reign of Ivan IV, "the Terrible"**	

217

1536–41		*The Institutes of Christian Religion* (Calvin)
1540		Foundation of the Society of Jesus
1545–63		Council of Trent
1546		Death of Luther
1547	**Ivan IV crowned Tsar**	
1551	Council of the Hundred Chapters (Stoglav) on the Faith	
1553	Richard Chancellor arrives in Russia by the White Sea	
1555–59	Building of the Church of the Intercession (Vasily the Blessed) to commemorate the taking of Kazan (1552)	
1562–98		Religious wars in France
1564	Publication of first book known to be printed in Moscow *(The Acts of the Apostles)*	
1581	Beginning of penetration into Siberia	
1589	The Moscow Metropolitan becomes Patriarch	
1598	**End of the Rurik line. Election of Boris Godunov**	

■ ■ ■

■ ■ ■ SEVENTEENTH CENTURY

1605–13	Time of Troubles	First part of *Don Quixote* (Cervantes)
1613	**Election of Mikhail Romanov: Beginning of the Romanov line**	
1616		Death of William Shakespeare
1626	Birth of Simon Ushakov, "modern" icon painter (d. 1686)	
1631		First French newspaper: The *Gazette*
1633	Foundation of Kiev College	
1634	First Primer printed in Moscow	

1635		Foundation of the French Academy
1637		*Discourse on Method* (Descartes)
1642–60		Revolution in England
1645–76	**Reign of Alexey Mikhailovich**	
1649	New Code Smaller Catechism, first popular textbook of religious instruction	
1651		*Leviathan* (Hobbes)
1653–54	Council on correction of church books; beginning of Schism	
1654	Union of Eastern Ukraine to Muscovy	
1667	Anathema on Schismatics	Building of Versailles for Louis XIV (1668–78)
1670–71	Uprising of Stepan Razin	
1672	First theatrical performance for Tsar Alexey Birth of Peter I	
1678		Congress of Nimeguen: French becomes the language of diplomacy
1682–96	**Reign of the half brothers Ivan V and Peter I**	
1686		Foundation of Saint-Cyr school for girls of the nobility (France)
1687	Foundation of Slavonic-Greco-Latin Academy in Moscow	
1696		The first Russian grammar, written by H. W. Ludolf, published in Latin at Oxford
1696–1725	**Reign of Peter the Great**	
1697		*Historical and Philosophical Dictionary* (Bayle)

■ ■ ■

■ ■ ■ EIGHTEENTH CENTURY

1700	Introduction of Julian Calendar
1703	Foundation of St. Petersburg The first Russian newspaper

1708	First printed calendar	
1711–12		The *Spectator* (Addison)
1714	Compulsory schooling for children of nobility and officials	
1714–25	Building of Petropavlov fortress (Trezzini)	
1715		Death of Louis XIV of France
1721	**Peter takes the title of Emperor**	
1722–24	Table of Ranks	
1725	Opening of the Academy of Sciences	
1732	Foundation of the Cadet Academy	
1738	First ballet school	
1741–61	**Reign of Elizabeth I**	
1748–55	Cathedral of Smolny Monastery (Rastrelli)	*The Spirit of Laws,* (Montesquieu, 1748) *The French Encyclopedia* (1751–80)
1754–62	Winter Palace (Rastrelli)	
1755	Founding of Moscow University The first Russian grammar in Russian, by Lomonosov	
1756	First Russian Imperial Theater	
1757–62		*History of Russia* (Voltaire)
1758	Founding of the Academy of Fine Arts	
1760	Lomonosov named rector of Academy of Sciences	
1762–96	**Reign of Catherine II**	*Social Contract* (Rousseau, 1762)
1764	Foundation of Smolny Institute on the model of Saint-Cyr	*Philosophical Dictionary* (Voltaire)
1768–78	Statue of Peter the Great (Falconet)	
1773–75	Pugachev rebellion	
1774		*Werther* (Goethe)
1775, 1793, 1795	Partitions of Poland	
1776		Declaration of American Independence

1781		*Critique of Pure Reason* (Kant)
1783	Foundation of Russian Academy Decree allowing private printing	
1787		The Constitution of the United States
1789		The French Revolution
1789–94	Dictionary of the Academy	
1790	*Journey from Petersburg to Moscow* (Radischev)	
1793		Execution of Louis XVI
1796	Institution of censorship Prohibition of private printing	
1796–1801	**Reign of Paul I**	
1799	Birth of Pushkin (d. 1837)	

■ ■ ■

■ ■ ■ NINETEENTH CENTURY

1801–25	**Reign of Alexander I**	
1801–11	Building of Kazan Cathedral in St. Petersburg (now Museum of History of Religion)	
1812	Birth of A. Herzen (d. 1870)	Napoleon's army in Russia
1814		Occupation of Paris by allied troops
1816	*History of the Russian State* (Karamzin)	
1823		Monroe Doctrine
1824	Foundation of the Maly Teatr (Moscow)	
1825	The December uprising	
1825–55	**Reign of Nicholas I**	
1830	Polish revolt	July Revolution in Paris
1835	"First Philosophical Letter" (Chaadaev) *Ivan Susanin* (A Life for the Tsar, opera by Glinka)	
1840	Birth of Pisarev (d. 1868)	

221

1846		*The System of Economic Contradictions* (Proudhon)
1847	Belinsky's letter to Gogol on the Russian people	
1848		Revolution in France *Communist Manifesto* (Marx and Engels)
1849	The Petrashevsky affair (arrest of Dostoevsky)	
1851	Opening of St. Petersburg-Moscow railway	
1854–56	The Crimean War	
1855–81	**Reign of Alexander II**	
1857–67	The *Bell* (Herzen)	
1859	Foundation of Russian Musical Society (St. Petersburg)	*Origin of Species* (Darwin)
1860	*The Thunderstorm*, play by Ostrovsky	
1861	Emancipation of serfs *Fathers and Sons* (Turgenev)	Beginning of Civil War in America
1863	Polish revolt	
1864	*What To Do?* (Chernyshevsky) Judicial and administrative reform	
1865		Assassination of Abraham Lincoln
1866	First attempt on life of Alexander II Foundation of Moscow Conservatory	
1867		*Das Kapital* (Marx)
1870	Association of "Peredvizhniki"	
1872	*Boris Godunov* (Mussorgsky)	First Russian translation of *Das Kapital*
1873	*The Onega Byliny* (Hilferding) "The Volga Boatmen" (Repin)	
1878	Populist movement Height of Terrorism	
1881	Death of Mussorgsky Death of Dostoevsky Assassination of Alexander II	

■　■　■